Da Capo Press Music Reprint Series

General Editor: FREDERICK FREEDMAN
University of California at Los Angeles

LESCHETIZKY
AS I KNEW HIM

THEODOR LESCHETIZKY
Elderly study by Ferdinand Schmutzer

LESCHETIZKY
AS I KNEW HIM

by Ethel Newcomb

With a new Introduction by
Edwine Behre

DA CAPO PRESS • NEW YORK • 1967

A Da Capo Press Reprint Edition

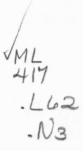

OUR LESCHETIZKY HERITAGE

Keine Kunst ohne Leben, Kein Leben ohne Kunst. No art without life, no life without art. This was the simple credo of Theodor Leschetizky, written with his autograph on photographs he gave his pupils and remembered by them as his favorite saying. It gives the clue to magic that enthralled us. It was the faith by which he lived.

His life was not only devotion to the musical art but to all art—above all to the art of living generously, amply, with wide interests, deep sympathies, constant friendships, delight in beauty, and courage in grief.

This art in life is not common or easy today. Probably it never was. But wherever it can be brought to pass or taught as Leschetizky taught it always with the art of playing the piano, it answers a deep need in these times of massman and adman, confusion and violence, cynicism and frustration, times when the individual is assailed on all sides by forces inimical to life as it should be and could be lived.

So here is this memoir by Ethel Newcomb of her years with Leschetizky as his pupil, teaching assistant, and great friend, written at white heat while she still was under his spell.

For students of the history of music and for musicians, both performers and educators, the book is a window opening on scenes from the life and work of one of the most productive teaching geniuses of any time.

It has the ring of truth. Miss Newcomb's account is set down from her diaries and her memories. It is free of self-glorification—written from a devotion to her teacher and to music so real that nothing but complete candor would do.

You participate in affairs that went badly, in scenes of failure and disappointment, of explosions of temper, of merciless labors for excellence, of times of success and delight. You hear the pithy speech of "Professor" on piano playing and teaching, and his convictions on what the life of a responsible artist should be.

The dates of Miss Newcomb's association with Leschetizky in Vienna, and by correspondence during her stays at home in Whitney Point, New York, are 1897 to about 1913 —more than fifteen of the seventy years of his life in music. He began to teach as a slender boy of fourteen, already known as a pianist *wunderkind*. He received pupils, not as a seeker of pocket money but as a serious professional pedagogue with his own studio. From the beginning, he taught with zest and fascination.

"Teaching was fresh air to him," said Benno Moiseiwitsch in a London newspaper interview. "His pupils were his great act of creation."

Considering the nature of Leschetizky's involvement with pupils—individual lessons lasting an hour and a half and even longer, often leading to lifelong friendship—the number of his studio graduates is astonishing. The late Edwin Hughes, in a paper published in the *Leschetizky Association News Bulletin,** refers to a list of twelve hundred pupils taken from Leschetizky's lesson books dating from his St. Petersburg Conservatory years to shortly before his death in 1915. And even this lengthy enrollment Mr. Hughes considered incomplete, for missing from it were the names of several pupils known to him during his association with Leschetizky as pupil and teaching assistant.

Mr. Hughes wrote:

> American audiences began listening to piano recitals by pupils of Leschetizky well-nigh 90 years ago.
> It was in 1876 that Annette Essipoff, his brilliant pupil and afterward his wife, was first heard in America. Fannie Bloomfield Zeisler returned from Vienna and began con-

*"The Leschetizky Heritage," by Edwin Hughes, *Leschetizky Association News Bulletin*, January, 1963.

certizing in the eighties. The advent of Paderewski came in 1891 after four seasons of study with Leschetizky and a series of unusual successes on the Continent and in England.

There followed Ossip Gabrilowitsch, Mark Hambourg, Artur Schnabel, Katharine Goodson, Arthur Shattuck, John Powell, Elly Ney, Ethel Leginska, Ignaz Friedman, Heinrich Gebhard, Richard Buhlig, Ethel Newcomb, Alexander Brailowsky, Severin Eisenberger, Martinus Sieveking, Gottfried Galston, Paul Wittgenstein, Frank La Forge, Eleanor Spencer, Mieczyslaw Horszowski, Benno Moiseiwitsch and others.

Wassily Safonoff and Ossip Gabrilowitsch, two of his best-known pupils, also became famous conductors, the former leading the New York Philharmonic from 1904 to 1909.

These, mentioned at random, and many more who spent student years with Leschetizky in Vienna, are familiar names to anyone who has listened to concerts in America during the last 50 years.

A list of Leschetizky pupils who were still playing and teaching in North America and overseas in May, 1942, when the Leschetizky Association was organized, would be very long. But such a list would still lack the names of musicians of known Leschetizky descent—Leonard Bernstein, Clifford Curzon, Rudolf Firkusny, Witold Malcuzynski, Guiomar Novaes—and the names of eminent pedagogues and cultural pioneers; such as Lyell Gustin of Canada. These important figures are not Leschetizky pupils. They are pupils of pupils. These with *their* pupils (for Leschetizky pupils, such as Heinrich Gebhard and Artur Schnabel, taught almost as long and extensively as did the master himself), number many thousands, a company far too numerous to be identified and indexed in this volume.

The magnificent line of Russian pianists stems from Leschetizky and his fellow-teacher and great friend, Anton Rubinstein. Both were on hand at the founding of the St. Petersburg Conservatory. Annette Essipoff, Leschetizky's pupil and his second wife, had, after their divorce, a long career of teaching in Russia that paralleled Leschetizky's in Vienna. Prokofieff was one of her pupils.

The tours made by Leschetizky's great pupils throughout the world revealed an array of diverse keyboard personalities—performers of such dramatic individual differences that it was hard to believe they were taught by the same master. Yet beneath these contrasts was an identical idea of what beautiful piano playing should be. Memoirs of Leschetizky pupils—Schnabel, Gabrilowitsch, Gebhard, Powell, and others—express this common conception, often in the same words. It boils down to something like this: Playing the notes right, the greatest technical virtuosity, is not enough. If that is all you have to offer, better leave the keyboard alone. There must be warm, expressive, living beauty —tonal loveliness, sculptured phrasing, a fine sense of the proportions and meaning of each composition, and, above all, vital dynamic rhythm. Music must *speak*—or it is nothing.

A teacher, Leschetizky held, should be an artist and a player. He himself had behind him a far-flung playing career, second only to that of Liszt and Rubinstein. His absorption in teaching lessened his interest in public appearances, and his fame as a pedagogue swallowed the memory of his career as a performer. Not so to his students. We continually heard him play at lessons, illustrating points in the works we studied. His knowledge of the piano as an expressive and dramatic instrument was uncanny, his tonal palette contained every shade and color, his rhythm was infinitely subtle, infinitely flexible, and his pedaling bordered on the miraculous. All this in the service of the composer, his music, its understanding, and its truthful transmission to the listener.

The slow movements of Beethoven as played by Leschetizky remain in my memory as unequaled for depth and beauty. Once at a lesson on Op. 57, he said of the slow movement, *"So sitzen die Götter auf dem Olymp"*—thus the gods sit on Olympus. And truly the gods were present, all the gods of music in their glory.

Leschetizky told in my hearing of his discovery of the piano's capacity for tonal variety and beauty. At the age of eighteen he was a young virtuoso, much sought after for his flashy, brilliant pyrotechnics. Such keyboard acrobatics

were then the order of the day in Vienna. He was at a
gathering of music lovers when a new pianist named Schulhoff played in a manner that was strange and not appreciated by his listeners. Instead of astonishing by speed,
dash, and virtuosity, he made the piano sing in an almost
human voice. Such beauty and communicativeness was then
unheard of. Leschetizky was overwhelmed. Ashamed of his
own playing when called on for a show-off performance that
would put Schulhoff in the shade, he hurried home, shut
himself off from public engagements, and worked with every
resource of ear and mind to produce the Schulhoff tonal
magic. Only after many months did he succeed, but this
lonely, stubborn struggle, he told us, was his real birth as
an artist.

"Above all, there was his tone," reminisced Benno
Moiseiwitsch in a newspaper interview. "No one had a tone
like his. He never taught us any 'secret' there: one just
picked up something of the lustre from him. At 76, he still
played beautifully—luscious tone and wonderful scale
passages."

"Leschetizky had a holy horror of anything that smacked
of the pedantic attitude in teaching," wrote Edwin Hughes.
"He consistently refused to write a book on piano playing
and never made use of or reference to books that several of
his pupils wrote on the so-called 'Leschetizky Method.'"

Repeatedly he said to pupils: "There is no Leschetizky
Method."

His genius lay in his skill in discovering and developing
the individual capacities of pupils, inspiring and directing
them to attain their highest potentiality. His way of han-
dling each one as an individual, of finding individual and
highly original solutions for difficulties, was of constant
amazement to the listener. (Those of us who had graduated
from the "vorbereiter" stage had access to the studio as
listeners. Professor enjoyed an audience, old performer that
he was!)

Any gifted pupil who found his way to this one-man
school was welcomed by its benevolent despot—whether

sent and supported by the Queen of Rumania or arriving in borrowed boys' clothes as a runaway from the Frankfurter Conservatory. Ethel Leginska, the runaway, told me this story which is not in Ethel Newcomb's book, though it should be. Leschetizky not only taught her without pay but even paid Miss Newcomb out of his own pocket for the lessons that prepared her for study with the Master.

Generosity to pupils with more talent than money is in the Leschetizky tradition. from Professor himself to his pupils and pupils of pupils. Lesson charges were low or nonexistent to the impecunious and brilliant. In Vienna, an evening suit with proper accessories would arrive mysteriously at the address of a penniless boy about to make a début; or, on the day of a concert, an evening dress would be delivered to a gifted girl from a provincial village facing her Vienna bow without appropriate apparel. An ambiguous "From a friend" would be written on an accompanying card.

Leschetizky's great pupils followed his example. Paderewski, at the height of his first London success, supported the *wunderkind,* Mark Hambourg, during three years of study with Leschetizky. Harold Von Mickwitz who, according to his pupil, Helen Norfleet, came to Texas when its frontier towns resembled a cowboy movie, taught the needy and gifted without fee. Young Cecile de Horvath, after her last lesson with Ossip Gabrilowitsch, received from him on the homeward-bound boat a steamer packet containing his photograph and a check for the amount she had paid him for lessons. "A young artist at the beginning of her career always needs extra funds," he wrote. "Perhaps this amount will help you to give an extra concert in New York or Philadelphia."

Vienna in Leschetizky's day was marked by *laissez faire* gaiety and ease. Culture was widespread, music flourished, students came to Professor from all over the world. In this atmosphere, our master's famous *Class* presented to an intimate gathering of about 150 musically aware listeners the first appearances of scores of young men and women destined to be the carriers of musical delight to their day and generation.

Most of Leschetizky's pupils—those of world-wide concert artist fame and those known mainly as regional pianist-teachers, carried on not only Professor's approach to playing and pedagogy, but variants of his *Class* and of his studio atmosphere—the stimulation, the laughter and companionship, the wide horizons. Memoirs of the pupils of pupils sound alike, whether Clifford Curzon describes his musical life at its dawn as student and concerto accompanist in the beautiful London home of his teacher, Katharine Goodson; or Leonard Bernstein writes of leaving the Brookline, Massachusetts, studio of his boyhood teacher, Heinrich Gebhard, "not on two feet but floating on air"; or Carol Robinson and Grace Potter Carroll reminisce about the Chicago salon of Fannie Bloomfield Zeisler.

Nostalgic clouds drift down the years from musical evenings of Leschetizky pupils arranged for *their* pupils in Minnesota, Texas, Michigan, Oklahoma, Missouri, or Western Canada. For that matter, New Yorkers regret the passing of the annual May Sunday on the Long Island estate of the late Paul Wittgenstein, an affair consciously modeled on Professor's *Class*—the elite of young talent from Leschetizky Association studios chosen to perform, food that was perfection, leisure to chat with friends, enjoy the apple blossoms, and sniff the spring.

Thinking of Leschetizky, one wonders how this genius would have fared in our times of industrialization and bureaucratization. Can one imagine him a student in a present-day university school of music or a great conservatory, industriously accumulating credits for degrees, toiling on his Ph.D. requirements in order to be assured of a post with tenure on a faculty of some institution of musical learning, there to pilot young talents to *their* doctorates and so on? Can any of his pupils who experienced years of his inspired guidance picture him harnessed to a set curriculum, hemmed in by big organization procedures, distracted by administrative diplomacies and politics?

The master teacher, the original, his personal relation to the development of the student part of the creative process, finds up-hill going in this era of mercilessly increasing population, crowded schools and universities, TV courses, teaching machines, and various computerized ways of human processing. From Socrates, through the ages, the great teacher has persisted in all branches of the humanities and the arts, a nourisher of all that pertains to civilized living. Despite all pressures and obstacles, the tradition of Leschetizky and his great artist-teacher pupils must continue if we are to enjoy the piano, not as an instrument of percussion, but as the voice of great music as Paderewski, Schnabel, Friedman, Horszowski, Firkusny, Novaes, Curzon, and many fine but less-well-known artists have shown it to be. Otherwise, keyboard magnificence in the grand manner will be lost to the world of music.

In closing, I would like to give you an impression of Leschetizky which will bring feelings of recognition to his surviving pupils, those who came in childhood or early youth to the teachings of his richly experienced old age. I quite from a book, now out of print, by Annette Hullah, a student:

> Leschetizky is a most delightful host, the very embodiment of fun, his presence entertainment enough. As a raconteur, he is unrivalled. His powers of mimicry are in themselves sufficient to justify a career. He is the most appreciative of listeners and the easiest of guests, charming and genial, finding pleasure in everything.
>
> Aristocrat in life as in music, he exacts from those around him gentle manners and delicate observances. The rough diamond does not attract him. His natural love of order desires everything to be in its place and suitable to the moment.
>
> He is of small build, wiry, highly strung, magnetic from top to toe. The whole man seems charged with electricity which sparkles from him whenever stimulus evokes it. He gives the impression of being the essence of nervous force rather than an embodiment of physical energy. A certain aristocratic spirit reveals itself in the fierceness of his eyes and his short quick step. He knows what he wants and intends to have it.

He is a man on whom has flashed at times a comprehension of the unfathomable tragedy and mystery of life and would fain turn away from its sombre to its lighter aspects.

Transparent as a child, his face is the index of his mood. In two or three moments he will become as many different people, dry, derisive, dejected, earnest, gentle, even tender. His waywardness is difficult to follow: yet beneath this kaleidoscopic surface lie those qualities that have made his work what it is: unfailing patience, inflexible will, unswerving concentration, his whole being bound up in his music. It is this firm belief in the necessity of his work and his devotion to it that has made him the greatest teacher of piano the world has ever known.

There is a story, possibly apocryphal, of the manner of Leschetizky's death that is so much in the style of his genius that it would be a pity not to record it. I had it from Louis Finton, long-time student and billiard-playing companion of Professor, an American resident of Vienna, who was caught in a roundup of enemy aliens and interned there throughout the First World War. I have never doubted the veracity of the account, given him by Professor's servant, Pepi, a peasant woman, too simple, it would seem, to invent such a remarkable tale.

The time was November, 1915. The guns of August had long thundered away. The international assemblage of Leschetizky pupils had scattered to their homelands. The master, desolate from the breakup of his class of gifted young people, his sight impaired from an unsuccessful cataract operation, and with the infirmities of his eighty-fifth year upon him, traveled to Dresden to visit his son, taking Pepi along to care for him.

Finding his son seriously ill, he took lodgings at a hotel. One evening he said to Pepi:

"Heut' nacht werd' ich sterben." (Tonight I'm going to die.)

"Aber, Herr Professor, don't talk like that. You're no sicker than you have been right along."

"No, no, I'm going to die. Go down to the Maître d'Hôtel and get me a bottle of champagne."

In fear and trembling she went. Professor drank and said: "Jetzt bet!" (Now pray.) Pepi fell to her knees. He drained a glass, a last toast, as it were, and died, one hopes, in a champagne glow of his long faith in life in art and art in life.

EDWINE BEHRE

THE LESCHETIZKY ASSOCIATION

The Leschetizky Association, Inc., its membership open to pupils and musical descendants of Leschetizky, is chartered under New York State law as a nonprofit membership corporation, its purpose "to perpetuate the principles of Theodor Leschetizky in teaching and playing and to honor his memory." Its activities include a triennial New York Début Competition of qualified artist students of members, cooperative recitals of young students, in New York monthly recitals by an adult players' group, and, through Leschetizky Association member Herman Newman, music director of WNYC, the New York municipal broadcasting station, radio and TV appearances of students and members.

The Leschetizky Association publishes an annual news bulletin. This volume is its first venture in publishing material on Leschetizky in book form.

Membership of the Leschetizky Association numbers about 370. The majority live and work in the United States, although the Leschetizky Association is active in the principal New Zealand cities, and members are also enrolled in Austria, Great Britain, Canada, France, Egypt, and Poland.

There is a companion organization in Richmond, Va., known as the John Powell Foundation and composed of John Powell students who perform and promote his compositions and cooperate in recitals.

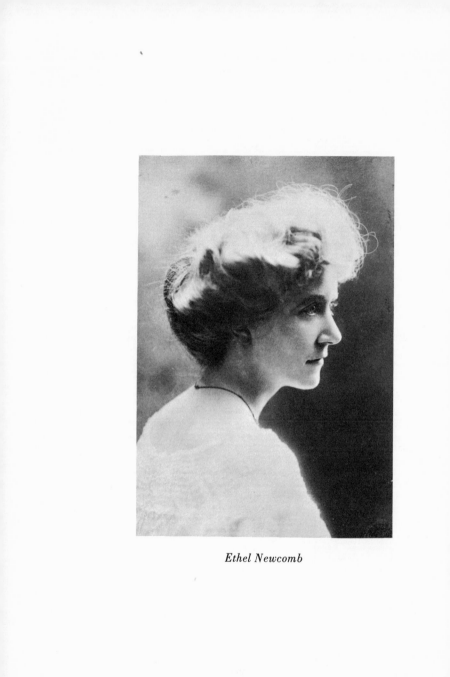

Ethel Newcomb

ABOUT ETHEL NEWCOMB

Ethel Newcomb (1875–1959) first came to study with Leschetizky in Vienna in 1897 after a series of odd incidents described in her book. She was the beautiful and gifted daughter of a prominent upstate New York family who wished to give her a year of study in Europe before launching her social career. She remained abroad two years and returned launched as a serious student of the piano with a concert career in mind. Thereafter, in spite of family traditions and plans, her life was music—performing and teaching—until her death at eighty-three at Whitney Point, the family estate near Binghamton, New York.

Ethel's relationship with Leschetizky was threefold: pupil, "Vorbereiter" (teaching assistant), and close personal friend. Its special quality can be glimpsed in extracts from the letters Leschetizky wrote to her over the years—letters bequeathed to her publisher, who in turn gave them to the Leschetizky Association. Résumés and translations of this correspondence have appeared in the Association's *News Bulletin.*

The earliest letter, dated July 1, 1899, "at night," is a touching farewell, sent the day before she embarked for America after her first period of study. *"Meine liebe, gute theure Ethel"*—my dear good precious Ethel—Leschetizky used the formal "Sie," though later it was "Sie" or "Du," the intimate form, and often both in the same letter—"Sie nehmen ein Stück meines Innern mit."

> You take a piece of my inner self with you. You know that I am not such a fortunate man as people imagine. . . . You have promised me that you will be true to Art, and under

all circumstances. Keep your word and try to grow in Art, *ever* and *ever*. You also will not always find yourself on a bed of roses—then you will discover what comfort music can provide in life. You will think of me. Amen! Now dear Ethel, I embrace you a thousand times in spirit. May all good spirits [alle guten Geister] go with you and protect you. In true devotion and friendship, your Theodor Leschetizky.

Later he wrote:

I was so happy to hear that you have appeared twice successfully in public. Art is a grateful friend—the more one devotes one's self to her, the greater return she makes. Don't let yourself be taken up by an empty life. It would be a pity, dear Ethel. You carry in you a rich, warm musical sensitivity. Don't drop this. Develop it more and more. There is energy and rhythm in you. Technic and power always increase with industry when one knows *how it is done.*

In 1901 Ethel returned to Vienna. Two letters from Ischl, Leschetizky's summer home, were full of anticipation. Her début in 1903 is described vividly in her book. A long letter from Ischl in 1904 was full of advice about playing in London and Berlin—what pianos *not* to use, what halls to play in, possible programs, and so on.

Ethel seems to have remained in Vienna quite steadily for some years for concerts and as Leschetizky's assistant. About 1906, when I lived in the same house with her in Vienna, she was a slim, arresting apparition with her marvelous pale gold hair (in one of his letters Leschetizky calls her "Elfe"), beautiful clothes, and a pale gold Russian wolfhound that accompanied her everywhere and once saved her life when a gas pipe broke in her room while she was asleep.

During another period in America, Ethel received his letter urging her onward as an artist:

Ethel, you must not be too modest. In America there are few who do as well as you—so go forward, go ahead! I hope you will come to Vienna covered with success instead of dissolving in the family, which after all, doesn't give any real satisfaction—unless a true marriage for love is in the picture—it cannot be otherwise for an Ethel Newcomb.

After this American period, Ethel was again in and out of Vienna, a fleeting figure, sometimes a guest at classes. She especially loved to play Schumann.

I vividly remember being at Leschetizky's the day after Ethel again left for America—it must have been about 1910 —and hearing "Professor" tell with great emotion how she had wept—"Sie hat so furchtbar geweint"—, saying she felt they would never meet again. I believe they never did.

From that time on, Ethel Newcomb made her home in New York, combining teaching with a modest concert career. Pupils came to her from the United States and Canada; and they followed her to Whitney Point when she retired from New York and public performances.

At Whitney Point, Ethel continued to teach and to play weekly recitals for pupils and music lovers almost up to the beginning of her last illness. In a small simple house on the family estate, surrounded by a few devoted pupils, she lived the life of music. Leschetizky would have approved and applauded. There was about it all a suggestion of his own life in the Karl Ludwig Strasse in Vienna. Faithful to his precepts and example, she spent her days with music to the end.

Her book about Leschetizky, a true, unadorned portrait of a great man, is a precious heritage to the many thousands who have come under his influence, pupils and musical descendants "unto the third and fourth generation."

E. B.

CONTENTS

Introduction: "Our Leschetizky Heritage"
by Edwine Behre VII

The Leschetizky Association XVII

"About Ethel Newcomb" by Edwine Behre XIX

Leschetizky, As I Knew Him, by Ethel Newcomb 1

Plates I-IV 297

Theodor Leschetizky: A Bibliography 301

Theodor Leschetizky: A Chronology (1830–1915) 309

Works for Piano by Theodor Leschetizky 311

Index I: Leschetizky on Piano Playing 314

Index II: Compositions Discussed 316

Index III: Persons 318

LESCHETIZKY
AS I KNEW HIM
By ETHEL NEWCOMB

D. APPLETON AND COMPANY
NEW YORK : : LONDON : : MCMXXIII

PRINTED IN THE UNITED STATES OF AMERICA

DEDICATED
TO
M. L. R.

FOREWORD

The bare facts of Theodor Leschetizky's life are well known. His distinguished personality has been the subject of several books and many articles of merit. One book is by the Countess Potocka, his sister-in-law, another by Anette Hullah, his pupil.

He was born in Poland, at the Castle of Lancut, near Lemberg, June 22, 1830. His father, a Bohemian by birth, held the position of Music Master to the family of the Potocka. His mother, Therese Von Ullman, was a Pole. Leschetizky died in Dresden in 1915.

Much besides has been said and written of him as a teacher, and of his manner of instruction, and a great diversity of opinion expressed concerning the so-called "method." Madame Breé, and Fräulein Prentner, two of his most experienced assistants, have written admirable books.

To the reader, who may wonder what I could possibly add to this material, a word of explanation is due.

I have not intended to write biographical facts, already many times rehearsed, or to defend the sane and broad principles of beautiful piano playing, which were the basis of the master's teaching, and are far beyond the scope of any such limiting term as "method."

During several years of association with Leschetizky, first as his pupil and later as assistant, a great many interesting and amusing experiences were impressed on my memory. Many of these have an interpretive value, in helping to a more intimate knowledge of the man and teacher; and it is in the hope that they may fulfill this purpose that I have felt encouraged to relate them.

Every one knows that the career of a pupil studying with a great master is a stormy and difficult one, and never easy, especially if that master be a great one. For that reason I hope that no reader will be hurt or displeased on finding his own experience, or perhaps one that resembles his own very closely, brought to light. My best justification for these personalities is that I have not spared myself. And if in the opening chapters I have dwelt on my youthful impressions, and told in too much detail the story of my own musical development, it is because I have found it easier to illustrate in personal terms one of Leschetizky's most conspicuous traits—the profound interest which he felt in his pupils.

LESCHETIZKY
AS I KNEW HIM

LESCHETIZKY
AS I KNEW HIM

CHAPTER I

WHEN I first went to Europe, I was taken by my aunt, who had studied piano with Pruckner in Stuttgart some years before. We had really gone abroad to visit my uncle in England, but I had my father's permission to spend a year on the Continent to study music or anything else that I liked. One year was thought enough, of course, to make a finished artist!

It was my aunt's idea that I should take up the study of piano. On both sides my family were musical, but my aunt was the only trained musician among them. In her opinion, I was nothing less than a prodigy. I had played by ear as long as I could remember, but there was nothing I hated so much as learning notes, and so, until I went to Europe, I played mostly by ear, and used to imitate my aunt's playing as well as I could. I was also brought out on several occasions to play at her pupils' recitals. My father, however, had old-fashioned prejudices against artists, and desired nothing less than that one of his children should become a professional musician.

We already knew of Leschetizky, but my aunt, who was somewhat Puritanical, and was alarmed at certain rumors she had heard about the great pedagogue of Vienna, had decided that our year could be more profitably and safely spent in the conservative atmosphere of Stuttgart. The hands raised in horror there at the mere mention of Leschetizky's name only confirmed my guardian in the opinion that she had chosen well for me. He was, they said, the last person in the world to whom one should take a young girl for lessons.

All this only stimulated my curiosity and desire to go to Vienna. One day, oddly enough, after I had begun my lessons in Stuttgart, a letter came from my father informing me that he had heard of a good teacher in Vienna. His name was "Leschetizky." He had been Paderewski's teacher and might be worth going to, he thought! If I were going to study music at all I should go to the best!

In Stuttgart the kind and distinguished Professor Pruckner had pronounced me very musical, but was doubtful if I could ever acquire enough technique to play well. He was a delightful pianist himself, and had been a pupil of Liszt. He told me many things Liszt had said to him about the piano and concerning the relation of art to life, and very generously gave me autographs of Liszt. But, while I was very sorry to part with this interesting and valuable teacher, I was only too eager to get away from the stuffy air of Stuttgart. With my father's suggestion to give emphasis to my pleadings, I finally persuaded my aunt to write to an acquaintance of hers in Vienna, and ask him how we might best approach Leschetizky.

This acquaintance had been a colleague of my aunt during her student days in Stuttgart. He had since married another pianist, and was well established as a teacher in Vienna. After hearing from his wife that they would undertake to put us in touch with Leschetizky, we started. To improve our chances of an introduction to the master we provided ourselves with letters from ambassadors and other persons of importance—a precaution which must have caused him some amusement!

The friends to whom we had written met us at the station and conducted us to a small hotel in the outskirts of Vienna. I began to study with them, believing, of course, that I was being prepared for the great teacher. We had not thought to find out who the master's assistants were; but after a time it occurred to us that we were never meeting any of his pupils, or any one who seemed to have any connection with him.

After studying three or four months we began to inquire when we could go to Leschetizky, but there was never a definite answer, and, one day, in my aunt's absence, I was asked to sign a legal-looking document requiring me to agree that for a period of two years I would not study with any one in Vienna but the man from whom I was then having lessons.

Naturally, the paper made me suspicious, and I refused to sign it, saying I preferred to wait until my aunt's return.

It was only then that we realized in what a neat trap we had been caught. But we at last managed to meet a real pupil of Leschetizky, who told us that these teachers were in no way connected with him, and that, on the contrary, they had a working system of keeping pupils away from him by pretending to be his assistants, with a preparatory course stretching indefinitely into the future. It was hearsay that other people were involved in their scheme of intrigue; hirelings, who met strangers

at the stations, and a certain well-known clergy-
man, who always recommended this couple when
people wrote him for his advice about studying in
Vienna, at the same time warning them against
Leschetizky. We found it very difficult to leave
these people, and so bitter was their resentment that
it was not until years afterward that they would
condescend even to greet us when we met in a concert hall.

It was really very easy to get an appointment
with Leschetizky for the purpose of playing to him
—once at least! We had not needed the ambassador's letters, and could have gone by ourselves, if
we had only known it. Through the pupil of his,
who had helped us to escape from our first teachers
in Vienna, we met Fräulein Prentner, one of his
real preparatory teachers, and it was she who took
us to Leschetizky.

It was his dinner hour when we arrived at the
house—about five o'clock. From beyond the doors
connecting the music room with the dining room
came sounds of festivity, and my first impression
was that a very gay party was going on. I remember thinking how amusing it would be to meet all
those people, and I felt rather sorry that Leschetizky had to leave such pleasant company to hear
me play. There was a great deal of laughing and
talking during the few minutes that we waited; then
the doors opened, and the great master stood before
us, amiable and smiling. There was nothing of the
elderly pedagogue in his manner of receiving us,
but such a quality of friendliness that I was at once
at ease with him. Nor did he appear old to me,
for all the more than sixty years he counted at that
time. Even my immaturity recognized the remark-

able, enduring youth of Leschetizky's personality, and I recall my wonder at his alert step and his active, supple, and astonishingly young-looking hands.

After chatting with us for a few minutes, he inquired how long we intended to stay in Europe. I told him we had already been there six months, and had just succeeded in getting to him. Then, after a short interview, he asked me to play. When I had finished, his comment was that I probably played a great deal by ear, and did not read well. The criticism astonished me, and I wondered how he could possibly have known this. To be able to play by ear, Leschetizky explained, was really a talent in itself, but something that one dispensed with the more one studied. Then he tested my ear, and smiled at me in a still more friendly fashion, but, when he gave me something to read, it was done so badly that I was convinced he had discovered in me an abyss of ignorance, at least in so far as the theoretical knowledge of music was concerned.

However, my playing as a whole seemed to please him, and he asked if I could arrange to take four lessons from Fräulein Prentner before we returned to England. Then he puzzled me very much by asking if I could settle down seriously and devote an hour a day to the piano during the summer. My idea of serious study was sitting at the piano many, many hours a day, and I wondered what he could mean by this. I had heard that Leschetizky's pupils studied eight or ten hours a day, and that they were only too easily recognized in Vienna by swollen muscles and bandaged hands. It was concentration and right habits of study that counted more than the time spent, he told me, and then, smiling whimsically, said he supposed it would be very hard for me to give up my good times.

"Still," he added, "you should learn to feel that your music is a good time."

While we talked, Leschetizky regarded me with a sort of gentle and kindly amusement. A silver buckle, which I was wearing, seemed to attract him particularly, and, even when I questioned him about my study, I noticed that his eyes wandered admiringly toward the buckle. At last he asked me where I got it, adding, "A young lady who dresses so tastefully should learn to play well."

Encouraged, but with great trepidation, I inquired if he would have me for a pupil.

"Certainly," he responded, to my aunt's great relief, "I will teach you."

Then he became very earnest and told me that I must strengthen my fingers. While I showed a very promising natural talent, in his opinion, I had neither strength nor technique. Even when he spoke in criticism, Leschetizky's manner was so gracious that I instinctively felt I had found a friend.

All this had not been quite formal enough for my aunt, who was also hoping for lessons and realized far more than I the tremendous importance of getting to Leschetizky. I had been excited, but not at all overawed by the interview, at the same time conscious of a certain glamour and fascination associated with so celebrated a person. My rather casual attitude had not been disturbed by any formality on the part of Leschetizky, while, it must be admitted, my aunt was distinctly surprised and a little shocked by his lack of ceremony.

My aunt was always very much in earnest about everything, particularly her music. When she told Leschetizky she wished to play for him, he, too, became quite serious — too serious even for her! Leschetizky knew far better than my aunt that she was too settled in her way of playing to be influenced by him, as he liked to mold a pupil's style to his ideas. She was, however, a woman of distinction and some attainment, and Leschetizky recognized in her a personality that could not easily be dismissed.

He expressed his willingness to hear her play. My aunt went to the piano. Tremulous with excitement, her hands fluttered over the keyboard; in her nervousness she could not even find the place to start. After a few minutes' agitated searching of the keys, she began the "Barcarole" of Chopin, and proceeded very shakily as far as the difficult passage in trills. Here her fingers failed her entirely and the "Barcarole" collapsed.

"But you see, madame," Leschetizky commented, not unkindly, "to play a piece one must be able to do even the hardest measures in it." And then, gently pulling a lock of his own white hair, he said, "but one can always learn—I learn every day of my life."

Always afterward Leschetizky spoke of my aunt as "Tante Palpita" (di tanti palpiti).

In justice to my dear aunt, I must add that, in spite of mature years and many discouragements, she progressed enough to have a few lessons with Leschetizky, and, as time went on, the palpitation was less in evidence.

We talked again about my studies and the lessons which I was to have with Fräulein Prentner before returning to England. I promised to study well, but, at the same time, the absurd notion possessed me that I had already accomplished the most difficult part—I had played for Leschetizky and had been accepted as his pupil. In the autumn I would return, and, by virtue of some miracle, he would in a short time make an artist of me!

If I had gone to Leschetizky as an older or more advanced musician, there would doubtless have been quite another impression to record. Then, perhaps, I should have had a presentiment of the formidable old man and critical master, who often reduced prospective pupils to such a state of terror that they never dared appear before him again. His mood was kindly that afternoon, and I felt that he had petted and indulged me as a child. Small wonder that no shadow of future struggle cast itself across my dreams! It would all be so easy, I thought, under such a genial and kindly master.

As we left the master's house I felt myself in a glow and daze of happiness, which no sternness on the part of my aunt or of Fräulein Prentner could disturb.

CHAPTER II

DURING June, already a year since I left home, I studied with Fräulein Prentner, covering, however, only the most elementary principles of technique in the few lessons which I had before we left for England at the end of the month, but I had high hopes of overcoming the weakness of my rather frail and undeveloped hands, and spent a great deal more than the promised hour a day at the piano during that summer. The people with whom we had studied before this in Vienna had, indeed, many good ideas, but I realized that now I was beginning at the foundation, and that I should have to show myself a diligent student.

September found us in Austria again, this time at Altenmarkt-on-the-Triesting, a little village about two and a half hours from Vienna. Fräulein Prentner had a few pupils there, and my study began in earnest, while all the time I was eagerly looking forward to the day when I should see Leschetizky again, and should have made enough progress to begin lessons with him. Altenmarkt eventually became a place of real importance to me. It was a charming hamlet of about two hundred peasants, all very curious about the little foreigners who had come to this remote place to study music. Why had we come there, and who was the great man our parents had sent us so far to know? They were sure that there were men in Vienna who knew a great deal, but they supposed there were some in our countries who knew a lot more. But surely there could not be a place more beautiful than Vienna! Later I used to leave Vienna, when I had special studying to do, and go out to the cottage of these hospitable people, where there was actually a good grand piano, the wedding gift of the father of the girl who had married a man from a much larger village in Austria. This stranger had a great reputation in Altenmarkt; he read books, and, according to his admirers, knew some of them by heart. However, a few years later he utterly disappeared, and when I appeared at the familiar door one day, after sending telegrams that I was coming, and receiving no answer, I found strange forbidding-looking faces instead of the kind ones I had known. The belief was that the burgomaster had gone to America to join his summer guests! As a matter of fact, his wife had not heard from him for two or three years and believed he was dead. Many of the peasants in this little place had suffered greatly from the disappearance of this man — the burgomaster, who had taken all the money from the town with him, and as they were suspicious and superstitious, as well as ignorant, they treated his wife unkindly for a time. She asked me if I would walk down the street with her to convince the people that her husband's whereabouts were unknown to us Americans. In seven years he had not returned; but the peasants, seeing their mistake, grew to like and trust us again.

But that first summer, when everything was serene and beautiful, there were three of us who studied the piano, and we vied with one another in making as quick preparation as possible for the lessons with Leschetizky.

Three months of preparation brought me to that

coveted goal. Late in November we went back to Vienna, and the lesson was arranged, to which I brought the first three Czerny studies, Op. 740, and three small pieces. To my delight, the lesson went off successfully.

"You have shown temperament," Leschetizky told me; "now we will see if it is your own, or if it is due to the teaching of Fräulein Prentner; at any rate, you need not continue any longer with an assistant, but come every week to me."

In the then uncertain and undeveloped state of my musical training those first lessons seemed to focus about one important point which illumined everything I studied. This point was impressively put to me the first time I played those three Czerny studies for Leschetizky. Much piano technique was contained in these Czerny studies; but technique, he explained, was of very little value in itself, and was useful only as a means of expressing beauty. He talked at once of a threefold process of mind, eye, and ear; the lack of one of those essentials of talent was a serious matter in the development of an artist. Some had a good memory, but the ear was either naturally deficient, or was not trained to listen; others had, perhaps, great powers of expression in tones, but with no "keyboard sense" whatsoever, and this he attributed to a lack of training of the eye. He used to say also that getting to the bottom of the keys in playing was a question of eye as much as of touch. The real pianist, as distinguished from the "piano player," had these three qualities, either naturally or developed. But Leschetizky attacked them separately.

He began to teach me where to look in learning a piece; and then, when I had become familiar with all the positions, he would call upon me to try to hear at last what I was playing. I supposed, of course, that I had heard, but according to his meaning of the word, I may have never really heard at all.

In all my lessons there was never much said about technique. On one occasion, where I lacked tone and asked him if I should use the thumb, "Of course," he said, "use the thumb. Use the finger that is the most suitable at the time. Learn several different fingerings, and then judge which is the best one. One only helps the other; but I should say, at this particular place, that if you had ten thumbs, you should put them all on that one note. This is the way it should sound," he would always say, and then play a few notes himself. "Train your eye and ear," he always reiterated, "and the rest will take care of itself."

In time one became accustomed to trying to imitate him. If the ear were not trained well enough to accomplish this at once, he would advise with great patience trying again slowly — "at a snail's pace." Sitting at his piano, perhaps without even looking up, he would say, "The third finger is too loud; I would take the thumb there," or, looking at the hands, "The fifth finger is not yet strong enough."

If these ideas of his about learning to play were more generally understood, it would silence, once for all, those critics who have judged Leschetizky from the reports of his untalented and unobserving pupils, and those who claimed that his title to fame was derived more from his ability to give a technical equipment to the student than from his skill in developing the means of musical expression. In

Stuttgart they had talked to me about technique, but in Vienna I heard very little about it. Technique seemed to be only a clever and intelligent way of doing things. Strong fingers, Leschetizky claimed, could be acquired in many ways besides thumping the piano. As for that hard and fast Leschetizky method of which we heard so much, I soon discovered its very elastic texture.

While living in Altenmarkt, I had formed a life-long friendship with two American girls, two sisters from Winchester, Virginia. One of them, Virginia Cover, a most talented and accomplished girl, who all too soon gave up her music for marriage, was also being prepared for Leschetizky. We each had our peculiar difficulties. I had to make my hand heavier; she had to make hers lighter. We tried all sorts of tricks to hurry up the process; paper wads between the fingers while we practiced, and, in my friend's case, a strap, which she wore every night on her double-jointed thumb. Our hands were quite different, but we studied along the same lines, not guessing what significance this physical difference would have for Leschetizky, when we should come to him for lessons.

We finished our preparation at about the same time, and at the second lesson each was given a Beethoven sonata to study. Of course we set out to help each other. My friend had her lesson first and told me everything she could remember about it; I even appropriated the fingerings. When my turn came and I began to play the first movement, Leschetizky looked at me in surprise and exclaimed, "What made you do a thing like that? It is not necessary or becoming to you at all. And your hand will never do it." Then, seeing my pages black with pencil marks, he laughed, and told me he was afraid I had not understood him at the last lesson. "It is not always easy for two people to come to the same understanding of terms," he said, "we must learn to understand each other at the piano." As he went back to his piano I heard him say, "Really, must I do that all over again?"

In amazement I explained that I had never played the sonata for him at all. It was then that he recalled my friend's lesson, and instantly there came to him a picture of her heavy, strong hand. Although annoyed with himself at having confused us, he at once took the greatest interest in showing me how differently I must attack every difficulty in the piece. Not only must the fingering be altered, but even the tempos and shadings. My friend had undertaken to write down all his suggestions of interpretation, and these I had conscientiously transcribed to my own copy and put them in practice as well as I could.

"Oh, yes," he said, "you have 'stitched' in these expressions," and, taking a pencil, he erased every mark on the page. "If one wishes to remember some special point," he said, " it is better merely to put a cross over that place in the music as a reminder. Always ask yourself questions, and try to find out for yourself what is the best way."

Here, then, for me were two illuminating ideas: one, that the ear must memorize, and the other, that a piece should require even different interpretations by two people of contrasting physical characteristics and temperaments.

The first of the celebrated "class" meetings was held that year early in December. It would be quite impossible to exaggerate the importance of

these occasions to the students or to Leschetizky.
We met at about five o'clock in the afternoon, and
so far from there being any real formality, the atmosphere was very festive and exciting. Leschetizky was happy on those occasions, and always appeared with his white hair beautifully dressed and
curled for "his family," as he called his pupils.
Nothing was allowed to interfere with these
Wednesday afternoon private concerts, called the
"class."

It was the master's purpose to make the conditions as difficult as possible for those who played.

"Learn to play in public here," he said, "and if
you can do it here you can do it anywhere."

He said that for twenty-five years he had kept a
record of every piece played in the class and the
name of every student who performed. About one
hundred and fifty students made up the class, and
from them a half dozen or so, who had good lessons,
or who were preparing for concerts, were asked to
play. I had heard rumors of some who had actually broken down there; and this, I discovered, was
as great an offense and affront to the class as it
would be to an audience.

I was a bit overwhelmed, knowing the brilliant
students who were part of that season's class,
when Leschetizky asked me at my second lesson if
I did not wish to play. Ossip Gabrilowitsch was
there; also Katherine Goodson, George Proctor of
Boston, Arthur Schnabel, and Bertha Jahn, the
class prodigies. When Wednesday came and the
class assembled, Leschetizky made out a list of those
who were going to play, and, pointing his finger at
me, said suddenly, "You are going to play to-day."
To my inquiry as to what I should play, he rejoined

mischievously, "Oh, you have so much to choose from?" I gave him the names of the three pieces I had played in my lesson that week and waited my turn to play. The first went well, and I was about to go on to the second, a mazurka of his own, when he stopped me.

"Wait a moment. Can't you make a little modulation from the first piece to the second?" he asked.

I told him I was afraid I could not.

"Have you never studied harmony?" was the next question.

"Not yet, Professor," I answered. Whereupon I was painfully aware of amusement in the class. There were gasps in one corner, commiseration in another, and all around me a buzz of speculations as to how Leschetizky would receive this announcement.

"Not yet," he repeated, "but you have played Liszt rhapsodies; that is real American."

Turning to Arthur Schnabel, who was then a boy of eight or nine, Leschetizky asked him to come forward and make a modulation for the lady. The use of the word "lady" made me realize in a moment that I was a grown-up beside this boy, who made my modulation with the greatest ease and beauty, and that I must have cut a ridiculous figure in Leschetizky's eyes by playing Beethoven sonatas and Liszt rhapsodies without a knowledge of the barest elements of theory.

That first trying experience in the class stamped on my mind the conviction that there were other elements in the education of a musician besides technique. As I look back upon my first two years in Vienna, I know that a great deal of the subtlety and finesse in Leschetizky's teaching were lost on me. I was young and impressionable; and the many-sided, highly-colored Viennese life had an irresistible fascination for me. Just to be there was delightful; the splendor of royal and military functions thrilled me; it was all like looking on at a colorful and absorbing play, and though visions of handsome officers and brilliant cafés sometimes interfered with complete concentration, an awakening imagination must have compensated Leschetizky for my lack in other directions, else he never would have shown such wonderful patience in reiterating those principles which lay at the foundation of all beautiful piano playing as he taught it. "To listen," "always to listen" and "to open one's ears," were phrases he used again and again.

"Play the first half of your phrase," he would tell me, "then stop and listen to it over again without playing it. When you crossed the ocean, did you not often go to the stern, and look back upon the track that your steamer had made; there is really no track, but you know exactly the course your ship has taken. And you know how, when you have said an emotional thing to a person, it becomes clearer and clearer as you reflect upon it; you remember the tone better than anything else. Then, perhaps, you will run back and apologize for your remarks if the tone has been unwarranted. Or, if you have spoken weakly, you wish you had been more forceful. If you study the first part of your phrase, trying to hear over again the exact tone you have used, you will always know what to do with the second half."

There was a little game to which Leschetizky often resorted to help one learn how to carry a phrase in one's mind: on one side of the piano he put a plate of beans, and on the other an empty plate. First one had to idealize the phrase—hear it played with all the taste and beauty imaginable. Then, if it was played correctly, a bean was transferred to the empty plate. Another attempt, if successful, brought a second bean to join the first, and so on, until all the beans were transferred to the once empty plate. But if the phrase went badly just once, all the beans had to go back, and the process began afresh. It was a splendid lesson in concentration and worked beautifully, not only with children, but with grown-ups as well, who were in the habit of repeating a phrase over and over again, never stopping to think of improving it before repetition. This game brought about great respect for the beans, which, in the end, were treated as solemnly as an audience.

If humor could press home a point, Leschetizky never failed to make use of it. I can never forget my surprise and chagrin when he came into the room one day, apparently ill, and gave me this reproachful greeting, "You, my dear pupil, are to blame for this; you played so coldly at your last lesson that you have given me rheumatism."

Leschetizky never missed an opportunity to impress upon me that one's best study could be done away from the piano. He habitually carried some phrase in his mind, and would often go on a long walk to study how best to play the piece. One could more easily imagine the beauties of music, he said, than one could reveal them in actual playing. Tempos and shadings could be learned away from the piano, much time could be saved, and the repertoire could be extended by studying while walking or seated in a train. Listening to the inward singing of a phrase was of far more value than playing it a dozen times.

Nothing annoyed and disappointed Leschetizky more than the failure "to open one's ears" and listen. There was one pupil who had studied with him for several years and had developed a conventional big technique, coming at last to the stage where the master was willing to hear him play the Schumann "Fantasy." That was really a point of arrival, for the "Fantasy" was a great favorite with Leschetizky, and he would tolerate nothing but the most beautiful performance of it.

He listened intently to the first phrase, and, stepping to the piano, said dramatically, "Good-by." The pianist was too much amazed to comprehend his meaning, and Leschetizky repeated, "Good-by—I really mean it," he said, "and we shall never meet again at the piano; a man who would play that first phrase like that would murder his mother."

Of course, as the time approached for me to go home, I tried very hard to remember everything Leschetizky had told me, because I had little hope of ever coming back to him. The three years which I had spent in Europe seemed to me a very short time, but my parents considered it altogether too long. Fearing I might become too much the European, my father had sent my sister Mary to join me at the beginning of the third year, with the message that we were to enjoy ourselves that last year, go to Italy if we liked, but, above all, return to him happy and content to remain at home.

My sister began to study the violin, but gave it up for the sake of her voice, which a good teacher in Vienna thought very beautiful; and Leschetizky, who was very critical of voices, encouraged her. In consequence, she, too, became very serious in her attitude toward a career of music.

At the end of the third year my aunt, my sister, and I went home, and, as I expected, my father met every word about further study in Europe with utter disapproval. We were pale-looking; we were becoming foreign in our ways; we spoke of careers, and of royalty; and, worst of all, I had returned with feelings of veneration and awe for my master, Leschetizky! I had also returned bitterly dissatisfied with myself, and, it must be confessed, my playing was anything but enjoyable to listeners. I was overcome with a sense of my own deficiency; I had tried to gain strength and technique, but my few big pieces remained in a half-learned condition. Two or three small compositions were really all that I had to show for three years' study in Europe. These were either thoughtfully and timidly played, or else in a style too hard and unwieldy. It was not possible in two years' study with Leschetizky to get the best from him, unless one were far advanced. If one had learned to listen to tones, that was in itself a great lesson, but rather discouraging in the process. Nobody approved of my playing; my father did not like it at all, and took a very resentful attitude toward "that old man in Vienna," as he expressed it. He could have throttled Leschetizky for every word of discouragement, or, indeed, anything he had said that was not complimentary. But my mother, who was very artistic herself and had great sympathy with our tastes and aspirations, now quietly paved the way for us to return to our studies.

We at last managed to sail, after a few months at home, with the promise of one more year in Europe.

CHAPTER III

On Thanksgiving Day we reached Vienna, my sister to study singing, and I for one last year with Leschetizky. We were happy, indeed overjoyed, as we arrived there in a beautiful snow storm, and went at once to the Embassy to celebrate Thanksgiving and to see our friends.

Of course, I was all eagerness to see Leschetizky again, and to go to the house, with which I had so many pleasant associations, all the more valuable to me now, since I had had such difficulty in coming back. He lived in the Währing Cottage. His villa was large and roomy, and, on entering it, one had the impression of intense activity within.

To the right of the entrance hall was the dining room; straight ahead the large music room, and a smaller room filled with shelves of old music. In the music room, at the end next to the dining room, were two large grand pianos, side by side, one furnished by Bösendorfer of Vienna, and the other by Bechstein of Berlin. They were covered with piles of music kept in perfect order by Leschetizky, according to a system of his own whereby he could instantly find any composition he wanted.

Here were famous old copies with marks by the composers themselves, precious documents to Leschetizky. Near the piano were the marble busts of Annette Essipoff and of Chopin. Whenever the pianos became worn in the slightest degree by usage, they were quickly exchanged for better ones by the manufacturers.

The pupils sat at the Bösendorfer and Lesch-

21

etizky at the Bechstein. If any pupil were unfortunate enough to break a string, Leschetizky, however displeased, would himself instantly put a new one on, and tune the instrument.

Beyond the music room was a balcony with steps leading down to a lovely garden, thick with trees and shrubbery, and far away, down a path, could be seen a large bust of Beethoven. During the hours of the classes one often awaited one's turn to play, pacing up and down this garden, hoping that no one would come to interrupt the misery.

In the rooms on the second floor, where Madame Eugenie, his wife and former pupil, had her rooms and practiced, were pianos of other makes — a Blüthner and a Steinway, the best instruments these firms could furnish.

On the third floor lived Leschetizky's old friend, Mr. Minkus, a Russian violinist, whose public career was ended. His health was failing, and Leschetizky had invited him to spend his last years under his roof. He played most beautifully, and I was often sent up to him for practice of chamber music.

Downstairs, to the left of the hall, was a small room, called the "torture chamber" by the students, where they waited their turn for lessons. The hours spent in that room were filled with varied emotions. If one heard shouts of rage from Leschetizky, one shuddered for what might possibly be his own fate later; and listening outside, one was almost as alarmed to hear playing that made him cheerful and happy, or so far beyond one's own present possibilities that there was great danger of not being able to prolong his good mood. The shouts of rage usually meant that the pupil was

playing unrhythmically. This had the worst possible effect upon Leschetizky. As he came downstairs one morning, a pupil was heard inquiring of
the butler if the Professor was in a good humor.
Leschetizky overheard and stepped quickly forward. "My dear girl," he said, "my humor depends
on the playing I hear. I hardly think I could live
through the kind of day I had yesterday—every one
unrhythmical." There were naturally all kinds of
lessons: poor lessons by good pupils, good lessons by
pupils he expected little of; but if the pupil had no
rhythmical sense, it was better to study with some
one else, unless he had real heroism. In after years
I learned how much tact and sympathy and discretion were needed in that room, to greet the returning
pupil, elated or despairing, as the case might be,
and also to appreciate the kindness and sweetness
that had been shown me in my various moods on
returning to that room for my hat and coat.

After several trips to the Währing Cottage only
to find that each time Leschetizky was too busy to
see me, I soon suspected that something was wrong.
However, the delight of being once more in Vienna
mitigated any feeling of uneasiness, and, with my
sister, I sent out invitations for a large "At home."
Of course, most of the pupils made it a point to be
in Vienna early in autumn, and it did not occur to
me that Leschetizky might be annoyed at my late
return. Our social activities must have seemed to
him very foolish; and, without knowing the difficulties I had overcome in returning to Europe to
study again, he denounced me before the class in a
way I have never forgotten.

Before I went home I had had weekly lessons
from him, but this time it was January before I

found it possible to get a lesson at all. Just before
the first class of the new year one was arranged, and
it proved to be a memorable affair for me. I expressed myself as very happy to be in his rooms
again, and he said he was very glad to see me, but
his manner was so cold that I was utterly bewildered.

"Sit down," he said, "and let's have a little talk.
Now, you are a very charming girl, and I like you
very much, but I have found another teacher for
you. You know, I am too difficult for you to study
with. You should be able to have a good time here
in Vienna, and not have to study so hard as you
have to study with me. I hear that Alfred Grünfeld is a little more lenient toward his pupils than I
am. He is a very agreeable person, plays beautifully, and is a splendid teacher. You will have far
more time to enjoy yourself and to give teas in
Vienna."

For the first time I found Leschetizky thoroughly
cross with me. My heart sank with every word he
said, and I was very much overwhelmed. Finally
he did consent to hear me play, and promised to
think over the matter of giving me further lessons
if I really felt serious about it. I had prepared the
Schumann "Concerto" for this lesson, but nothing
about it pleased him. After the first movement he
closed the pages, told me to put the "Concerto"
away and not to bring it to him again for at least
two years.

Then came the first class. We were all assembled.
Leschetizky entered the room, scratching his head
in a way familiar to those who knew him well. It
always meant trouble of some sort. He made a
short speech.

"This is the first class of the year, and I hope in this year to accomplish great things. Let us begin at once. Who is going to play?"

Somehow every one seemed petrified, which only increased his nervousness.

"This is all nonsense," he continued. "I want those who are going to play to-night to give their names at once."

Seven or eight arose at that, but, as I was not going to play, I remained seated.

Turning abruptly to the whole class, he said, "If there is any one here to-night who has been in the habit of playing and does not give his name at once, that person may leave the room and not come out here again, where there are serious people."

Gradually I became aware that every one in the room was looking at me.

Half dazed, I arose to my feet, and said, "If you mean me, Professor, I have nothing to play."

"Of course I mean you. I want this company to know that you have come to Europe to drink tea. You have been spoiled by me; you have been spoiled by everybody. Now there is something else in life besides being spoiled."

I sat down in the bitterest confusion and dismay, but Leschetizky knew that he had hurt me enough, and that was all he wanted.

At that instant I resolved that my study should turn toward some point and purpose. It was one thing to resolve, and another to accomplish. My attitude had changed, but he was still suspicious of my real seriousness in study. It was not long after that painful experience in the class that he told me I forgot half the fine points in the lesson by meeting people on the way home, going out to tea, or amusing myself in some other way, when I should go quietly home by myself and think over the lesson. There was a little chapel about ten minutes' walk from his house, and after that I formed the habit of stopping in there until there was no more danger of meeting my friends.

A lesson with Leschetizky was highly instructive in many ways. Often there was very little playing in the lesson. Sometimes he would hear a piece through in silence, and then quietly remark at the end, "Well, do you like it that way?"

More often a great deal of the time was taken up with conversation. It was always a disappointment to him if the pupil failed to grasp his meaning and apply it to the music. If a piece was really well played, one would usually hear from him, "Don't you want to play this in the class?" And if one demurred, "Well, you should want to, it is good practice. It is like walking up to the cannons to play a piece the first time before an audience. The wise one will gather his friends, and also his enemies together, and try to please them. Yes, before a concert it is necessary to practice before people. Make them listen to you whether they want to do so or not. Scratch on the doors to be allowed to play. You may think you have a piece learned, but you never know until you have tried it in public. Of course, if you had imagination enough this would not be necessary. You might fancy yourself before an audience at home, come out and bow to it, and then see how nervous you would be. Even then, you never know what kind of audience you are going to have, or how it will affect you."

One pupil took exception to this advice, believing that a piece properly learned would go just as well in public the first time as after repeated tests. She was expecting to appear with orchestra in Germany at the end of the year, but persistently refused to try the concerto before the other students.

"Well, let her see," said Leschetizky. After a very unsuccessful performance on account of nervous strain, she returned, and humbly begged to be allowed to play the Heller "Preludes" in class. On the other hand, it was only when the piece had been brought to a professional standard that one was asked to play in the class. I once brought to him a very difficult composition which I hoped to have ready for the class in a few weeks. It was quite unfinished technically. He threw the book on the floor in a rage, and exclaimed, "How can you be so foolish? That will not be ready to play in six months. You must not become one of those pianists who have to work themselves into a frenzy at the last moment."

I began to see that a great deal of one's happiness with him depended upon how one acquitted oneself in the class. He was then as much the critic as the master; and he was delighted if one succeeded, miserable and displeased if one failed.

The pupils who had played were asked to stay to supper, and the better one had played the nearer to Leschetizky one was allowed to sit at table. There was often enthusiastic reference made to the very good playing, or a kindly criticism of the playing less good. "Bertha Jahn is the only one to-night," he said once, "who succeeded in getting the touch of the new Bösendorfer piano. The rest of you failed," he said smilingly. "We are a truthful family here. It is good practice to criticize if we do it with intelligence and without prejudice.

Of course, it is human to be prejudiced and partial. I cannot help being so myself," he said. "How can I help liking to see a not ugly-looking young girl like Bertha, who half the time does not know how well she plays, go to the piano quite simply and strike first notes with such beautiful tones?

"Ladies and gentlemen," he went on, rising, "first let me tell you what great pleasure one or two of you have given me this evening. There is one down there hanging his head, but he need not do it, it was only bad judgment in taking too fast a tempo. That happens to every one; indeed, no less a person than Rubinstein made such mistakes, and told me once (you will excuse me) he could have spit in his face for beginning the last movement so fast. But another has suddenly begun to be artistic, and two or three are on the right road." Looking in another direction, he said, "We have in reality no shattered hopes here to-night. We have, moreover, very little chance here for jealousies and affectations, for we have to come forward every now and then and show exactly what we can do. It is easy enough to think you are a great man when you are not obliged to prove it." And so he would go on at these suppers.

Toward faults of memory he was more lenient than anything else. I have seen him sitting at the other piano running his fingers over the keys while the pupils played to supply the notes where a possible slip of memory might occur; but I have also seen pupils sent from the room after one chord which had been badly attacked. Wrong notes disturbed him greatly.

"Is there any one in this room who can play without striking wrong notes?" he called out one

evening. Then, turning to a row of long-haired
young men standing at the back of the room, he
said, "Come up here, one of you, and see if your
long hair will help you to do it any better."

What to him were probably the most serious
faults were bad phrasing and a failure to listen to
one's own playing so as to judge the relationship
of one tone to another. Before us all he knelt at the
bust of Chopin one evening, and exclaimed, "Oh,
Chopin, forgive us for what has been done to thy
music in this room!"

My most painful recollection is of the time when I
disappointed him in the Tschaikowsky "Concerto."
At one of my lessons he said to me, "Your technique
is now at a point where you can very easily learn
the Tschaikowsky 'Concerto.' That is one of the
easiest to play if one has technique enough."

The following week I brought it to the lesson.
He thought there was no reason why I should not
play it in the class two days later. I thought otherwise and did not intend to do so unless he particularly wished it. When Wednesday evening came,
I was startled to hear him begin a speech by saying
how quickly a thing could be learned, if the technique "machinery" were in order.

"It is perfectly possible," he said, "to learn a
great composition in a few days, as actors learn their
rôles overnight. One of us has prepared the Tschaikowsky 'Concerto' in a week, and will play it."

I said, "Ten days, Professor."

"A very quickly learned concerto," he rejoined.

Some of the artists who were present crowded
round the piano where I sat trembling so that I
could scarcely keep my feet on the pedals. He
began the orchestral part with great fire and car-

ried me along through the first movement. The
second movement pleased him too. He loved to
play this concerto, and plunged enthusiastically
into the third movement, where I suddenly left out
a whole page of repetition, and only great quickness on his part saved us from collapse. We finished
the piece, but the enthusiasm was gone. At supper
that evening there were no speeches! In the suc-
ceeding lessons I found him so depressed and disappointed that I was in a wretched mood for
weeks.

It was a long time before I succeeded in pleasing
him by anything I did. Some small, carefully
learned pieces for one lesson brought no encouragement to me from Leschetizky. I looked into
his face in vain for any sign of gratification or enthusiasm. Some time later, however, I pleased him
with an entirely correct performance in the class of
the Mendelssohn "Concerto in G Minor"; also by
my willingness to learn a long and difficult set of variations in manuscript by the Belgian composer,
Leopold Wallner. This manuscript had a curious
history. A musician, while walking along one of the
streets of Brussels, happened to hear good piano
playing before a certain house. She knocked at the
door and was invited to enter. Noticing a great pile
of music, all in manuscript, she asked the player if
his compositions had been published and received
the very modest reply that he had not thought it
worth while. One of these she sent to me, and
Leschetizky was delighted with it, considering it
pianistic and interesting in many ways. It was
such a laborious task to read this very illegible
manuscript that I think I won at last a bit of admiration from Leschetizky in this round-about way.

At a later lesson he turned quite seriously to me and said, "Who would think that a little blond American girl would be able to catch the rhythm of that part so correctly? It is one of the places that, if you imagine incorrectly, it is an all-day job to undo the wrong. It must be heard correctly the first time. You would be surprised if you knew with whom I spent one whole night trying to get the rhythm correct. We were tired, too, but toward morning we had it! You Americans are curious people; you have all kinds of good qualities, but they do not coördinate. You disappointed me in the Tschaikowsky 'Concerto.' No, no, not because you left out a part, but because you failed where so many fail! It was the first time I had heard you play with real freedom of rhythm and it was that that upset you.

"It frightens me, and I have yet to discover whether you can ever put freedom and sureness together. I want to know that you can," he went on, in almost pathetic tones, "for accuracy without expression isn't worth that," snapping his fingers.

"Our lessons from now on must have a different character entirely. You must play your pieces too freely for a while, and learn sureness from a different angle. Don't be afraid to express yourself. One player you may like to hear; the other, who knows far more perhaps, you do not care a bit for. Why is it? Your audience does not know either. They only know that there is something they like with the one; with the other they are more apt to say they never liked the piano anyway, and your audience longs to be pleased, and your uneducated audiences are also hard to please. They want emotion and expression more than technique. Educated audiences will give you credit for all kinds of things that the other audiences will not, and how every one loves beautiful tones and stirring rhythms! But you mustn't break down before an audience under any circumstances. They will always be nervous over you afterward."

"How easy it all sounds when it is beautiful," I said.

"Yes," he replied, "but the footlights make it difficult; and here you have them, so make the most of them, and go on playing in the class."

It was most difficult to play before these one hundred and fifty students, with Leschetizky himself sitting at the other piano. The teachers were there, who were the assistants of Leschetizky, and, of course, many of the pupils were learning the composition one was about to play. Leschetizky liked good manners at the piano, and a poor deportment made him either sarcastic or inclined to ridicule. One girl held her head too far over the piano. Leschetizky came up behind her at the end of every phrase or two and tilted her chin higher in the air. A specially confident bearing was also a dangerous offense to his sense of propriety, although he was never fond of excessive diffidence and lack of ease. If one demurred too long about playing, the second invitation from him was perhaps not forthcoming, unless there had been good reason for hesitating to play. But he was touchingly fond of supplying, himself, the deficiencies of pupils who were serious in trying to overcome them and who would not accept applause when it was unmerited. One rarely received a compliment from Leschetizky. A compliment was a great concession from him, and if one heard him say, "Not bad," it was something to be remembered.

Jan Sickescz related how miserable he was on one occasion after playing in the class, because, though every one else had seemed pleased with his playing and told him they were, Leschetizky did not say a word about it, and when he passed him, Leschetizky was silent and walked away, giving no sign of approval. Jan decided to go home and not stay to supper, and, feeling very much displeased and disheartened, he slipped quietly away without saying good-night. Some one remarked this to Leschetizky, who seemed surprised and touched. However, at their next meeting Leschetizky only scolded him roundly for his departure, and, on hearing that Jan had left because Leschetizky had not seemed pleased with his playing, went on with the scolding, telling him he must not be vain. He had received compliments enough that evening and hadn't needed any contribution from him. He had heard them all pay him compliments. "If you expect me to pay you compliments here," said Leschetizky, "well, you have come to the wrong address."

The classes were great occasions in many ways. Singers, actors and painters were usually present. Madame Frances Saville sometimes came. Therese Leschetizka came from Russia with her husband, who sang in the Opera at St. Petersburg, and one day Loie Fuller introduced her protégé, Isadora Duncan, who at that time was just beginning to dance in Europe. She arrived at Leschetizky's house after her first performance in Vienna. Leschetizky was immensely interested in her appearance that evening. She went upstairs at once and asked for lamb chops, at eleven o'clock.

"She shall have them," said Leschetizky. "Run and try to get them, some of you; be sure to get them!" he ordered, "for we must do our part this evening."

Her bare feet were a sight new to Vienna and to us, but Leschetizky begged her not to mind our levity, saying that he would turn us all out if we displeased her. Then he sat down at his Bechstein and played for her to dance as long as she would. Her manager made the fatal mistake of asking Leschetizky to sign a contract to go as her accompanist around the world, and we were all rather sorry for this *faux pas,* as we had considered it the greatest honor that he had played so long and so beautifully. He played Chopin mazurkas and his own mazurkas, followed by most beautiful improvisations, so that her great dancing became almost a secondary affair. Leschetizky was always quite willing and pleased to accompany singers. He was rarely asked to do so, but at his own house generally volunteered. Alice Barbi, whose singing Leschetizky loved, used to like to come to the classes at times, and, if she could be prevailed upon to sing, he felt greatly honored. On one particular evening she was going to sing some new songs, and, besides, wished to have some of them transposed. I happened to be the only one of the pupils she knew so she looked around and asked me to accompany her and to transpose the songs. I was embarrassed, and Leschetizky evidently noticed it, for he walked over to her instantly and asked her if she would like him to play her accompaniment. Of course she had not thought of asking him. After she had sung and had moved every one greatly with her marvelous voice and interpretation, the thought evidently struck Leschetizky that perhaps some one else had noticed my embarrassment, so he said quite loudly to me, "Did I not recommend a sonata to you to play sometime with the violinist who is coming soon?"

I started to say that he must have forgotten that I had played it to him two days before, half learned, but he gave me a sign to keep silent, and went on, "I should like to hear that sonata. Some parts of it are very beautiful, and I think the notes are here. Of course, you are only reading it, but you read well, and can give a good idea of what it is."

So I sat down and "read" the thing through beautifully; at any rate other good readers in the class crowded around us to congratulate me and said they had no idea I read so perfectly. The most difficult passages were read as well as the easy ones, and any one might have noticed the twinkle in Leschetizky's eye. Just as we were leaving, Leschetizky gave me a wink and a nod, and whispered in my ear: "Now go home and learn to read."

There was indeed not much tendency in the Leschetizky class toward superficiality or conceit. He was always quick to detect anything artificial in our behavior. The slightest evidence of conceit was noticed by him, as well as the opposite traits of diffidence and sensitiveness. He had an excellent memory for little traits of character, expression, or tones of voice; but once he became convinced of seriousness and sincerity, one felt friendship behind even the severest words.

A lack of vital interest in study and improvement was incomprehensible to him, and he was patient with, and admired, only those whose energies were equal to their desires in fulfilling their duty to their talent.

CHAPTER IV

THERE were some lessons that might be called typical lessons and this is one of my own that I well remember.

"Well, what have we to play to-day?"

"The Schumann 'Carnaval,' Herr Professor."

"Really, the Schumann 'Carnaval'! Learn the Schütt 'Carnaval' sometime too. That is also a real Carnaval. People don't play it enough—there is a very good reason why; it has to be played well, as the Schumann has to be. Nowadays it must be *more* than well played. You know, I have been talking about you to-day; Martha Schmidt was here, and we spoke of you. She says she met you in the Prater the other day, and her account of the conversation with you is not quite satisfactory." This he says laughingly, and I begin to be a little disturbed. "Oh, don't take it too seriously, or I shall think she was right. She says you were offended because she made some criticism of your technique. You were not offended, were you?"

"No, I was very much obliged to her."

"Well, she thinks you resented it, but Martha is probably right—she knows a great deal. You must remember, too, that she expresses herself more freely than you do. When you are really serious you are quiet and uncommunicative. You should be more expressive, and say what you think. People should give the correct impression of themselves. There is generally no reason for being misunderstood in this world. Of course, that is not the Viennese temperament. Now, there is Schütt, for instance. He is expressive, and sometimes might be a little less so in public. In the Bösendorfer Hall, for instance, if something delights him he begins to make love to the performer. No one is expressive enough for him. But he has written many beautiful pieces, and his 'Carnaval' is one of them. Perhaps I say too much, but parts of it to me are more beautiful than the Schumann 'Carnaval.' And how I wish I myself had written that little 'Prelude in D Major' of his! Learn to play Schütt's music as it really is, and you will become more expressive at the piano, perhaps too much so. Americans might go too far if they really got started; but I think there is not much danger of that."

This I find ambiguous, and he smiles at my confusion. Leschetizky has often said that our Puritan background has stamped us all with too much rigidity in our bearing as well as in our souls.

"But Martha told me other things, too. Martha says you have now in your repertoire three ballades of Chopin and only one Bach fugue. If I can ever find your specialty in music, I shall thank Heaven, but up to now I have not found it, and we must not become unbalanced. Better one Chopin ballade and three Bach fugues. And then, my dear child, you never learn things like the 'Etincelles' of Moszkowski. Don't be too scornful of that sort of piece. You need those pieces to complete your repertoire. You know a dinner must have the accessories. That is a piece you hand out to your audience like sweets wrapped in silver paper and served on a silver plate. There must be nothing about it that isn't perfect to the last detail. Study like Fannie Bloomfield Zeisler, who, when she has something like that to learn, extracts everything from it; she presses everything out of it—like juice from a lemon. She misses nothing. And you must also take pleasure in studying such things. They are not thick with music as is the Schumann 'Carnaval.' There is nothing special there, you understand. *You* must make them interesting and beautiful yourself.—Well, now the Schumann 'Carnaval'; we must not talk too much, some one is coming afterward.

"Do you know, this life is really killing me. I suffer so in some of the lessons. I give my heart's blood. They say 'yes,' but they play 'no.' Perhaps you will brighten me up now with the 'Carnaval' of Schumann well played. You are going to play it in the class surely."

I have just noticed a little unusual disorder in the room. Leschetizky always smokes a great deal during the lessons, and to-day there are many cigar ashes around the pianos. The chairs on one side of the room are pushed away from their usual places, which all means to me that Leschetizky has been giving a difficult and tiring lesson before mine, or perhaps more than one. He has evidently been walking also, as he often does, to indicate graceful tempos, or to show the pupil what awkward ones he is using; or he has been correcting bad pauses; or showing by suddenly plunging ahead, or drawing back, the way the pupil is playing. A glass of water near by makes me suspect that he has been tiring his voice and has probably been shouting. If a pupil played unrhythmically he generally did stop him with shouts. This is not all conducive to my happiness at the moment, but I get myself together as well as I can, and begin the Schumann "Carnaval."

"Ho, ho," he says, "well now, a little more courage to begin with! More festive than that! I was very much pleased the other night on entering the house of a friend of yours to hear a piece very well played, which I didn't know at all. A waltz of Moszkowski, you say. Well, I apologize—you *do* learn the side pieces, since it was you who were playing it. Very good—sentimental; well, the 'Carnaval' of Schumann is sentimental in places. Where one learns the true spirit of the 'Carnaval' is here, in Vienna."

I try again to make the opening chords like his. When I say I cannot, I receive a long lecture on the changes that have taken place in my tone and touch lately, especially about the fingers, which Leschetizky thinks are not now strong enough to "temper" the muscular force that my arms have acquired. He has noticed this before, he says, and I would give anything I possessed if I had not been slighting my finger technique so that my chords could roll out in the smooth way that his do without any apparent effort.

"You see, Martha Schmidt was perfectly right," he goes on. "Martha is now the best in the class." Again Leschetizky launches forth in a description of the things she has just accomplished. "She has a real interpretation for everything she plays. She goes to every concert, and comes away with an intelligent criticism. Why don't I accept a position as critic on some small newspaper in Austria or in France? Write as correspondent for Viennese concerts? Excellent practice," Leschetizky says. I begin to think that we shall not be able to play much of the "Carnaval" to-day, if we get so far afield, and I put my hands on the keys again.

"There you are, in a hurry—always in a hurry," he says. "You play hurriedly sometimes, too. And your pauses are not good." Here he compares relaxing all the muscles to the deep breathing of the singer. "And take long breaths," he says, "you will relax the muscles better then." He tells me what deep breaths Rubinstein used to take at the beginning of long phrases, and also what repose he had and what dramatic pauses. "There is more rhythm between the notes than in the notes themselves." He reminded me that Liszt used to say this. "Paula Szalit is the only one who ever asked me to tell how Rubinstein breathed. No one else ever seemed interested to know.

"Well, now once more, and go on."

I get to the second page when Leschetizky's posture at the piano attracts my attention. He sits there forlornly and really looks as if he were going to weep.

"I thought you were going to make me happy to-day," he says. And then, most dejectedly, "Really, to-day, if you do not play that part with warmth, I cannot bear to hear it. If you knew how often lately I have heard the Schumann 'Carnaval.' Play me the Schütt 'Carnaval' instead—that's fresh—that's new. I am tired of the Schumann 'Carnaval.'"

I hardly know what to do myself at this point, so I ask him if I may try it once more. The pedal is wrong.

"My dear child," he says, "God won't help you. You have to hear that yourself." This makes me laugh, and my laugh for the moment saves the situation.

"There is great charm in this part, but with you it is all lost. I admit this first part is also the most difficult. In the rest of the 'Carnaval' the expression is given, so to speak. With understanding one can play the rest better."

We proceed to the Pierrot, but I have not succeeded in dispelling his depression. Some moments of a lesson with him are very long, and he has stopped me at the first chord, and shakes his head mournfully.

"You ought to know better than that," he says. "You did the same thing at your last lesson—you do not even know what," he says. "That must not be told you twice. You must *hear* it! If a stranger heard you play that way he would say you were a very talented person, but you had a bad teacher. It isn't your strength at all, it is your ear! Why the bass so loud?" he says, coming over to my piano. "Never cover up the top when it has anything to say. Yes, that one note one calls bad, really bad," he says. I try again.

"Stop!" he calls. "Wait!" "You do not have to catch any trains, have you, or *have* you perhaps?" he said, going back to his piano. "*I* haven't any to catch, and here I sit, waiting to hear a plain A flat played with tone. I tell you, you would be the first to criticize if you heard some one else play like that! You go to a concert to have pleasure in the music, don't you? Well, it is no pleasure hearing it played that way. Now, I notice that you can learn a piece quite perfectly at first, but then you let it go, and sometimes in the end, it does not sound as you think it sounds, or the way you mean it to sound, and believe that it does sound. The right sound must be kept, and also brought out. Yes, you smile, but you should not smile just this minute. Don't you think that Mr. Sauer would have studied a whole hour on these two or three bars to bring out clearly the meaning of the notes, if he was not satisfied with them? You are not always clear, besides sometimes you must even underscore. For you it is clear, of course, because you know it, but not every one does know. Besides there will be some who know it so well that they suspect you do not. You have a brain for this purpose, and you must not be satisfied because you understand the notes yourself. The other one must understand them, too. On occasions one uses the brain, you see."

"Yes," I say, and try to smile.

"Until you learn to think an hour for every hour you play, you have not learned to study.

"We have come to the end of the Pierrot. You mustn't distort him," he says. "Just the same Pierrot had some noble instincts; he was a loving creature, too."

We get over to the Eusebius, and I cannot please him. Every phrase seems to depend on the way one plays the one preceding, and every time Leschetizky plays the whole so differently that I am discouraged, and beg to be allowed to leave it until another time.

"Not at all. Not at all," he says. "You will go home, and think and think, and come no nearer to it. This is a question of touch and tempo, and if you will only listen better! Why, some people learn a language by listening, and never see a book. The grammar will not teach you how to play this part. Stop thinking now, for a moment, and listen." Leschetizky plays this part again, but still very differently.

"It cannot be the same every time," he says. "Don't try so hard, but let your good ear direct you." In the second half he jumps impatiently from his chair and shows me by stiff and jerky motions what my rhythm has been.

"I would like to let it go as well as you would," he says, "but we must not leave it this way. It must be richer and fuller. There are no bare branches here. You must have the leaves on the trees. One does not become an artist in a day," he remarks. "There are so many qualities that go toward the playing of this one part: warmth, abandon, and fine shading, and intense listening, and will power—all those things besides the notes."

I have not even followed the marks of shading in the good Peter's edition. "It would be so much easier to be more attentive to those marks," he said, "unless, indeed, one could make better marks oneself, and some do not even take the trouble to find out the meaning of the names—Estrella, Florestan, etc."

Leschetizky hates nothing more than dejection on the part of a pupil. I start out as bravely as I can with the next, and also finish the one called Coquette.

"Deceiver!" is his one word when I finish. A smile or a laugh or a pleasantry always made everything better in the lessons and, when he reiterates "Deceiver," I think the best thing I can say is, "I believe you are right," which brings a smile to his face.

"Of course," he says, "you know the meaning of coquette as well as any one. Well then, since you have understood me, let us go on."

I realize now that I must play and not be stupid, and that if I have studied the piece well at all, I must at least do something that will show a little spirit and initiative.

"Yes, I know you can do it," he remarks, "but then, why so timid in the beginning? Timidity in feeling is no good. The tempos are the manners, in one sense, and your manners in playing are too timid."

In another place I have tried to make a difficult technical passage easier by playing some of the notes with the left hand, which belong to the right. The change is too conspicuous and makes it appear that my technique is not adequate.

"Play it as it is written," he tells me. "This is a General's piece, and you must play it like a General."

I ask him if it is good at another place.

"No," he sings out. "You lost some of the tones there. Begin at the eleventh bar."

At my failure to do this instantly he laughs at some thought of his own.

"Must you begin back at the stove?" he says.

"Stove?" I repeat. He only laughs the more.

"You do not want to be like the dancer.—Yes, there was a dancer once who always had to begin back at the stove when he broke down, because he had always started at the stove."

I see the application of this, as I am unable to begin at any bar, and have to go back to the first.

"You must be able to begin at any measure," he says, "or you will always be nervous over slips of memory. When you make a mistake, study it. The mistake makes the right way clearer."

"Why did you stop?" he questions me at another place. "It was good. Go on, go on! Play ideally, child, *ideally*. That is all that is required of one."

We now have a long conversation about the different interpretations that have been given the Reconnaissance. Paderewski had once played it, so, Rosenthal and D'Albert in another way, and one or two of the pupils had actually done something unusual and beautiful. The fingering made some difference in interpretation. As we proceed, he criticizes my pianissimo. It is not singing enough. One place should be piously played. He turns to me with a sly twinkle in his eye, and asks if I do not know what it is to be pious.

"Well," he goes on, "I am not afraid of the Davidsbündler. Your rhythm is all right. Those are the easy things for you, but there is the danger. They must be well finished, too, or else you will disappoint your good friends. You must surprise rather than disappoint. Never disappoint an audience. You have studied well this week," he says, "and learning to study well is the main thing. It is half the battle."

I am overjoyed to hear this from him, as my last lesson was rather a mystery to me.

Some one comes in to ask if the pupils who have waited so long shall continue to wait. Leschetizky apologizes and says, "No, I cannot do any more to-day."

We go into the dining room, and I am invited to have dinner with him, all the conversation turning toward Schumann and Schütt and the various artists who have interpreted the Schumann "Carnaval" to please great audiences.

CHAPTER V

"Well, it will be good to hear some Beethoven," Leschetizky began, at a particular lesson. "To-day I have heard nothing but waltzes, mazurkas, capriccios. Besides, I have had—you cannot imagine the people that have come to me during the last few days, wanting to know *exactly* how this and that was done. One even asked me what program for my feelings I had in certain pieces. If he could know *that,* he said, he would not ask for any other instruction. They all wanted names for pieces; they wanted names for all the emotions: one does not know whether to laugh or cry. There have been some singers here. One tenor left his book of Schumann songs here on the piano, and I looked it over because he had written down a great many words to indicate what feelings were proper. I must tell you this, and you will laugh. Look at this: 'Tears of joy.'

> Whenever I gaze within thine eyes,
> All care and sorrow swiftly flies.
> > (*Feel happy, and look rapturous.*)
> And when I kiss thy lips so sweet,
> My cure is perfect and complete.
> > (*Shake yourself a little, and look heavenward.*)
> And when I lean upon thy breast
> > (*Fright.*)

"Wonderful!" Leschetizky exclaimed.

"Now, the pianists try to do the same in a different way. This is no joke at all. There are many who spend valuable time tabulating their emotions, and inventing a story to tell the music by, instead of letting the music tell the story. It is all bosh!" he said. "What would such a one write for the 'Sonata Appassionata,' for instance?

"You will have an experience to-day," he said. "There are now some teachers here who want to listen to lessons. There are two very dignified ones coming to-day, if you do not mind, two ladies highly recommended as teachers, but yours is the last lesson, and I have plenty of time with nothing to think of, nothing to worry about until to-morrow. What are you going to do this evening? Are you tired, or are you going to be tired? Get the beautiful Elise, and we will go somewhere—somewhere, I don't know where; does it matter? We will go to Pötzleinsdorf to supper, where there's the little garden and we can talk. Oh, I've forgotten: I thought I was free now for the rest of the day and night. But no, Madame —— is here, and we are going to one of her twenty-course dinners. All champagne, no beer at all! I like beer also at the dinner. But all those twenty courses, or so—it's really too tiresome. I won't go! I will tell you now what we shall do. I shall be ill and suffering, and in need of rest and a walk into the country. I'll steal out to Pötzleinsdorf, and if you and Elise, or Schütt, or Jane, or Mary should happen to be there,—well, it will not be our fault if we are not unhappy! We could meet out in the other direction, and walk over the road Beethoven often walked. Have you ever been to the Central Cemetery? You know the tragic story of the Theater

an der Wien? Years ago they were giving a performance of the 'Tales of Hoffman,' when a fire
broke out. As the poor people tried to get out, the
big front door fell in—pushed down by the people
outside trying to open it to save them. It made the
theater nothing but a trap, and nearly every one was
burned to death. There are hundreds and hundreds of little graves in the Central Cemetery, and
the opera has never been performed since that time.
The Emperor forbade it. Some one ought to go to
the Emperor and ask him for permission to have it
brought out again. I think I will go to him myself. The Emperor is a wonderful man in many
ways. Beethoven would have respected him. His
Majesty does not know much about art, but then
he does not pretend to know. However, he is
proud of some accomplishments, for example, of
his skill at billiards. One of his friends was ban-
ished last summer for having once allowed himself
to win a game from the Emperor. But the Emperor is, on the whole, not unkind; and you and
Elise will have seen for yourselves how he can
smile and return your curtsies with a charming bow
and salute. In Ischl, of course, he is free and happier, and likes well enough to see pretty ladies
dropping him curtsies on the woody road.—You
had the white dress last summer, and Elise the blue,
or gray, no, it was blue—her eyes were not so blue
as the dress. What a pity that she gave up her
piano! She who had leisure, good taste, personality, and great beauty of person and character.
Oh, I weep to think of her! Only courage she
lacked. She played the Mendelssohn 'Concerto'
very well, very well indeed. It was the first time

that she had played in the class. She closed her piano the next day, feeling that she could never be an artist. You remember, the cartman was ordered to take her piano away as soon as possible. Really, it is too sad; but, of course, one must realize how necessary it is to get accustomed to playing before people. That is always an ordeal at first, and has to be studied as well as anything else. But now I never speak to her about it, and we remain the best of friends even without the piano—perhaps really better friends, because I know her better. I see her whole character. She is a noble soul. Oh, if more pianists had her qualities! We'll meet to-night, I hope. . . . One thing more I had on my mind. I want to get the 'Tales of Hoffman' unearthed, and I think really of going to the Emperor about it. When are you going to study the 'Appassionata?' You must have the notes of that learned for a long time. It is not difficult to learn, but you must be able to think over the phrases and parts for a long time. This part—the middle movement—is not your pleasant walk in the country. Beethoven was walking up to the altar—in his imagination, at least—and he didn't crawl, not he! He walked with his head up. It's all religious— every bit—but pagan, you understand, not too Christian. It's not humble; it is beautifully proud. Go into the Votive Kirche on your way home, and walk up the aisle in this spirit, and you will know how to play this part. There's more tenderness in the first movement. Paderewski plays that movement better than any one else in the world. He puts something in it—I do not know what—but— well, you feel glad you are alive! You know I was curious to see him again after he first went to America, England, and France. I thought the success might spoil him, but it only made him play better. At the first chords he played me when he returned, I said to myself, 'No, he's all right.' Nothing will ever hinder his progress. And he has fantasy. He is far from tabulating his emotions, far from that. He is free of all that nonsense. There is not one of these Beethoven sonatas that should be limited to a program of feeling. Read carefully the Hanslick book. It is not infallible, but you will find valuable suggestions well worth thinking over.—But to play that first movement well, you must have a love for all the world. It does not matter for what part of the world you have the greatest affection and longing, but it must show in your playing. Hanslick speaks of an adjective playing, and his ideas are sound. This is a tender passage; this is a noble sentence; here are proud crescendos, the tones march on proudly; then you are depressed and languid. Give yourself to these sonatas. . . . Now, play me the theme of your sonata, the 'A Flat Major.' I used to play this sonata a great deal."

He listens as I play him the theme.

"It is too torn up," he comments, turning around; "it lacks what the Italians call *desinvoltura*. Why is that in your playing, I would like to know. You have two or three poor qualities that we will speak about. They exist more in your playing than in your manner otherwise; I do not notice them in your personal bearing. I wish you would talk more about yourself; it is good practice, and helps me too. I do not know whether your life has been sad or merry. You do not smile any too much.

Your sister smiles more. But even if you smiled all the time, I should not know whether it disguised your real feelings or not. Some people smile when they are sad; others look serious when they have not a serious thought in their heads and never did have. You have friends with sour faces, one in particular. I am sure he does not smile in his soul. One must smile in one's soul. That is everything. I am afraid of those people who never smile. Your friend sometimes comes to see me, but he looks as if he had nothing but enemies. He is very polite. Do you like him, really? You can say anything you like to me.

"You have two or three little habits also. Don't be shocked; they are not very bad ones." I cannot help interrupting him, "Did you mean to imitate me the other day, when you held your right hand across your waist as you walked across the room?" "Yes, I did," he answers. "There is something about that little mannerism of yours that I do not like. Let me see your hand. Let your hand lie in your lap. Well, you have been studying hard I see; your hand has taken on strength and character, and begins to look like a pianist's hand, but, when you hold it up that way (that has become habitual with you), it looks weak and white and ineffective. It disturbs me always, excuse me, but it does, and I can't deny it. It is a good thing always to have about you a certain amount of self-criticism, not too much to make you self-conscious, but a good, wholesome, running criticism with humor. Humor, you understand. You remember the opera singer who was dismissed, not because she sang badly, but because she rubbed her nose so much that it became fiery red, and she didn't look well.

"I notice you have a way of covering your face when you laugh. It is only a little thing, but it is not specially becoming, and you are not a Japanese, so why form the habit? But there are little habits in playing that you must constantly recognize and criticize as good or bad. The fingers are nothing but little trained animals and know nothing themselves, so that everything depends on your direction. You are sometimes halting in your rhythms, and I do not understand it. You must cure that at once," he says. "It can be cured by thinking correctly. Some people talk about feeling in playing, and get themselves into a labyrinth of thought and calculation and program-making that only spoils the playing. Then there comes along a little person who has rhythm, and can make beautiful tones, and perhaps knows very little, but can think to some purpose. You have to study sometimes years to get beautiful tones; some people never get them. Rhythm is your feeling, and you can put it instantly into your playing, now, this minute," he said. "You can conquer the world with rhythm and beautiful tones. You can think of rhythm as the conduct of life. As for technique—that is different. If one studies with intelligence, it is a small matter. Any one can get it who studies well. But to put those finishing touches to technique, so that it is a 'beautiful technique' is different. There's that little sonata, 'Scarlatti,' for instance, very easy to learn to play at first. It lasts three minutes played in tempo, but it takes six years to learn to play it well. My little 'Arabesque' is one of those difficult pieces to play well. Play that legato and flowing in a small room, but crisp and clear in the big hall. There are two interpretations for that."

He went on for a long time showing me pieces that could be interpreted in two or three ways.

"What is my bad habit in rhythm?" I asked.

"No, I haven't forgotten," he replies, "but I do not know the exact words to express it. It is something inborn, I should say, but you only show it at the piano. Perhaps you study with too much interruption of the ideas. I listened once for an hour behind your door. Your *Hausfrau* gave me a comfortable chair and let me smoke. You stopped too often. I wonder just why you do that."

"When were you listening?" I asked.

"The evening you were studying the Chopin you played in your last lesson. Think it over and see if you can find out the cause for yourself, and let your melodies become more singing, and your tempos smoother. You must put more joy in your playing. You must be happier in your study and in your playing before people. Take all the rules of singing for your melodies. I leave you a legacy of these little rules," he says, scribbling down something on my notes, "but get more happiness into your tempos: that will be your own study and duty.—What do you think," he said suddenly. "Yesterday I had a pupil—I think one of Frau Breé pupils—excellently taught. Frau Breé is writing a book—a book about my (long pause)—about my method. One has to call it something, if one must write a book at all about the way to study. It is the most difficult thing to write about; and most books are worse than useless. But hers will be good—as good as a book can be; but method—well, method depends on the person you have before you. Now, no one could be better prepared for the life of playing than this pupil of hers. But I heard him play five pieces straight through, and noticed that as he approached the end he became very nervous. With every piece it was the same. I began to think—what is this man? What troubles has he had? Or doesn't he study a piece to the end? So I tested him. He could play the piece backward, if necessary. He knew every bar. I said to him, 'Play the fifteenth bar from the end.' In an instant he did it. That means that he knows his piece. He sees it like a picture that you once shut your eyes before, then look at again, and always remember. Some people try to remember their pieces by making the harmonies stand out as colors. Too many of these extraneous things are never good. Look at the different methods all over the world for learning the piano. All of them have something good about them, but they are all bad, too. Your memory must be mostly a musical memory.

"But what then is this man's particular trouble? 'Would you read me a poem that you don't know?' I asked him. Very much amazed, he opened this little book here, and read it, but before he had finished, his breath seemed to come with difficulty, and he became agitated. 'You are an intelligent and strong-willed man,' I said to him. 'What makes you so nervous? You are young, too, and cannot have had great anxieties in your lifetime!' I tried to make him tell me about himself, and he finally did, but with an expression of defiance on his face. At school he had always failed when he was made to speak a piece. He nearly always burst into tears and left the stage. Then they tried to teach him to make a speech—did everything to help him to overcome his nervousness. Finally he gave up going to school, and went to a conservatory of music in another place. There his reputation had not followed him, and he took a new start. He succeeded in music, but when the final examinations came, and he expected to be able to play his piece to the end without breaking down, there seemed to be a fatality about it, and he did go all to pieces, and gave up, feeling himself an utter failure.

"Now, he came yesterday. I have told him all kinds of things. I have told him he must learn to swim, learn to fence, learn to ride—do things—become accomplished until he gets confidence in himself. This is one way of overcoming nervousness.

"I want you never to have a failure," he said to me; "you are the kind of person that gains much by successes and loses heart by failures. It is perhaps a certain confidence in life that is lacking in you that shows in your tempos. Keep the joy of life in you. Look at me," he said; "it is only by not allowing myself to think of disagreeable things that I am here to-day. You know, troubles do not make Christians of every one."

A knock at the door was heard. We had already talked a long time, and it was five o'clock. Leschetizky had forgotten that the two people were coming to listen to my lesson. Often he permitted this kind of thing to teachers who could stay in Vienna only a short time and who were not prepared to play for him. At this lesson the arrangement proved as instructive to me as to them, I am sure, for their few questions and their way of understanding his teaching brought to light such different interpretations of ideas, that some of the questions I had always vaguely wanted to ask were answered. Leschetizky loved to have questions put to him in the lessons, and really begged the pupil to ask them, but irrelevant and unintelligent questions with a lack of humor affected him as disagreeably as speechlessness, so one did not lightly ask him questions. And his pupils did well not only to show a variety of feeling, but to preserve a great deal of cheerfulness in all their lessons.

The ladies entered ceremoniously. They were evidently very correct in everything, and in art, surely, of the entirely cerebral persuasion! This contrast with Leschetizky would lead to something interesting, I was sure.

Now we had to play more and talk less, and all that Leschetizky said was directly applicable to the music I played.

I started the first bar of the first variation slowly, and then brought the third bar into tempo. This I did, I think, quite unconsciously. It furnished the master with a pretext for a long talk to the teachers about knowing the musical values of a piece.

"You see," he said, "she knows what she is doing." (I didn't really.) "The motive resembles so closely the last bar of the theme that she feels the comparison and allows for it in the playing. It is a great thing to realize all the little points that are similar, and to make these comparisons in music; that, after all, makes the music, doesn't it?" he said. "Beethoven knew what he was doing, I can tell you, and one must play as if one understood

him. The unmusical person is like the man that
takes you canoeing and does not know the river.
You may paddle over it without any trouble, but the
one with whom you feel safe is the one who knows
all the peculiarities, difficulties, and also danger
points. Your phrase is endangered where the first
cadence occurs. There you must keep up the row-
ing steadily, or that little current will swerve you
around, and you may upset." This was a gentle
reminder to me of what he said when we were alone,
about the theme and keeping smoother tempos, and
I realized that it was only kindness that made him
speak so impersonally now.

In the variations with the octaves I found another
valuable point to remember. It was the first time
that I had put into practice something he had told
me many times about taking single notes. He recommended *saying* the note just as one was about
to strike it. It saved me a top F before the teachers, and I saw that Leschetizky was smiling.

"A good technique," he said, " contains many
tricks." Leschetizky was speaking in French to the
teachers, who had come from Paris, and I saw their
amazement to hear this word from him. Their
amazement was so great that he supposed they had
not understood him.

Tricks," he repeated in several languages, "you
must try all kinds of ways, and try to study from
editions with the fewest fingerings. What bad
players these men are generally! You can tell by
the fingerings they put down, and the pedal, too.
Why does one need pedal marks? It is the people
who don't listen who need the pedal marked for
them! And it is so simple generally! If you had

only heard Rubinstein," he said; "you seldom heard
the pedal with his playing, but it was always there.
He was sensible. Common sense," he said in three
or four languages again—"that is a great word
'common sense.'

"After all, you do not need your foot and your
hand both. If the hands hold the note you don't
need the foot to hold it, and if the foot holds it, then
why the hand, too?" he said. "And just let the air
through!" he said laughingly. "You don't need
rules for the pedal—you need common sense and
your ear to direct you."

"May I ask a question?" said one of the teachers.
Leschetizky bristled. "What is this going to be?"
he said in an undertone. One of them went to the
piano to ask him about the phrasing of a well-
known melody. Their amazement increased in
leaps and bounds when Leschetizky asked them
what they were playing—he could not remember.
To think that Leschetizky did not know what it
was! Then they spoke of an opus, and, to their
blankest astonishment, he said he could almost
never remember an opus.

"I know very little," said Leschetizky seriously.
He was also taken very seriously by the teachers.
One said that it perhaps was not so surprising after
all that he did not know the melody they had played,
and that an opus *was* a very difficult thing to
remember.

Leschetizky seemed to be growing good-humored,
instead of otherwise, as might well have been, and
my lesson proceeded with perhaps more ease than
usual. One of the teachers was complimentary of
my technique, but asked with some temerity if it

was allowed to play the second variation so fast. "I am glad you have asked me," said he. "It did sound too fast, because she played with too much tone. A little less tone," he said, turning to me, "so that it will sound a grade slower." The significance of this answer passed over the heads of the teachers evidently, but to me was most illuminating, as I had lately joined a small class for the study of acoustics, in order better to understand some of the statements he made in the lessons.

"Here comes a beautiful variation," said Leschetizky, and when I started to play it, he stopped me instantly. "No, no, no," he said. "You must be more serious," he said, looking at me and laughing. "There is a variation similar to that in the Beethoven 'Variations in C Minor.' I always think of my grandmother when I hear it," he said. "It is a little weird and unearthly. It is calm. Play it calmly," he added. "It is as calm as death." One of the teachers asked at this point if he had known his grandmother. "No, I did not," he replied. "We are getting far away from the music," he said, "and the time is short. Let us forget our emotions, and begin to play."

I had now reached the last variation but one, and was scolded a little for using too much motion of my hands. This light scolding did seem to make the teachers very much animated, and Leschetizky's good humor and talkativeness, as well as theirs, increased. When I came to the last variation, he said laughingly, "Now you can have your up and down motions all you like," and the teachers thought this a great joke.

Then, at the end, it became more difficult, and I

had to try to hear exactly, note for note, what Leschetizky wanted me to do, and to try to copy him. He played the phrases many times, and for a few moments became stern and thoughtful, which puzzled the teachers. I suppose they wondered if I were going to cry or become confused, but I already knew Leschetizky too well for this. After having spent weeks of daily playing to him of the Schumann "Fantasie" in Ischl and never pleased him at all, going home sadly, day after day, believing that I was never meant to be an artist and never could be, and after hearing from day to day from Leschetizky that it was no better, that I had not understood him and that I was not even on the right road—at this, in comparison, I experienced only a slight moment of anxiety. I was more sorry for the teachers, who looked very much agitated and as if they would like to run away.

"You see," said Leschetizky, "you must turn completely eloquent at this moment, and every tone must be in its right place. That is a sentence that must be studied so that it will never fail you. It is dramatic, and every tone must mean something. Your mood is prayerful at this moment, and you must not become distracted."

"What did you mean there?" asked one of the teachers. "That means prayer?"

"Yes—no—yes—of course not," said Leschetizky. "Don't ask me what it means—the music means what it says to you. Do you need to put anything more into this than there is there? Isn't it beautiful enough without putting anything into it? To you it may mean something more or something different from what it does to me. One never knows. I cannot tell exactly what it means to you, and you will probably never know what it means to me.

"She smiles," said Leschetizky, speaking of me, "and I do not know exactly what that smile of hers means always, but it means something. Now she cannot smile at all," said Leschetizky. "So it is in life. One smiles where another is serious, and this is interpretation. Don't you think so?

"You have come here very seriously to listen to a lesson," said Leschetizky to one of the teachers. "I see that you have brought the Beethoven sonatas, and have been writing down words very often. It would interest me greatly to look them over and to see if your words express my real meaning, for if they do not, the words may not really help you. I may have said some things that were perhaps not clear to you. May I look at what you have written?" said Leschetizky.

"Certainly, Professor," replied one of them, but with some embarrassment. "Oh, no," said the other, "please don't! please don't!"

"As you like," said Leschetizky, "but it would interest me very much," and the book was handed to him.

I could see how he was trying to conceal his astonishment. He also left the room for a few moments, and I heard afterward that he sat down in the little room beyond the hall and laughed. "What next!" he exclaimed. "Now I shall have to be serious, if I ever was in my life!"

He returned to the music room polite, but very bright-eyed. "You have a large class of pupils in Paris?" he inquired. "Yes, Professor," they

replied, "and we are there together—we collabo-
rate." This word almost upset Leschetizky.
"You are acquainted with those two famous teach-
ers in Paris, Mr. Diemer and Mr. Philippe?"
"Yes, Professor." "Why do you not go to listen
to some of their lessons, they are great pedagogues.
They know many things. They are emotional, as
we are." "Yes, Professor, but not so much."
"Oh," said Leschetizky, "how do you know that?"
"I am sure," said one, "they cannot indicate so exactly to their pupils the way to play emotionally."
"Nor can I indicate the way to my pupils to play
emotionally. That is impossible," said the master.
"They must be emotional themselves. If you ask
me how to play emotionally, then my answer will
be, 'If you have to ask me that question you can
never play emotionally.'"

One of the ladies was apparently very nervous
and appeared to be weeping. "We are very much
fatigued, Professor," she said; "we have had a long
journey, and have been very much depressed in
Vienna. We have also been very much disappointed and discouraged." "Why is that?" asked
Leschetizky. "I cannot explain," she answered,
"but we find the atmosphere here not so serious as
we expected." "There are very serious people
here," replied Leschetizky, "but in an artistic way.
They do not wear their seriousness on their sleeves.

"Now, let me take up the points of your writing
that you have allowed me to read. You have written down: 'You do not upset, but go safely on.'
'If you want it to sound faster, play louder.' 'Listen here, no horse play here.' 'Be a musician as
well as a pianist.' 'Play with joyous motions up

and down, and laugh a little.' 'Be calm and unhappy!' And in parenthesis, 'Feel as you felt
when grandmother died.' Some of these indications
I can understand," said Leschetizky, "but others
are entirely unintelligible to me. What, may I ask,
does this one mean to you: 'You do not upset, but
go safely on'?" "It means, as you said, Professor,
that one feels very safe and comfortable, as one
would feel canoeing, or, possibly, you did not mean
just canoeing—we have never been canoeing, so we
do not know—and canoeing with some one who
is agreeable to you (or else you would not be with
him), and that you have a feeling of security with
him, and do not upset." "Now," said Leschetizky,
"do you think that your audience or your listeners
are going to be able to understand that?" "We
thought, Professor, that you meant us to feel that
when we played. There is another, but not well-
known, teacher in Paris who has the same ideas.
We thought possibly he had been a pupil of yours,
Professor." "It may be," replied the master, "but
I hope not."

"Now, this other one here," he continued de-
terminedly; "let us take them all in order. 'Listen
here.' Why particularly there?" he asked. "Because you meant, we thought," one of them answered, "that that part was so beautiful." "No,"
said Leschetizky, "I can dispose of that point very
quickly. Good pedaling, good style, good taste all
depend, for the most part, on listening to your own
playing. Piano playing is not all emotion, by any
means. You must use your senses, and always have
them with you, or your emotions count for very

little. If you listen well, that in itself is a means of attracting many emotional qualities."

Before the third variation in A flat minor they had written: "Feel as you felt when grandmother died." How was Leschetizky going to control his face, I wondered, but there was not a sign of amusement, as he asked them how that title would help them to play that variation. "But you distinctly said, Professor, that you always thought of your grandmother when you heard something like that variation." "So I did," and here was an outlet for his laughter. "But I would be sorry," he said, "if I always thought of her at the time of playing this sonata. Mesdames," said he, "did you ever hear of the actor who had no expression in his voice and had never been successful? He had only technique and skill. He was cold, and, of course, could never get any applause from his audience. He almost lost his position in the theater, when one evening, as he was going on to the stage, he received a telegram that his best friend had just died. He had to play a happy and humorous part that evening, but was overwhelmed with grief. But he suddenly knew how to put such ardor and feeling into his voice, that he spoke with warmth and color. His audience liked him for the first time. Some one asked him years afterward what had changed his whole career in acting, and he answered that for the first time in his life that evening he had learned what suffering was, and then his joys meant something to him after that.

"If I am going to give you anything of value to take back to Paris, it is my advice to study and teach to bring out the beauties of the music, and enjoy yourself more in your playing, and let your pupils do likewise. If you label your phrases you will have to instruct your audiences in these names, and then, where is the music? Way in the shade! Besides, you will play no better. I hope you will not go back to Paris saying that Leschetizky told you what to feel at every turn. There are good teachers there who would disagree with me.

"Fantasy," he said, "is the word, and fantasy means absence of rule. You must try to play from the heart, and use your mind for your study, which is way behind you when you come to play. The music is the emotion itself, if you like.

"Would you like to hear this sonata?" he said, as the teachers heaved a sigh, and looked rather crestfallen. Then he sat down at his piano and played the "A Flat Sonata" with that intensity of poetical expression that belonged only to him. He tried to teach this quality, but evaded all rules and intentions. The teachers were not hanging their heads in sorrow (or they had perhaps forgotten to do so) as he played the funeral march; they looked rather uplifted and ecstatic than otherwise, and Leschetizky played it very softly and tenderly. At the last movement they became quite happy and cheerful.

Then they said good-by. He escorted them to the outside door, then went quietly to the window and watched them as they went away.

"They mean well. How very little a teacher can do for some people!

"Oh, let me get out to the country, which is not so complicated," he concluded, "where I can recognize myself, and where I do not have to account for every word or every smile."

CHAPTER VI

ONE day I went out to Leschetizky and found him in one of those moods that I had heard about but had never witnessed. His face wore a dark look, and he was making no attempt to conceal his feelings. "One mustn't be a bit afraid of making enemies," he said. "Make them all enemies sometimes; they come back again when they see how little you care."

I was surprised to hear him say this, for only a week or two before he had expressed an entirely different view in the presence of several people. He had talked a long time about the efforts one should make to be fair in one's lifetime, and he had used the English word "fair"—he thought the word very beautiful.

By this time I had heard all kinds of rumors and gossip about Leschetizky, but I observed that no two people ever seemed to hold the same opinion of him. He was becoming to me an amazing and almost incomprehensible person. He had a different word and different advice, it seemed, for every pupil. One thing only could be counted upon—his guests and pupils had to be lively and not dull. His speeches after the suppers at the classes were as different in character as his lessons; but let a stupid or dull or easily shocked person show himself, and we all knew what was coming from Leschetizky. There was an Eleventh Commandment that he spoke of: "Thou shalt not be stupid"; and upon this text he would often deliver sermons.

I had heard stories of his apparent cruelty, but I knew him to be a man so full of tenderness and consideration that I despaired of being able to reconcile these conflicting estimates of him. Much of the gossip had its origin, of course, in jealousy. Pupils "finished" at other schools and at conservatories of music generally found their way to Vienna and Leschetizky; and frequently much well-meant advice was vouchsafed by incredulous people who were sure that students could find more sentiment further south, more dignity further north, or more accuracy in Paris, and that Leschetizky himself was impossible. It was a common occurrence during the inevitable conversation that Continentals start while traveling, to be asked pointedly if one was studying with "that terrible Leschetizky." This comment was only too laughable to any one who knew him at all, or who understood in the slightest degree the artistic atmosphere of Vienna.

It was very unfortunate for the Americans that an important American musical periodical chose to publish a series of articles criticizing Leschetizky's private life. Every American in Vienna looked upon this ill-advised policy with great resentment. The Europeans thought we should make a public statement on his behalf. Leschetizky had just married for the third time and had been twice divorced —something that can hardly be called exclusively European; and any one seeing Leschetizky at all as he really was would not be likely to think of him as a trifling and unprincipled person. He himself ignored these attacks at first, but when one day a

long, particularly vicious and untrue article reached
him, he lost his fortitude and took occasion during
a class to express his feelings.

He first made a count of the Americans present,
then asked them to rise and hear his view of the
matter. He began by quoting this journal, to the
effect that his class was made up mostly of Americans who were misguided in coming to him to
study the piano.

"Look around," he said, "look at yourselves; are
you not only a handful in this class of pupils? Are
there more Americans here than people from other
countries? The majority of my pupils are, I think,
proud and happy to be here, even if they have to
go through many trials and tribulations under this
roof. We can thank Heaven that the trials are for
art's sake and for nothing less than art! Here you
few Americans rank the very poorest of all in art,
as well as in human understanding, and you spend
your time in making private affairs of which you
have no knowledge conform to your perfectly artificial code of morals—at least if you feel as your
editor feels! But," continued Leschetizky, looking
sadly and wearily away, "I have loved some Americans; and some of my real friends are living in
America—Madame Helen Hopekirk and Madame
Bloomfield Zeisler, for instance. But now if you
feel as your editor feels I want to tell you few
here, Go back to the place you came from, for I
can do without you—all of you, every one," he said
with emphasis. "I do not mind if I do not see one
left."

This rebuke was, of course, particularly hard to
bear for a few of us, and for me especially. I had

just begun to feel myself progressing in music; and only the week before I had had what was called a very "good lesson." I was learning to think of Leschetizky as the best of friends to go to for advice on all subjects.

I had had two or three proofs, besides, of his good offices in connection with certain little troublesome affairs that might have ended in bad feeling and gossip. These things he stamped out as quickly as possible, and the instigators were punished— sometimes all too severely.

But no two people seemed to think alike about him. One young man proclaimed himself disgusted with Leschetizky's idea of music and life altogether, saying he never would listen to him again. "You will never be an artist with your creeds and doctrines," Leschetizky had told him. "You are a thousand miles away from expressing your true self in music. You must live; you must be lively; be gay—learn to dance. You must get yourself out of your sordid and distorted atmosphere." The father of this youth had written finally to Leschetizky to say he was sorry his son had ever for a moment come under such bad influence.

Another young man continued to fare ill in the class because of the particular kind of conversation that seemed most natural to him, a kind which Leschetizky detested. "You will always be a nobody," Leschetizky said, "if you choose such themes to dwell upon. You already have the atmosphere about you of coming up the back stairs; and by and by the back stairs will be too good for you."

He had shown great concern over a young girl in his class who had just made the acquaintance of a celebrated singer who was about to go to Paris. The latter had wanted the young woman to go with her for a fortnight to be present at her concert, and to meet Massenet and Saint-Saëns. "It was alluring, of course," Leschetizky said, "and would be an interesting experience to a little Viennese girl to go with the brilliant artist to Paris; but I am uneasy about it. There is something in the eye of that singer that I don't like; and the young girl has a foolish mother and father. They know nothing of the world. At any rate," said Leschetizky, "I have taken the liberty of telegraphing to Munich to her to come back—that I want her to play at a concert." But they had already left for Paris. At the end of the week the young girl did return very much disgusted with her disagreeable experience. "But the best of it is," said Leschetizky, "the mother and father took *me* to task for letting her go at all. How can they possibly blame me, for I did not even introduce their daughter to the singer? Now, what can I do with these mothers and fathers?"

Such things constantly irritated him. Only a short time before he had had a serious quarrel with the mother of a young man who was very anxious about leaving her son amid the dreadful pitfalls of Vienna. "He will go to cafés if I leave him," said the mother. "Most certainly," Leschetizky replied. "But, Professor, he will become fond of the ladies." "I only hope so," remarked Leschetizky. Finally the poor mother had to leave. Leschetizky would not hear of her staying.

Just before one of my lesson days his troubles and responsibilities seemed almost too much for him to bear. When the day came I had no lesson at all. He began by telling me how angry he was at a disagreeable piece of gossip he had heard about me. At a certain point he stopped, and said, "I see the whole thing—you needn't tell me anything."

He abruptly left the house and must have spent several hours in seeing people, for, during the next twenty-four, I had no less than eleven visitors—all ordered by Leschetizky to apologize to me for a misstatement. First he had gone to ten of them separately and had asked if one certain girl had ever said such and such a thing. They had thought it wisest to admit that she had, and tell him the truth.

"Now go and get your leader," he ordered, "and hurry as fast as you can spin to apologize, for I never want to see such an expression on any lady's face as I saw upon Miss Newcomb's this afternoon when I told her what you have dared to say."

For the next few months relations were very strained between the "leader," as Leschetizky had called her, and himself; and I think she must have profited by the experience. It would be amusing to know what the feelings of the other ten were on seeing Leschetizky at their door in a state of ill-concealed wrath over a remark that I am sure was not maliciously repeated by most of them.

During those first years in Vienna I kept, school-girl-like, a diary; and as I look it over I find surprisingly little in it about music; it is mostly taken up with stories about Vienna. There is an account of parts of a conversation at a dinner table where Leschetizky was present. The friend and companion of a young pupil of Leschetizky's had just returned to Vienna, after an absence of three years. During her absence the young pupil had lived alone. She had undoubtedly had a very hard time when they lived together, for the companion had all sorts of strict ideas about living that were difficult for a young student of music to follow, especially in Vienna. They were Americans. The young student was not on any account allowed to go to the Philharmonic concerts on Sunday. She was to teach a Sunday-school class; and was forbidden to speak to Austrian gentlemen, particularly officers. They had come to Vienna to study music, and for nothing else; nothing must be allowed to interfere. The companion preferred them to pose as poor students, as this was a worthy object in life; and she told every one of their spending most of their money to come to Europe to study. Money was very important to the companion, who had plenty of it, and any one who did not respect money for its own sake was incomprehensible. She loved to say, "That old crank, Ibsen, says he would be ashamed to have a lot of money, but it only shows what a worthless person he is." The girl wished to take fencing lessons and to ride at the famous Spanish riding academy in Vienna, but the companion wrote to her father and got him to forbid it. They were in Vienna for one purpose only, and must not spend time or money for foolish, unimportant things. They had their days most rigidly mapped out, without a moment's recreation, or even time to think. Study hours were determined by the companion, and only books on music were allowed in the house. Leschetizky had been greatly amused by these facts, but had been rather inclined to agree with the companion in one or two respects. He expressed the opinion that the companion might now treat her charge a little more respectfully, since she had grown older and had studied to great purpose. Now, wishing to make amends, if possible, for her previous uncongeniality, the young pupil asked her friends to meet her dignified and intellectual companion while she stopped in Vienna. The companion was planning to go round the world alone, to study, with special designs on Greece and Persia. To please her young friend, Madame von —— invited Mrs. T—— and the others to dinner at her house and Leschetizky promised to come. A famous archæologist and two well-known painters of Vienna were present. Parts of the conversation at this amusing function it was impossible not to overhear, as Mrs. T—— had a very penetrating voice and a very decided way of speaking.

Archæologist: "How interesting, Mrs. T——, that you are going alone around the world to study."

Mrs. T——: "Thank you very much; but I know perfectly what I want to do and see, and as not every one feels as I do about these things I think I'm glad I'm going alone. Yes, I'm sure I'm glad."

Archæologist: "You American ladies are very strong-minded."

Mrs. T——: "Well, we have to be. There are all kinds of people in this world; the only thing is to be always sure you are right, and leave the rest to the good Lord."

Archæologist: (*After a pause.*) "Are you going to remain long in Vienna?"

Mrs. T——: "Not any longer than I can help. You know I told my young friend's father that I would stop here and see what she was up to." (*In a stage whisper, behind her fan.*) "She thinks Leschetizky is a great man. Between you and me, I do not. It's curious how many people get that notion into their heads. *I think he is a very dangerous person to associate with.* And you have such stupid customs here in Vienna—this kissing of the hand, for instance. They used to do that when I was here five years ago, but then Europe was somewhat new to me and I did not mind so much; but to have every one—why, three different men have kissed my hand since I arrived."

Archæologist: (*Rather long silence.*) "Of course Master Leschetizky is one of your young ward's friends."

Mrs. T——: "Yes, and I don't approve of that friendship. And she would improve more in her music if she had fewer friends and did not think of things outside of her music."

Archæologist: "Don't you believe in being a many-sided person?"

Mrs. T——: "I dare say what you mean by many-sided person and what I mean, are two totally different things."

Archæologist: (*With a smile.*) "Yes indeed, I am sure they are. I have been digging near Athens for a good many years. If you like I can get you permits to see things that are otherwise inaccessible to tourists."

Mrs. T——: "No, I thank you, I have come to

Europe with a list of the things I must see. You know, in art one must choose well the things one really wants, and stick to them. I do not intend to turn to the right or to the left; but to be able to write a good lecture, when I get home, on the things most worth seeing in Europe."

"And do you think, Madame," said Leschetizky across the table, "that you can come to Europe and judge so easily which are the only things to 'stick to'?"

"Most certainly, Mr. Leschetizky, one knows the good from the bad, as well as the right from the wrong. I make it my first duty to be always right. One can always know that if one stops to think."

"Black and white," said Leschetizky, "no colors."

"Yes, there are only two ways in this world—one is right and the other is wrong," replied Mrs. T——.

Leschetizky: "Your young artist friend here might think otherwise and know far better."

Mrs. T——: "I have no doubt, Mr. Leschetizky, that my friend has become so Viennese that her ideas are not those we have in 'God's country.' They have become distorted." (*A slight pause.*) "Every one becomes interested in Leschetizky's face."

"No," said Leschetizky, with an expression of determination, but of distinct hilarity on his face, "it is quite the contrary, for she has a great amount of that discrimination which is inborn in some people and which enables her to put a question mark after every thought." Everybody laughed, and the situation was saved. The famous archæologist now gave up entirely, remarking to some one near by that "the lady didn't need him at all, as she had the double stars of Baedeker to go by." While the companion talked complacently to her hostess, Leschetizky drew his pupil into the next room. "I was wrong, indeed," said he. "I thought you had probably been a naughty child five years ago, and could now well afford to make amends. But, my dear child, get as far away from such people as possible; they are not for artists; such people drag you down. An artist must look up and not down. If art is worth anything it is to keep you from becoming sordid and narrow. Get as far away as possible from such people."

"She will," said one of the painters, "don't worry about her, Herr Leschetizky."

"How do you cope with all these duennas and guardians of your pupils?" "I would not have them come near the place," said another. "They only distract the poor, struggling students. We all have to struggle and mustn't be bothered for a moment; besides they sap one's vitality."

"Weren't we polite though?" said another. "Didn't we please you?" they asked. "You see, we Viennese, although wicked, are nice polite people, aren't we?" Leschetizky's pupil said she felt wicked too. "No, you don't," said Leschetizky, "you have serious things to think of, and I wouldn't feel too much if I were you. Never think of that person in your life again."

The companion then thought it was time to go home. She did not believe in keeping late hours, and they said good-night, but the others stayed. Leschetizky, the celebrated painters, the archæologist, who was giving lectures at the university in Vienna at the time, stayed until nearly morning. Madame von —— went to bed about three o'clock; but the others all stayed until the bell struck six, and talked. Leschetizky talked for three hours on a stretch. He said he had come to the end of his patience with families and guardians and companions of artists. They stood in the way of pupils' development, and generally blamed him for all their difficulties, musical or otherwise. If his pupils were sometimes unwise or stupid, he was called to account by the guardians; but the guardians themselves did such unwise and foolish things. It was the rumor in Vienna that one mother gave her little boy prodigy all kinds of strong drinks to stunt his growth. She thought he would attract more attention professionally in this way. He was a tiny boy, only nine, played beautifully, composed, and, Leschetizky said, could direct a full orchestra any day, if he had to do so. He was a genius. Certain it was that they made the poor little thing work like a slave. Leschetizky was determined to get to the bottom of this rumor; however, he did not believe that it was true.

He showed them all the little muscle that sometimes connects too firmly two fingers in the hand, and needs long training to develop rightly. One of his pupils found great difficulty in training these two fingers, and the father, who is a doctor, wanted the muscle cut. Leschetizky forbade it, but the father insisted. Leschetizky then refused to teach the girl any longer; but the family visited him continually to talk the matter over. They made it very disagreeable for him, telling him he was obstinate and wanted nothing but his own way.

The conversation then turned to principles and morals. All five gentlemen expressed themselves freely. Two or three times they apologized before the ladies; but they all talked for an hour or so, and finally Leschetizky laughed. "Go on, go on," he said, "please go on. I wish you had for one day in your lifetime, any one of you, the responsibilities that I have; oh, it is wonderful to hear you!" And he would laugh again. He was sorry that his wife was not able to be there—she would have enjoyed this conversation. He spoke very beautifully of his wife, Eugenie, in that talk of his, and one realized how well she must understand him and how sympathetic and helpful she must be.

There is another story in my diary about a mother who always accompanied her daughter to the lessons. "I am afraid," she said, "that he will say something that my daughter ought not to hear." Often she coughed or interrupted, and showed agitation when he began to criticize her playing, or when she expected him to say something shocking. The girl was not untalented, and Leschetizky gave her frequent lessons. After three or four he decided upon his course—by that time he knew the pupil and the mother better. "Why are you here?" he asked. "Does your daughter want you?" "She needs me," said the mother. "I think not," said Leschetizky; "she has had you over her too long already. I do not approve of you—I have observed you for some time. You have not even had the sense to bring up your daughter properly. She enters the room ahead of you. She interrupts your conversation. I am perfectly sure that you quarrel when you are alone; and do you not write back to America and say that your daughter is a favorite pupil?"

"No, indeed," protested the mother.

"Well, here is a paper," he said, producing an American newspaper, and showing her one of her own published letters.

"Oh, these mothers and fathers!" said Leschetizky. "They drive me insane! I don't mean only the American parents—they are peculiar (smiling) in that they always appear to be so glad to get away from their husbands. In Europe the husbands come along, too, and I generally have the fathers as well to attend to. To think of all these husbands left for so long in America, a whole ocean between them and their wives! And the American girls don't seem any too respectful toward their mothers. Perhaps it only seems so. . . . There's another here that will have to go. She's English. She's very intelligent, but, oh, so easily shocked! Everything is shocking her. She makes you want to say shocking things."

However, Leschetizky easily changed his mind. And at the last class of that year this dear mother was present and was invited to stay with her daughter to supper. She had perhaps been forgotten or forgiven. There was an unusual number of guests. The playing of the evening had satisfied him, and Leschetizky was in one of his gayest and most genial moods. "Just don't let me think too much," he said, "I feel happier when I can keep myself from thinking. I am not the happiest man in the world," he said, looking serious for a moment, "and

when I look at you young people I think so much
of the difference in our years; but if I do not think
too much I can be happy." On seeing the stately
and thoughtful mother halfway down the table, his
mind took a different turn from what we expected.
He first asked Schütt, in a stage whisper, to tell
his neighbor to behave more properly, please to put
his hands in his lap where they belonged instead of
on the table; and then, in hard, peremptory tones
he called us all to order in a way that puzzled us as
to whether he meant it seriously or not. His face
took on a most terrible expression; and rising at
the table, standing stiffly, as he never stood before,
he delivered a lecture with a monotony of voice
never before heard from Leschetizky. One guest
was laughing a little too much. Leschetizky suddenly became the irritated schoolmaster—he
brought his fist down on the table and scolded; then,
to our astonishment, he began, in the grandest
style, to talk about the church. This amazed and
interested the mother, who undoubtedly began to
realize that there was some unusual cause for mer-
riment. She very tactfully began a spirited and
serious conversation with Leschetizky, which surprised and delighted him. He put aside at once
his pompous style of speaking, and turned to simplicity and plainness. His guest surprised every
one by her ability to talk with Leschetizky, and in
the end we found ourselves listening with greatest
interest to a long conversation about religion. On
leaving, the mother expressed herself as charmed
with Leschetizky's hospitality, his frankness and
freedom, but, above all, with his ideas on religion
and the church. "Your master knows everything,"

she said. "I had no idea he was so well informed on subjects outside of music." "That mother is an intelligent mother, and sympathetic also," said Leschetizky afterward. "I had no idea she was as artistic as her conversation showed her to be."

CHAPTER VII

THE one last year in Vienna to which my parents had agreed lengthened into two, and at the end of the second season I said a very sad and final good-by to Leschetizky. This would really be the end of my study in Vienna, I believed, and I was desolate at the thought.

Meanwhile, my sister, who had made excellent progress in her singing, decided to remain, and it was comforting to leave her in Vienna, as hostage for a possible return. Leschetizky had greatly encouraged her in her studies. She and a little band of friends stood mournfully on the station platform, saying good-by to me, repeating their invectives against parents who did not encourage their children to become artists.

On my way to Bremen, and across the ocean, I had ample time to meditate upon these things, and I am happy to say that by the time I saw my father's dear face at the piers, I had come to a better understanding of the sacrifices which parents on their part were called upon to make.

At the steamer my drooping spirits were revived a little by a beautiful letter from Leschetizky in which he said he hoped very much that it would be possible for me to come back, and, if I did, I might play as often for him as I liked, but there would be no more *real* lessons—no paying for lessons. This I cherished as an argument I might one day use with effect upon my father. Leschetizky had also written some touching and serious things about parents; and his words taught me to realize the difference between those who deliberately hindered the artistic development of their children, and those whose motive for keeping them at home was only affection and love.

"You must show your parents that now you can do something well," wrote Leschetizky; "if you play well I judge from what you tell me that they will know it; if your coming back is a question of money, you can tell your father from me that you are able to earn money yourself. I understand such parents as yours," he went on, "and such relationships as yours are. No one in the world ever had a more devoted mother than I had and no one ever loved his mother as much as I. One time when she was very ill I had a concert that would take me from her for many days. My friends said that I should not leave her, but she was the one who made me go away to carry on my career. She died during those days and I never saw her again. You will see that if you are serious in your music your parents may become your best friends."

And so I came home, and played often for any one who cared to hear me, also a few times in public. During that year I was happy to receive many letters from Leschetizky and to hear also that he hoped I would return before long. He liked occasionally to have an American newspaper sent him, but took far too seriously the great headlines telling of damage done by lightning, the great floods we had, the terrible heat and fires. Often several pages of his letters would be taken up with expressions of commiseration for the intense heat that was reported in

America. "Do not go near New York," he wrote, "but stay quietly in the country and keep yourself rested for your studies in this hot weather."

He had a romantic feeling for the sea and would write how he tried to imagine the highest waves: "No picture could give any idea of the sensations one would have on passing another steamer in mid-ocean." He wondered if it did not take real courage to put one's feet on the gangplank and separate oneself so entirely from the land.

Some years before this the little town of Whitney Point, New York, where we lived, had been nearly destroyed by fire. Leschetizky never forgot the time in Altenmarkt when I received a newspaper with an account of the disaster. Very shortly a letter came saying that the fire had not extended as far as was reported and that our old house was still standing. His disgust for the exaggerations in the newspapers was most amusing.

In the meantime, my mother had gone to Vienna to join my sister, and Leschetizky wrote to me a great deal about Mary's singing. This is one of his letters:

DEAR ETHEL:

"At last, at last I am able to write about your sister Mary. I have heard her twice during the past week; once in her apartment in the presence of her teacher and last Wednesday in the class when her mother was present—something which you probably have heard of already. Well, it took no little trouble to get Mary to sing, particularly in the class. I can say now that since last year she has made great progress, particularly in regard to technique. For example, she often sings difficult coloratura passages most excellently, and in her high register she has, for the most part, a brilliant attack, even in piano, also little turns and embellishments come out quite deliciously. Furthermore, the spirit is not lacking, so that she sang Rossini's. aria from 'The Barber of Seville,' *Una Voce Poco Fa,* in the class, with great success, in fact. On the other hand, the 'Traviata' aria, which has more dramatic content, was not so good. In my opinion her weakness lies in the fact that her voice in the high register is sometimes, indeed often, somewhat sharp and thin, and that the lower register is not cultivated enough, so that she seldom brings forth the so-called 'dark' tones, and her execution is lacking in *portamento.* I like her lower tones especially, more than the high ones, and I think it would be good if Fräulein Mütter would have her sing more legato things in addition to those with technical difficulties—something that I already hinted to Fräulein Mütter. In regard to technique, the trill must be improved, as it is not on the level with other technical accomplishments. As I always have it in mind that you could give joint recitals with Mary, she should cultivate the lyric element more and develop greater warmth of expression; and to this end, naturally, the voice itself must be made warmer. I am of the opinion that this is possible, and I hope that Fräulein Mütter will follow this course more. Now you know pretty much all that I think about Mary's singing.

"Well, I am curious as to what further decisions will be made in regard to Mary. Her mother wants to take her to Italy. That is all right, but Mary must, in any case, not interrupt for too long a time her instruction, which, as a whole, is being conducted very well. I hope that this will not happen.

"Now I will tell you something about myself.

In about fourteen or sixteen days I will leave here, that is, about the 14th of June, and therefore I will give up my work with the students in about a week. My liver gives me considerable trouble again, and first of all I must have rest, and it is high time that I go to Carlsbad. After three or four weeks of the cure in Carlsbad I shall go to Ischl for about two months, and then, perhaps—yes, probably—to Paris, when I have become completely rested. In Paris I want to stay three or four weeks and then go to Wiesbaden for eight or ten days, or perhaps first to Wiesbaden and then to Paris.

"Your successes in your own country have given me the greatest pleasure, as you can well imagine. Meanwhile, I hope for early news of you, and remain your true old friend.

"THEODOR LESCHETIZKY."

In another:

"Now about your sister. From a letter which I received from her I take it she has had some disappointment, but the cause she has not told me. I have only heard about that from you. Frankly, I am not sorry that it has turned out this way. If Mary fulfills that of which she gives promise perhaps it is the best thing that could have happened. Sorrow and suffering, if they are really deeply felt, are factors which often form the greatest inspiration in art. She is young and beautiful and will forget.

"I would wish that the American 'flirt,' which is cultivated over there in your country entirely too much, will not prove the cause of her forgetting but rather that it will be art instead.

"In about two weeks I shall see her again. I hope she will be frank and truthful with me as I shall be with her, and, on my side, I will not let her lack for encouragement. In any case, I do not think it would be well for her mother to be with her in Vienna. Mothers and fathers are usually in the way in the artistic development of young people, even though they are artists themselves— something which is not the case with your parents. I must add that I find your mother, who, as you know, spent the evening with us after the class, a very charming and sympathetic person. I am heartily sorry that I was not able to talk with her because I am such a stupid fellow (*Trottel*) in English."

And when I wrote to my adored master that I could probably not return, I received the following from him:

"Art is a grateful friend; the more you dedicate yourself to it, the truer it is to you. Do not allow yourself to lead an empty life. You have promised me that you will remain true to art under all circumstances. Keep your word, and try to grow more and more in art. You will not always have a bed of roses to lie upon, and then you will sometimes think of me. Amen."

When I was most despairing of going to Europe, one of my aunts came to my rescue by offering to take me back to Vienna as her guest. My father then resigned himself to the sad conviction, as he expressed it, that we were never going to be with him again for long. He would not even go to the steamer to say good-by, declaring that he would go to those piers only when we came home again.

It pleased Leschetizky immensely to have old pupils return; and this time when I reached Vienna he greeted me with warmest words, adding that, after all, the Americans were serious people; we were not all of us living just for the "dollars."

In spite of his satisfaction, he told me he could hardly understand how I had the heart to leave my parents. One day, however, he brought me a slip of paper with a quotation from Grillparzer: "Where your work is, there also should your home be."

Soon after we had settled in Vienna for the season, he and Madame Leschetizka sent out invitations for a large reception in honor of Professor Leopold Auer, who was one of his old friends and had come to Vienna to visit him. My aunt, my sister, and I went. When supper time came, Leschetizky took his guest of honor to a smaller room upstairs, where he could have less formal conversation with him than was possible downstairs, among the many guests. He invited Miss Evelyn Suart, Mark Hamburg, my sister, and me to join them. We were already seated at the table when it occurred to me that we had been sadly neglectful of my aunt, who had been left downstairs among guests to whom she probably had not been introduced. Leschetizky realized that we had been rude, and, when I started down to her, he followed me, remorseful and apologetic. But we were very properly rebuked by her before Leschetizky for our neglect. Always antagonistic toward aunts and mothers, and guardians in general, Leschetizky did not receive this with good grace at all. I remember asking him if we could not get Edouard Schütt to take my aunt to supper, but Leschetizky objected, "No, no, Schütt is not to be used for such purposes, and probably he has selected some one himself, anyway." So we went back to the others and tried to forget our troubles.

Some weeks later Leschetizky wanted to know whether the relations between my aunt and myself had improved, and I had to admit that I was still embarrassed and miserable before her. Instead of the sympathy that I expected, he displayed a frank delight in my situation. It was high time, he said, for me to become independent.

"Your parents are making great sacrifices for you and your sister. She is going to Paris to study with Marchesi and will have to use a great deal of money in Paris. There is no reason why you should not earn your own living. You do not have to live in big hotels and fashionable places, encumbered by people to whom you are indebted. I have told you for two or three years that you could teach, and now, thank goodness, the time has come, when you ought to do it. Every pianist should have pupils. People forget the artists who have only played, but pupils carry on the teachers' memory. I shall be giving you something that will last you your whole lifetime. Now to-morrow I will send you six pupils, and announce in the class that you are to be my assistant."

This was the greatest surprise to me, and I was open-mouthed with astonishment. "I cannot do it," I said, but Leschetizky reassured me. I had never done any teaching and was frightened at the prospect of undertaking it.

The next day I did, however, receive four pupils, who must have had confidence enough in Leschetizky to overlook my unprofessional attitude. My sister listened behind the door to every word I said,

and now and then a giggle escaped her. This came
to Leschetizky's ears; he quickly came to our apartment and decided that my sister and I should be
separated by a corridor. Our dogs were to be kept
in the farthest room, or my sister could take them
out for a walk, while I was engaged in giving lessons. Meanwhile, Leschetizky had made arrange-
ments with Frau Breé, Fräulein Walle Hansen
and Fräulein Prentner, who had been my teacher,
for me to go to them and listen to at least one of
their lessons. It was most valuable experience to
observe their various ways of explaining his principles, and very useful in supplementing my lack of
training as a teacher.

Before long I had plunged into teaching in earnest, and had pupils, as did all the assistants, from
every country in the world. My first pupil was the
director of a conservatory in Germany, an excellent theorist, without much knowledge of the art of
piano playing. He wrote many austere compositions, and, in fact, did everything but play the piano
well. His tone was hard, and "matter of fact," but
he learned three or four pieces and several Czerny
études in so short a time that I could very soon send
him out to Leschetizky for a lesson. It did not occur to me to go with him. Afterward Leschetizky
told me he was excellently prepared, but I should
never have known just what happened at his lesson if two other pupils had not been present. From
them I learned that Leschetizky stood up after my
pupil had finished, and said, "Now, I want to tell
all of you here who has prepared this gentleman,
and ask if you do not think Miss Newcomb has ped-
agogical talent?"

So far, Leschetizky had not announced in the class that I was to be his assistant, probably because he wished first to test my capabilities.

This announcement was received with mixed feelings. One American mother whose daughter had studied with him for several years, expressed herself as very skeptical of my qualifications. She had the tactlessness to inquire of Leschetizky why her daughter could not be appointed assistant, if I could, to which Leschetizky sarcastically replied that she would have to ask some one else.

His three experienced assistants, however, were most kind and encouraging to me, and said it was very good and essential to have an American assistant among them. Frau Breé paid me the great compliment of saying she envied me the advantages I had as a teacher in having prepared myself to play in public.

And I had still another lesson to learn from Leschetizky.

The first money which I earned by teaching I used to give a little supper party for him. My sister and I invited him one evening, and when he came, we set out a most delicious little supper which we had ordered in from Sacher's. Leschetizky was in the habit of going to supper late in the evening, either after concerts or after his long walks. He loved to stroll about in the evening and amuse himself and meet his friends in the different cafés of Vienna, but about ten or eleven o'clock he was always ready for a little supper. My surprise met with little success. I told him I had just earned some money and wanted to spend it on him. He looked at me thoughtfully, shook his head, and finally remonstrated, "This is not good at all. The first money you earned should have gone into the bank for serious purposes.

"How valuable it would be for you," he continued, "to know what it is to be compelled to earn all the money you ever have; there are many things you would become more interested in. Supposing you had to make the dress you are wearing—how careful you would be to learn not to waste any material!"

And so he went on, to our amazement, taking the affair of our little supper very seriously.

It was very hard really to please Leschetizky. He now found fault with me for not being more professional, but I discovered, as time went on, that it was from kindness of heart and dread of the time when I might cease to enjoy myself as much as I had so far in the slight experience of teaching, that I had found such a pleasure.

"You must not think," he said, "that because you have had two or three agreeable and appreciative pupils that they will all be that way. They have liked you personally, too," he said, "but you will soon enough have some who will criticize you and your teaching, and then you will know what it is to give out your best energy in a long lesson that has not contained one pleasurable moment."

CHAPTER VIII

THE first lesson with the great master, after weeks or months of preliminary study, was an event for the preparatory teacher as well as for the pupil. It was customary to accompany pupils to the first few lessons as a convenience to Leschetizky, an arrangement from which the teacher often derived valuable hints for the preparation of later pupils, as well as, perhaps, a new direction for the future studies of the one already prepared. Sometimes Leschetizky inquired why the preparation had taken so long. On the other hand, he was apt to be skeptical about people who gained access to him very quickly. He judged his pupils from many standpoints, and so one never knew what the outcome might be. A lesson might be long or short, and every one was in reality more or less a reflection of the moment, according to the impression made upon him by the pupil. He liked to see good feeling existing between preparatory teacher and pupil. On one occasion he laughed outright on seeing his assistant and pupil come in together. "Really," he exclaimed, "you look like two school children, but that is not a bad sign!" So keen was his interest and curiosity in his new pupil that he would often go to the window to watch him come down the street. The pupil's manner of entering the room would be noted, and everything that had been observed or heard of him was taken into consideration. Good nature and self-possession on the

part of the pupil acted as a stimulant to Leschetizky in the lessons, as also courage in asking intelligent questions. Blunders were often cheerfully
overlooked if the personality of the pupil was at all
agreeable to the master. But, while the pupil's
personality was of great interest and importance
to him, the absolute correctness of every musical
as well as technical detail was the supreme test in
the first lesson. Every chord had to be understood
so well that its arpeggio could be played fluently
without hesitation. Moreover, the musical structure of the piece had to be so perfectly understood,
as well as visualized, that one could begin at any bar
or on any note. Until a few technical studies and
two or three pieces were mastered in these respects,
it was not possible to follow him freely in the de-
tailed study of tone and rhythm, which was so vital
a part of his marvelous teaching. The preparatory
course completed—it might be a matter of weeks
or years—it was possible for an assistant teacher
to broach the question of a lesson with Leschetizky on behalf of the pupil. He might ask the
pupil to play for him the fiftieth bar, for example.
This was a simple matter if one understood the
form and structure of the piece (which so many did
not) and much simpler than it seemed if one could
inwardly sing through the melody from a note near
one of the points of what he called *"Orientirung,"*
which he held that every player should have established for himself and visualized in the beginning, as
one visualizes the important features in a landscape.
He liked to have a pupil prove to him that he could
learn one piece exactly in this way, almost entirely
away from the piano, studying from the form down

to the details, instead of beginning to learn the piece by first listening to the playing of it, a method which he declared was never safe.

The lessons were often full of odd surprises for the assistant. The language was a hindrance, Americans being especially handicapped in this regard; and even if one spoke German and French fairly well, the exact value of Leschetizky's words was often lost. Naturally very few spoke Leschetizky's own language, Russian or Polish, and consequently German and French were most commonly used in the lessons. He himself spoke admirable French, which, however, he declared he had learned mostly in foreign countries, as he had never spent much time in France. He knew Italian fairly well, but very little English. He was an excellent Latin scholar and with him it was decidedly a point in one's favor if the pupil, whether man or woman, knew Latin. He was once heard to recommend to a young English girl to take the advice of her Ruskin who believed that every young lady should know the letters of the Greek alphabet.

Leschetizky has been described as moody, but he was not considered so by pupils who had known him best and longest. It is true that he was very susceptible to the atmosphere created around him, and was, in the lessons, as elsewhere, under the sway of varying emotions, much as an audience at a theater is under the domination of the stage, and he allowed his intuitions to guide him. In the lessons he rarely refrained from expressing himself with the utmost frankness and honesty, according to his impressions. Once he had consented to give a lesson, he gave his whole mind to it; consequently the assistant profited as much as the pupil by these first lessons. Often there were embarrassing moments, as when the pupil was criticized for something which was perhaps the result of an oversight on the part of the assistant. Every assistant, I think, dreaded the interruption of Leschetizky's flow of ideas by some trivial matter not at all worthy of the high standard he had set for himself in these lessons. A strange edition disturbed him. What he called artificial fingerings made him nervous—the position of the hand and the fingering should be different for each pupil. He often remonstrated or scolded—"Of course the fingering that's written there you wouldn't use. That is written by a man who is no pianist! But whatever makes you spend time looking out such absurd fingerings? Why not be simple, and take the fingers that lie most naturally over the keys? Your fingering has no connection with the shape of the group of notes you have to play or with the size of your hand either. You mustn't copy your assistant's hand or mine either." That was the time for the assistant to exonerate himself if he could. Leschetizky would then go to his piano and analyze, and dissect, and put together a difficult passage, with a view to adapting it to the hand of the pupil, and it was to be hoped that both assistant and pupil could fairly follow his method of procedure until he had made a finished product, or one that was at least ready at that moment for a public performance. And then he would tell you that the mastery of this difficult passage which he had selected was not at all a question of practicing; it all depended upon the understanding of it and the ability to see it plainly

—of making a picture of it in the mind's eye. After playing every note so slowly that one could memorize every detail and listen to the vibration of every tone, he expected the whole passage to move more rapidly the next time. The third time he expected you to play in tempo, and he considered that it all should go easily in tempo if you had understood his method of learning it. At an unsuccessful fourth attempt he would generally look the player in the face and take a new and ominous estimate of his talent and ability.

Whenever a pupil brought him a new composition and was unable to play some of the difficult passages, Leschetizky took time to learn these passages himself then and there. With a difficult piece he would sometimes spend the whole lesson hour in learning every detail. The form he remembered at first reading, or by even glancing at the pages. His first glance would be at the length of the piece, and he had the number of bars at once in his memory. The pupil sat by, usually amazed at this process and at his ability to make all the difficulties seem easy. But he considered it quite simple. As to method in teaching, he thought there had always been a deplorable tendency to found systems and methods upon one point of technique. How he himself had suffered from that tendency! People came to him who could only stay a year or two, and the haste to learn everything in so short a time resulted in peculiarities and affectations, as well as in the hardest and most inartistic manner of playing—a style that Leschetizky abhorred. He used to remark sadly to these frantic pupils, "Yes, I see, time is money!" Often a word dropped by him when it applied only to some special point, became the basis for a "method" by those students who tried to crowd five years' study into one. There was the case of a young woman who had studied with one of these ambitious and feverish pupils. She already had the "method," she said, and, incidentally, she had neuritis in her arm. Her teacher had taught her that it was Leschetizky's method to press the fingers on the keys until the nails separated from the flesh, declaring that Leschetizky had used the expression, "press until the blood runs." What probably happened was that he actually said this to a pupil with flabby fingers that never reached the bottom of the keys. One can imagine the pupil asking if he should press, and Leschetizky's bored and impatient answer, "Yes, yes, press until the blood runs." This teacher had been truly honest in her desire to learn everything in one year. She appeared in Vienna one winter, a tall, middle-aged woman, doubtless with her return ticket in her pocket. She had a fever for learning but probably in so short a time learned very little.

People who had been heard by Leschetizky only once or twice often begged for recommendations. Whenever it was possible to give them he did so. Nevertheless he was cautious. On one occasion when a pupil was departing and a friend interceded in her behalf, Leschetizky was unable to connect any playing with the name. "Bring her out," he said, "and let me see her hand." When she came a glance at her hand reassured him. She had played well in the few lessons she had had with him, and the desired credential was given her. It was an astonishing fact that Leschetizky could remember every hand he had ever observed at the piano. Hands were like pictures to him, and of paramount importance. He might forget faces, but hands, never. After years he was able to recognize a hand and remembered the pieces that had been played by it.

Leschetizky had many annoying experiences with students calling themselves his pupils after studying only with assistants. Once at my own house he met one of these would-be pupils who told him she was preparing for him. He graciously asked her to play, which she did. Afterward she exclaimed joyfully to me, "Now I can call myself a Leschetizky pupil!"

It was always a mystery to him how some of the hands in the class became lame and strained, as he was unconscious of the foolish practices in vogue among the students. He constantly cautioned against any stretching or pulling of the hand, and it was never his idea to practice with paper wads or a key pulled up between the fingers! He did not advocate doing unnatural things with the hands or trying to develop a style that was unnatural. Sometimes a pretty girl had to make too heroic attempts to play her pieces and Leschetizky would stop her with this advice: "That piece is not becoming to you. A woman should never fight the keys, particularly if she is good-looking!" It was a grief to him that Paula Szalit, one of his greatest pupils, did not follow his advice more closely in her selection of pieces, but insisted upon playing heavy pieces for which he thought her small hands unfitted. As an example of taste in repertoire he would often refer to that charming artist,

Clothilde Kleeberg, a great favorite on the Continent, who never attempted anything that her particular style did not allow her to play well. It appalled him to think that any one should strain a hand in studying technique as Paula Szalit did from time to time. Hands, he said, could be injured away from the piano and through carelessness, too; and in this connection he spoke of Katherine Goodson's unfortunate experience during her last winter in Vienna. One evening, after playing, with her hands warm with the exercise, she had gone to an open window where they became chilled in the cool air. A rheumatic condition of the muscles set in, and she had to spend the rest of the season trying to rid herself of it.

He continually cautioned against technical exercises the last thing at night. Far better, he thought it was, to play pieces with a variety of technique and touch; nevertheless, the study of that part of technique not natural to one was something upon which he insisted, and how such practice could be used to the advantage of one's health was a pet whim of his. I had the theory applied to my own case. Once, on the way back to Vienna, I had been obliged to remain several weeks in a rest cure on account of a cough. When I came again to Leschetizky he wanted me to see his own doctor in Vienna. All chord and octave playing the doctor firmly forbade, to Leschetizky's excitement and disgust. The master claimed that he had once cured a girl of consumption by the practice of octaves and chords. Countermanding the physician's orders, he advised the same cure for my cough. His instructions were that my piano should be moved to the window, and I, warmly dressed, should sit very low, or, preferably, kneel before it, breath deeply, and, reaching up, practice heavy chords and octaves until I was tired. My octaves profited, and the cough did actually disappear.

One evening, as Leschetizky was dining, an American lady was announced, who said she had studied with him twenty years before. At first he was not disposed to see her, but when she sent in the usual persuasive message that "she had crossed the ocean to see him," he laughingly consented to receive her. Twenty years was a rather long time, he remarked as he left the table, and he said he did not know what he could do for a person after so long an interval, if she was not even talented enough for him to remember. When he returned he inquired of me, "Don't Americans always tell the truth? I don't believe she ever studied with me, for I cannot remember her hand." All the time I could see that he was puzzled and moody over his inability to recall her hand. He was convinced that he had never seen it before. However, he told her to come and play for him. Before the day appointed for the hearing some malevolent person in the class informed Leschetizky that the lady had been advertising herself in certain Western newspapers as a "Teacher of the Leschetizky Method in Twelve Lessons." A number of trying experiences, with recommendations and demands, had thoroughly tried Leschetizky's patience. "Leschetizky Method in Twelve Lessons" infuriated him and induced him to make an example of this teacher who represented herself as a former pupil. On the day she was to play for him the assistants were all invited to be present. We sat there around the piano when she came into the room. She entered tremblingly, but even in that tense and ominous atmosphere she kept up her pluck and went directly to the piano. I think (I was so utterly confused and embarrassed by the situation) that she played the Bach "A-Minor-Prelude and Fugue." Leschetizky listened in silence—always a terrible omen. If he was interested he never allowed faults to pass unnoticed. When she had finished he addressed the assistants, "Do you see any of my ideas in this playing?" No one could speak. He then turned directly to me, "This is a fellow countrywoman of yours. Just the same, you have got to tell the truth, is there anything good about it? And you are the one who has advertised herself as a teacher of my method in twelve lessons?" he said to her. "Is that so?" She could only admit it, and, fairly annihilated, she left the room.

About a week later this undoubtedly well-meaning woman sent for me. I had been the only American there, and because my face expressed sympathy with her she wished to tell me the truth. Since that miserable day of the hearing, the San Francisco earthquake had occurred; and only that morning she had received a cablegram from her father saying that everything she possessed had been destroyed. She said she wished to make a confession. Twenty years before she had been in Vienna preparing for Leschetizky. At last she was ready to play for him, and a lesson was arranged just the day before she was to leave. There were several pupils ahead of her, and late in the afternoon he sent out word that he could not give any more lessons that day, so she had to go back to America without playing for him even once. He was right, he had never seen her hand. At home something had been expected of her and she had "stretched a point" to call herself a Leschetizky pupil. I took this story at once to Leschetizky. It distressed him, but he could not forgive her sufficiently to see her again. "Of course I have taken away her income," he reflected, "and now there is this terrible disaster on top of it. I can at least send her some money," he said, "but as for hearing her again at the piano, no, I can never do that."

Such instances were annoying enough, but not so trying to him as the rarer experience of finding disloyalty in a real pupil, who, through egotism, had set himself in opposition to the master's methods. There was one who thought Leschetizky's way too long and arduous, and set out to discover for himself some short cut to fame. His method was based upon the theory that in the past pianists had studied too much. It was not at all necessary to bother with theory, or to learn anything except the actual pieces one intended to play. "What is the use of being a good musician?" he asked. "When you come before your audience no one cares what you know if you play well. Pieces could be learned from hearing another play them, as a parrot learns to speak. There must be a method in everything," he contended, and he had a method that would never fail. Upon these principles he established himself in another city, and boasted, when he left, that he would send a pupil back to Vienna to play, that would excel any pupil that Leschetizky had ever had. Some one remarked to him that if he did, Leschetizky would be the first to recognize it. If there had been reason in the method of this pupil Leschetizky would indeed have been the first to listen to him. He was eager for new ideas—the reason, perhaps, he was so tolerant of all who asked to play for him.

Now that I had shown myself capable of teaching, Leschetizky was very serious about having me go to Ischl in the summer to study with him how to teach. Up to this time I had heard very little about technique from him, and it was only from studying with him how to train different hands that I heard his views about technique. In Ischl not a day passed that we did not take up some point of technique, for whenever any one came there to play for him with the hope of studying, he would send his servant up the hill for me. While the prospective pupil played I stood by. Afterward he would ask me what I thought of the hand. He would take up the question of the thumb of one hand, for instance. This thumb was a little longer than usual—what would be the position, then, of the hand on the keyboard? Another hand was heavy—he instructed me how to give it flexibility and lightness. And these points he liked to discuss. I often recalled that first experience of mine in the beginning of my own study, when I had tried to copy hand position and fingering from a friend who was studying the same piece, and how Leschetizky went over every technical detail, in a different way, with us. He advised me now to dispense with all rules for wrist motion. "There is no method for the wrist," he said, "except to get the easiest way to the next note." And in the years since I have tried to keep in mind the exact meaning of his words. "Books could be written about the motions of the wrist," he said. "And, although it often required considerable knowledge to cope with an individual hand, in general it was better to let the shape and size of it determine the action of the wrist. Anyway, you can get your softest as well as your strongest tones from the arm with a firm wrist," he went on; "so in any problem of finger or wrist or arm it is better to reckon with physical characteristics, and be guided by good judgment. I can tell you," he said, "that I am to-day a much better teacher than I was ten years ago. One learns from every new pupil, the untalented as well as the talented. Sometimes the pupil who seems stupid in the beginning becomes an interesting student under good training. Often the talented ones find many simple things difficult, so every day I learn something new. Don't have a method," he said to me; "it is far better to leave your mind a blank for the pupil to fill in. You will discover more easily, in this way, what he needs. Even in technique it is impossible to have a method, for every hand is different. I *have* no method and I *will have* no method. Go to concerts and be sharp-witted, and if you are observing you will learn tremendously from the ways that are successful and also from those that are not. Adopt with your pupils the ways that succeed with them, and get away as far as possible from the idea of a method. Write over your music-room door the motto: 'NO METHOD!'"

CHAPTER IX

WHEN foreigners or strangers came to Ischl and looked about for lodgings, the familiar greeting was: "Probably you have come to study with the Herr Professor!" Those who remained in Ischl through the summer, were, for the most part, attracted there by Leschetizky. In this little town, picturesquely placed among the mountains of the Salzkammergut, the Emperor had one of his summer palaces. Brahms was also a summer resident, but was not friendly to strangers or interested in them. He was reported to be irritable and impatient of many small things. "My dog Solo would have annoyed him terribly," Leschetizky once remarked, but he added quickly, "He loved the mountains, though, and preferred these near ones to the lofty remote peaks of Switzerland, a preference one would hardly have expected in Brahms." Many distinguished people were to be seen on the Esplanade at Ischl. Johann Strauss was often seen there. Edouard Schütt liked to come over from Meran. Rosenthal and Fannie Bloomfield Zeisler came often to Ischl. As for Leschetizky, life in this beautiful spot was thoroughly agreeable. "Ischl leads to cheerful thoughts," he said. He dearly loved Ischl and all its surroundings. The place put him at once in a happy mood. During the six weeks of the rainy season of the Salzkammergut he was never unhappy indoors or taking long walks carrying his umbrella. He was only moody when other people complained of the bad weather. He owned a small villa there, charmingly situated, with a beautiful view in all directions, and on one side was a meadow leading into the woods. He often remarked that he was blessed in having many things at Ischl, the meadows, the mountains, the walks through the woods and the seclusion of his own garden. There was a profusion of flowers everywhere, and in the distance rushing waters were to be seen and heard. This tiny place was complete in every detail even to the friendly little bench outside the hedge which he considered indispensable to hospitality. "Tired peasants coming up the hill are glad of that bench," he used to say. "Brahms has sat there many a time, and who knows but that the Emperor with all his troubles may have rested there some time. He is a tired man, too."

The people of Ischl knew Leschetizky as a kind, affable man, who was interested in them and ready to listen to anything they wanted to tell him of their affairs or troubles. The peasants all knew him and were proud to say that he had spoken to them as he passed by. He addressed them with a kind of fatherly solicitude that was charming to see. "It is a good thing to have their approval," he said. "They know as well as diplomats whether you mean what you are saying or not." One lady there with little tact or pliability in conversation who often saw Leschetizky talking with various people, especially the peasants, took her notebook finally and tried to classify his remarks and record his expressions. She soon gave this up in despair, however, remarking that at first she had thought the

charm lay in his words, but was finally convinced
that it must be his manner, which acted like magic
upon people of all kinds. Now she knew that it was
hopeless to try to imitate him. He must be a ma-
gician, she concluded. She related many stories
that showed the master in a somewhat sentimental
light. Indeed, on occasions, he could be sentimental and tender, as well as intensely practical. One
summer when he arrived in Ischl—so the story
goes—crowds of children, friends and citizens met
him at the station. This was shortly after he had
been given officially the freedom of the town. The
townspeople followed him in procession to the hill-
side field beyond the villa where refreshments had
been prepared. Children with arms full of flowers
followed the Professor everywhere, clinging to
his arms and coat tails, as he greeted each one
separately by name. All at once he stopped and
asked, "Where is little Tillie?" On learning that
Tillie, a small peasant girl, had been obliged to stay
at home because she had no dress to wear for this
occasion, Leschetizky slipped away unnoticed, went
quickly to Tillie's house and took her to a shop
near by. The woman behind the counter fastened
on a new dress. Leschetizky washed the child's face
and shortly after he and a very happy little girl appeared hand in hand at the welcome party.

During the time that the Palace was occupied
Ischl became a gay and festive summer resort, especially for Austrians. The Empress spent a great
deal of time there, as did also friends of the
Court, notably Madame Schratt, the famous actress, who had a house on one of the beautiful roads
a mile or two out of the town. The Emperor, it was

said, liked to play billiards every evening at her
house, where the best players refrained, however,
from winning a game from his Imperial Majesty.

The Emperor walked generally at nine in the
morning and at five in the afternoon. Often his
steps led past the peasant cottage where we were
living, and in response to our low curtsy he saluted
us with great ceremony and with an enchanting
smile, which suddenly transformed his habitually
sad countenance. He walked through the fields
and forests alone, or with a companion, safeguarded,
however, by detectives who stationed themselves at
intervals behind the doors of cottages along the
way.

The summer when the Empress was assassinated
she had just left Ischl for Geneva. The Emperor
had recently completed for her a beautiful road
around and over one of the mountains back of the
Palace where she could stroll alone and unobserved.
It was possible, by introduction to an official, to
obtain the key that unlocked the series of gates
along this road and to walk there after the Empress
had left. One evening, as we had just descended
this mountain and had come into the Palace gardens, we observed signs of the greatest agitation.
In a few moments the bells of Ischl began to toll. A
huge voice through a megaphone called the people
together who gathered from the neighboring hills
to hear that their Empress had been assassinated.
Until far into night they collected in the squares,
falling on their knees, weeping and praying. It
was a touching and pitiful sight to see these kind-
hearted, devoted peasants at that terrible time. Indeed, it was many a day before the people of this

quiet little place regained their normal composure. Some of them were strangely terror-stricken. Others became unbalanced and wild. One good peasant, who had been gardener at the Palace for a long time, was so profoundly affected by the tragic news that he became almost insane. The Empress had always spoken kindly to him, he said, and to think that he had failed her when bad people rose to do her harm! He threatened to shoulder a gun and find the assassin, but finally his horror subsided into honest tears. His wife went on a pilgrimage to a shrine thirty miles distant, walking all the way, to offer thanks for the preservation of her husband's mind. During the following summer my sister and I lived in a little cottage at the top of a hill called the "Doppelblick." The good peasant woman with whom we lived used to tell how on many a morning the Empress had come across the hill through the field with her magnificent braids of hair down her back, dressed in a simple white dress, to drink a glass of milk at her cottage. This happened generally very early in the morning, she said. She would point with pride to the bench where the Empress had sat. "Who could have wanted to kill that poor lady, our Empress?" she said, crossing herself. "She was all kindness and she had so many troubles, too. She lost her only son and used to tell me how thankful I should be that I had all my children alive and well."

The peasants of Ischl were for the most part good-hearted and pleasure-loving. They seemed to enjoy life immensely and were very kind to their large families of children. One of the happiest and

gayest had thirteen, worked in the fields until sun-
down, and danced a good part of the night with
much drinking of beer. On great occasions she ate
meat, but with good beer she considered that she had
enough for everyday life. She was very sorry for
ladies. Ladies were generally not healthy, she understood. It was difficult for them to keep well,
she was sure, and she had often heard that ladies did
not love their children. Over in America, across
the Danube, they threw them into the rivers, she
had heard. She knew that if she went very far away
from Ischl, they would laugh at her for having so
many children, so she was satisfied, and preferred to
stay at home.

Leschetizky was always interested in the attitude
of foreigners toward this class, and was especially
amused by stories illustrating any interest these
people took in things outside their own work. There
were those who could vouch for the fact that one
good peasant farmer of a town in southern Austria,
despite his ignorance of all other reading, knew the
Bible and Shakespeare by heart, and once he had
been heard to recite an entire scene from *Hamlet*.
Another peasant owned a good collection of oil
paintings and argued with the owner of the estate
about perspective. It amused and interested Leschetizky to hear this peasant speak of his pictures.
(In Austria it was not at all unusual to hear ladies
tell of their servants hurrying to finish their work
in order to get a few free hours at a picture gallery.)

For many years Leschetizky had spent his summers here in sympathetic Ischl. As soon as he arrived and was rested from the journey and had

played the piano a little, his first pleasure was to walk over the familiar roads that gave him so much to see and think about and, as he expressed it, to ponder whether he had anything new and interesting or worthy about himself to bring to them—his old friends. He liked to saunter on his walks, and would ask any one about to go with him, "Are you the kind of person that will not saunter or stop occasionally? I hope not, for perhaps then you might not enjoy my kind of walk." He was especially fond of the road over the hill, called the Sophiens Doppelblick, from which there was a good view of the snow-capped mountains and deep valleys. It led also to a remote coffee house where one could order, besides the best coffee, a delicious little supper. He liked to stop in the deep woods on the way and tell mysterious stories. One of his favorites was an experience in Finland when he was on a long, solitary journey. This story his sister-in-law, the Countess Potocka, has charmingly told in her book about him. On one occasion four of us were with him in these woods—Edouard Schütt, his great friend and pupil, Miss Jane Olmsted, a favorite pupil, my sister, and I. We were seated on the ground under the great trees, when suddenly, on the road below, we saw the Emperor passing with his friend Madame Schratt. Leschetizky was on his feet in an instant, "Get up, get up, my children," he said, "there is a piece of Europe walking by."

Further along was a little stone erected to mark the spot where the Emperor's son had shot his first deer. Leschetizky used to like to stop here to indulge in reminiscences. He had had many conversations with the Crown Prince, whom he admired exceedingly. He spoke enthusiastically of his great mind, his sportsmanship, and his attainments in literature and art.

With all his activities Leschetizky never gave the impression of restlessness. He loved his home and the quiet of his own garden, where he would sit for hours. It was incomprehensible to him that people should find no comfort in their own surroundings. "Oh!" he would exclaim, "you people who make hotels of your houses, a place to sleep and dress in and then leave, you are the people who have only acquaintances, you have no time for friendships."

The longer one knew Leschetizky, the more one grew to admire his unerring judgment in estimating character. He advocated the most searching analysis of people in general. He thought one should study the art of judging people and never ignore any one. He had remarkable patience with some apparently undesirable people and admitted that he had himself learned through making many mistakes of hasty judgment to take pains to discover, once for all, the possible good qualities of others, for to overlook these was to place oneself at a great disadvantage. One should learn to be finely discriminating with people and not pass them over.

He received a great many people in Ischl, whether of the artistic world or not. Many strangers and distinguished foreigners who passed through the Tyrol and Salzkammergut made a point of paying a visit to Leschetizky, who had a great reputation for illuminating conversation. He took much interest in foreign politics and was keen to talk with foreigners about their countries, speaking to them generally in their own language.

In recounting the amusing beginning of one of his great friendships, he said, "When I see my dear friend Professor Neusser sitting here in my garden, I say to myself every time, 'What if I had missed knowing him?' for I nearly did miss it, through my own stupidity." In his youth he used to meet daily in the Kärntnerstrasse, a man of about his own age, and every time they met, a feeling of intense antagonism swept over him. It was apparent that the feeling was mutual. In the then narrow street they often had to pass so closely that their elbows touched. Each time Leschetizky ground his teeth in rage and declared that if their elbows ever touched again he would do something violent. He would even have welcomed an occasion for a duel, he said, so intense was his aversion for this haughty-looking stranger. Some time later they met at the home of a friend and this antipathy turned instantly to mutual admiration. On hearing the man speak, Leschetizky recognized his great ability and warmth of personality, and set about to make the best impression upon him. This was the beginning of a lifelong friendship. Professor Neusser was a celebrated Viennese physician and a good musician as well, a thing not uncommon among the Viennese university professors. Through him, Leschetizky said he learned to love all doctors. "They are the best people in the world," he added.

He told of another friendship that began very badly, too. Early in the acquaintance there were large gifts of champagne made which were promptly returned. Excessive friendliness he had also objected to, but he soon discovered great diffi-

dence under these extremes and out of a chaos of
disagreement and misunderstanding that lasted a
year or two, he brought to light a real friendship
that nothing affected or disturbed. Superficially,
one had to win him anew each time, but his real
friendships were lasting and profound. He always
had time for them and liked to talk daily, if possible, with the same people. There was a great depth
of feeling in his friendships, and he used to say that
friendship was the most difficult thing on earth
to retain or to be worthy of.

Although he could have more time to himself
here in Ischl than anywhere else, he never took a
real vacation. He disliked the thought of vacation.
It was incomprehensible to him that a musician
could be without his instrument even for a day if
one were to be had; and it is certain that if he were
in a place where he could not have a piano, he would
have sought out somebody who had one on which
he could play, or he would have composed, or at
least would have spent some of his time in the study
of music. He could scarcely keep away from the
piano and was in such intimate relationship with
it that he sometimes played a chord on entering the
room, as if to say good-morning, or, on leaving, as
if to say good-by.

One summer, as my sister and I were packing our
boxes to go to the Island of Rügen, Leschetizky
came to say good-by to us, and, fearing that we were
going to be late for our train, he helped with might
and main to finish our packing. As we were leaving
he exclaimed, "You haven't said good-by to the
piano." Then, seeing how hurried we were, he
went to the piano himself and played us a joyous

little good-by, adding, "It will be several days before you can hear a piano again."

It always seemed to me that he felt the tones speaking to him, although I never heard him say so. He did say once, however, that it was difficult for him not to associate the expression of a face with certain tones.

He had time in Ischl to compose, and wrote many of his pieces there, confining himself mostly to the type of small lyric pieces for the piano.

But he generally arrived in Ischl with boxes full of new compositions by others to be looked over. He was decidedly interested in the length of pieces and considered the matter of the duration of any composition as highly important. Often he made cuts, or repeated, or added parts according to his sense of time, and while he was reading new compositions, his watch was usually before him on the piano. He thought that the greatest composers often made the mistake of spinning out the music too long. "Shakespeare never made that mistake in his tragedies or comedies," he said. "Young people don't make that mistake either, it's the old ones."

Young composers could always be sure of his interest and careful attention. Sometimes he offered a prize for the best composition written by his pupils; once in Vienna he offered a prize for the best lyric composition written between classes, that is, in a fortnight. Arthur Schnabel wrote three. One of them took the first prize, but Leschetizky gave two first prizes; Ossip Gabrilowitsch won the other.

He and Julius Epstein consented to look over about one hundred and fifty compositions in manuscript, which were written for a prize offered by the famous piano manufacturer, Bösendorfer. Leschetizky was red-eyed from reading manuscripts all day long and late into the night. He seemed depressed also, and it was altogether a bad summer for pupils. One day, however, he appeared in an entirely new mood. He seemed relieved and fairly inspired. "I have found a real composition," he said at last, "a real concerto, and I'll wager anything that a young man has written it; only a young man could have written it," he said. "It is too difficult not to show age in musical ideas. When one is aged," he added, rather too solemnly we thought, considering his youthful spirit, "it's the quality of this concerto that counts, and one feels happy and young at some of these phrases." There were about thirty compositions still to be looked over, but this he did cheerfully, delighted at finding a real treasure. When the judges finally awarded the prize to the composer whose concerto had so pleased Leschetizky, his name was found to be Ernst Dohnanyi, then young and almost unknown.

We had an amusing discussion one evening in Ischl about one of the motives of a phrase that Leschetizky was composing. One of us thought it was too much like one of the phrases in the Chopin "Fantasie in F Minor." The others thought not. Leschetizky finally decided it this way: "If you will convince me that you can make the same motion of hand with the same expression of face for both, then I will throw away my phrase as too much like the other. Oh, children!" he exclaimed, "how happy I am to be here with my family—my pupils are my family. It is hard to be serious in this cheerful place. I should be writing humoresques and fantasies all summer if we did not have serious careers to think about. Go home now and tell me to-morrow that you have learned something new and have not wasted your time."

That summer about fifty people came to play for him with the hope of studying after taking the usual course of preparation with an assistant. Invariably he was more interested in their intelligence and temperament than in any amount of finger dexterity or academic knowledge. He listened with greatest attention to every one and tried to discover evidences of talent, but his verdict was usually final and, alas, sometimes merciless. One instinctively felt in playing to him that he considered every possibility, for his greatest ambition seemed to be to develop any good quality to the fullest extent to which it could be developed. "Only natural qualities can become great," he said; "the acquired ones may become excellent, but never great."

If there was any doubt in his own mind about a talent, he was always generous enough to admit that he did not know to what degree it could be developed. A well-known teacher, of Atlanta, Georgia, brought several of her pupils to play to him; she asked him if he thought one of them had talent enough to go on. He looked at the girl thoughtfully, then touched his forehead saying, "I should first have to know what's up here."

A young man came out to Ischl to confer with Leschetizky for the second or third time about his career. He had played a long time, but showed little intelligence in his study. He was vague and visionary, and thought Leschetizky too severe altogether. The patient master advised him to give up studying music at once if he did not intend to make a success of his career, and when this youth suggested that it would probably kill him to give up the piano, Leschetizky answered, "Well, then you had better have done with yourself at once than go on living to be a failure."

Of the many who came to play for him at Ischl he accepted three or four as pupils. To the rest he gave thoughtful and sincere advice, either offering the possibility of a lesson with him after an indefinite period of study with one of his assistants, or advising them kindly but firmly to seek some other teacher, or suggesting that they give it up altogether. One young man came to get Leschetizky's opinion about his difficulties. He had a most unfortunate hand, his finger-nails were grown too far over the finger tips. It was his heart's desire to play the piano, and Leschetizky instinctively felt this. After studying with a great many teachers in Europe and then coming to Vienna, he went first to an assistant, thinking to better his chances with the master by a little development of his hand. After struggling for a long time to find some position for his hand on the keyboard without success, he finally came to Leschetizky, who agreed to spend any amount of time to help him out of his difficulty. This young man was rather exceptionally accomplished as a musician, but Leschetizky could find no way to develop his hand, and, regretfully and with tears in his eyes for the poor boy's plight, he told him it was merely a waste of time to think of playing the piano.

Another boy's career he felt compelled to decide. This young man had studied to the point of playing the greatest compositions written for the piano with what Leschetizky called, "not merely good technique but a beautiful technique," but he thought he saw a great turning point in his career. "You have puzzled me for some time," he said; "I hear you play and wonder just what is the matter; I notice when you are playing a concerto the moment you have to follow, your playing takes on character. You associate the music with scenes and words. It is a singer's talent," he said, "and it is clear to me that you would be a great follower. Would you not like to be a famous accompanist?" he asked, as though the question was settled, "for," he added, "it is an honor to accompany great singers."

However, he took to his heart the two or three talented ones and especially one young man from Frankfurt, Paul Goldschmidt by name. One morning we were surprised to see him hurrying up the hill to the Doppelblick with that elated expression on his face that he had when anything delighted him. His words about talent, as he sat on the little bench beside the peasant's cottage, I well remember:

"I have this morning found a talent," he said, his eyes sparkling; "he is a German, with an interesting but complex personality. He is oversensitive, very young, believes in his own talent, and expects everything of me."

Leschetizky made himself comfortable on the bench and talked with deepest seriousness and concern. "If only he can take the rebuffs that will come," he said.

"His is not the great, forceful talent, it is fine and spiritual, and he is spiritual himself, but everything he plays he makes beautiful or he *could* make beautiful.

"If only he had the power of that other one who was here yesterday. You only had to look at him—to look at his jaw—to know what he would do. Why can't I put them all together?

"Up there," he said, breaking off suddenly and pointing upward, "there is a great orb called talent shining down on us. There are a dozen rays from it; one person catches this ray, another that ray, and once or twice in a century there is some one who catches them all. This new one does not reflect them all, but several," he said, "yes, several. I shall not try to do the impossible, or try to make out of him something that he is not. There are many who might congratulate themselves if they possessed the qualities that he possesses and I believe that he has a sufficient number to become a great artist.

"My energy shall not fail," he said. "If only *he* does not fail in some way. Teaching is art, too," he added, "and the more talented my pupils are, the more I feel the need of those rays we were just talking about. If he will do his part, I shall do mine."

CHAPTER X

THE discovery of a really great gift was always an exhilarating experience to Leschetizky. He was on these occasions inclined to go into long disquisitions on the subject of artists and the traditions of music. He would describe the different technical equipments of players, whether unknown to the world or famous. One could do such and such a thing well; another had great individuality in phrasing; another could never relax enough. He quoted Madame Marchesi who declared that a certain kind of person could never draw a long breath in public. "They breathe naturally only when they are alone," she said.

These talks of his, which proceeded apparently from reveries and ever-recurring pictures in his mind, were exceedingly instructive, and he made the pictures so clear that they were easily remembered. Paul Goldschmidt's character was worrying Leschetizky not a little at this time. The young man had individuality, but seemed to lack the ability to make his gifts shine forth. As Leschetizky expressed it, "he lacked the glorification of his qualities."

He was due for military service the next year, so Leschetizky set about to secure his exemption and succeeded in doing so. He believed he saw every reason for Goldschmidt's becoming a great pianist, and thought it was decidedly necessary for him to have uninterrupted years of study.

He sent him to me for preparation, but warned me constantly against leniency and haste. He told me how every teacher must beware of talented pupils—that both teacher and pupil often went astray by not being practical enough, and he thought that one could not be too practical in the training of the hand and in studying technique. Talented people were like children, he said, and a teacher must express himself clearly and distinctly the first time, as children and the talented remember the first word spoken and the first efforts of the teacher to express his idea. They do not need to be told twice. He summed up the requisites for a preparation for lessons with him as the application of a very few sound and practical principles to the hand of the pupil.

He was very much pleased that without any evidence of method I had been able to prepare two or three pupils in Vienna to play for him, who had succeeded in qualifying for frequent lessons and had been able to understand him in these lessons.

If one was ready for lessons from Leschetizky, one could usually get them. He was even willing, on occasions, to read over a composition with a pupil who had been prepared technically, with the idea of improving the pupil's method of studying by noting the workings of his mind. He was keen in such matters, but he did not approve of studying technique at first in pieces. After scales and études had been mastered, it was a different thing; one's technique could then be maintained by reviewing the difficult passages that one found in pieces, after which the incessant repetition of scales and études might be discontinued. He considered it very unadvisable to attempt to learn pieces that were technically too difficult, as one too often lost all sense of the beauty of the music by playing in false tempos until the ear had become accustomed to the wrong interpretation. To those who repeated difficult passages fifty times, or practiced with a timepiece or a metronome, he would say, "Where is your ear? Gone forever probably; keep your metronome to bark at you sometimes like a watchdog, if you are not sure of yourself in tempos or cannot retain them in your ear. Forget about your watch and concentrate your mind on your own personal mechanism; the dampers of the instrument you are going to play will also take care of themselves if your ear is good enough.

"And talented pupils," he said, "are easily distracted. They ask you many questions, but their own minds lead them astray. Paul Goldschmidt is talented enough, but he has just as much to learn as some others."

He was indeed more talented than the pupils I had already prepared for Leschetizky in the spring before going to Ischl, but they had been more practical themselves and had easily and simply studied exactly as they were directed. The first time that I met Paul Goldschmidt he seized both my hands and said, "If you will give me technique, Miss Newcomb, I shall be the greatest pianist in the world."

Many talented people came to study with Leschetizky, but never had I heard one of them making such a statement. Paderewski had been in no hurry, it was said, to learn pieces, and had confined his studying for six months to technique.

Paula Szalit, they said, practiced Czerny études all
day long for months and kept her mind free from
all distractions of beautiful music. She had taught
herself to play these études in all tempos and with
all shades of expression, so that they at last
sounded more like beautiful pieces. Leschetizky
had asked her to play one of them once in the
class, so beautifully did she play it in every respect.
Another of the pupils, little Miecio Horzowsky, it
was said, ran home as soon as his mind grasped
one fundamental of technique or tone, and incor-
porated it into every piece that he knew, turning it
over in his philosophical little great brain until
every possibility was grasped.

I repeated Paul Goldschmidt's statement to
Leschetizky, who did not like it at all, and technique
at once became the basis of disagreement between
them. To me Leschetizky frequently said, "Poor
boy, such belief in his own talent may bring him the
greatest unhappiness." However, Leschetizky
seemed more touched by Goldschmidt's case than
annoyed with him, and had great faith in his
powers. He cautioned me about his frail hand and
gave me many directions in teaching him, frequently inquiring about his progress.

While Leschetizky always insisted that he himself had no method, he on one occasion seemed to
be thinking over his words, for he added, "If I had
a method it would be based upon the mental delineation of a chord."

Many times he would ask the pupil to make a list
of all the chords, as well as of groups of notes, to
make a picture of them in his mind's eye, and to
study the picture, at the same time shaping the

hand according to the picture, before touching the keys. He called this the "physiognomy" of the hand. Some pupils found this very easy, while to others it seemed curiously difficult. To one American in Ischl Leschetizky spoke of this as his method, and advised him to take a few lessons at once of his American assistant, who happened to be there at the time. This pupil's prompt refusal to study with an American may possibly have led Leschetizky to make the remark that "Americans were very quick to grasp this point of technique." At any rate, I have heard him say once or twice that Americans had a talent for visualizing.

Regarding the subject of memorizing, Leschetizky had indeed a method, and Miss Annette Hullah, one of his English pupils, has given a most perfect interpretation of this method in one chapter of her book, *Living Masters in Music*.

It rather perplexed Leschetizky that sometimes Americans did not want to study with me, and it amused him very much to hear me say that I could understand that they did not feel like coming to Europe to study with an American. This was the reason that at first most of my pupils were Europeans. They had no such contempt for the ability of Americans. Behind their backs, however, Leschetizky was tireless in his efforts to make me worthy of the position in which he had placed me, and he did not intend to make it easy for me either. One day he presented me with a long list of compositions, and asked if I was sure I knew every one of them. He said they were pieces every teacher ought to know. There was a list of pieces for children also, mostly old-fashioned humorous little compositions. He thought children should not play grown-up pieces, or play like grown-ups, and should not attempt pieces with emotion.

He wanted me to play the "Concert Piece" of Weber at the first class meeting in the autumn, and "From now on," he said, "you must not strike a wrong note. Don't take me too literally," he went on; "there are some who think you are too inexperienced to teach. I shall tell them to substitute the word 'modern' for 'inexperienced.'

"I am going to send you the little boy," he said, mentioning one of the most talented pupils in his class, "for a few lessons. I will tell you what to teach him, for it is an intricate little piece of technique that takes time, but I have an object in sending him to you; it is to make those two or three Americans ashamed of themselves, who find it so difficult to come to Europe to study with an American.

"There are no mysteries in technique," Leschetizky often remarked. "The mysteries and secrets come when you begin to play dynamically and rhythmically. When once you listen to your own playing as if you were listening to some one else, and find yourself unhappy and dissatisfied, then it is that your real study begins."

But even in Leschetizky's opinion the difficulties which certain pupils experienced in working out technical problems seemed to be due to a combination of traits or qualities that could almost be called peculiar to certain nations or nationalities.

For example, one of his assistants declared that no American knew the value of the short note following a dotted note, and that she had never known an American who could give the short note its exact value in relation to the notes around it. This seemed on first thought to be absurd. However, it really was characteristic of us to be technically proficient and able to play perfectly in time, while the quality of listening and memorizing sounds was more or less lacking.

In all my study with Leschetizky and in all my experience in taking pupils to him and hearing others' lessons, I do not think there was any technical point that gave him so much trouble and annoyance as this one of the real value of the short note—a sixteenth after a dotted eighth, for instance, coming before an accent. There seemed to be no end of difficulty in this one little motive,—relaxing, contracting the muscles again just in time,—preparation of the next group, and, most of all, rhythm, which meant listening.

I shall never forget that in one of my own earlier lessons all playing was suspended for the sake of one note which, according to Leschetizky, I could not play correctly. When time came for this lesson, I began to have a painful premonition of my difficulty. This was in the first two or three bars of the "Nocturne in G Major" of Rubinstein. What was the matter with that E at the end of the second bar? I tried again and again to play it as he played it and wanted it, but at repetition my hand would stiffen at the wrong time, and the tone would come too soon or too late, or too loud or too soft. The lesson had come to a standstill. I was convinced that the fault was not that I did not judge correctly the length of tone F sharp before the E, for I flattered myself that I knew by now how to listen to the vibration and length of tone. After each failure the master would throw up his hands

in despair or disgust, or sink back in his chair
flushing with impatience. On the verge of despair
I remembered the fate of some of his pupils, who
for lesser crimes had simply been turned out of the
house. It was characteristic of Leschetizky, however, that he became all the more interested if he
saw that the pupil was trying doggedly to overcome
a difficulty. His whole attitude of mind would
change and he would bring to bear upon the problem a complete concentration of mind, and all the
resources of his ingenuity. Time did not count
with him then. He only became more and more
determined to succeed in solving the problem. On
this occasion, after probably half an hour, the situation became decidedly interesting. It seemed to
me that he must be going to send me away forever,
even if I should finally play that phrase as he
wished it played. Instead, he walked to the end
of the room and seated himself there at a distance
to listen to my attempts at an E that he could
finally call correct. After a while there came the
well-known smile on his face, which meant that he
had discovered where the difficulty lay. "But I am
not going to tell you," he said; "it is your business
to find where it is." He sat there comfortably for
another half hour, smiling and often laughing at
me until I discovered a simple remedy that was
beyond all the rules of touch and technique. I had
really been observing a rule and my hand would
not obey this rule. Well then, according to Leschetizky, the rule for me was wrong.

But generally Americans were in too much of a
hurry to listen to tones in the sense that Leschetizky used the word "listen," and this I believe ac-

counted for the statement of one of his assistants that no American could give the exact value of the little note in connection with the long ones around it. It was characteristic of Europeans coming to study with Leschetizky that they could do this apparently simple thing; and when an American could pass over such a pitfall to suit Leschetizky's keen ear it was almost a matter of congratulation to both pupil and assistant. In speaking of a delightful American pupil, Jane Scotford, who had been studying with him two years, Leschetizky remarked, "A mass of yellow hair hides those little American ears, but they are surely there and quite as good as some of the big uncovered European ears."

But if we had generally to be taught to listen, I think Leschetizky found us quick to understand when he talked of the mental delineation of a chord. His principle was that one should not strike a note or a chord without thinking of, and visualizing, or sometimes even saying, the next one, and all of his assistants made this the basis of their teaching of technique.

When one spoke of exercises to Leschetizky he smiled and counseled working the fingers up and down until they were tired on a book or table, out of consideration for the neighbors. When one asked what he meant by listening that seemed so obviously simple, he would tell you to try, first, taking one sound, either a tone of an instrument, or a tone of voice, or a knock on the door, or a word in a language one did not know, and try to repeat this sound exactly, with long pauses between, so that no sound was produced for the second time but al-

ways for the first time, as one would have to do
before an audience. "You must remember," he
said, "that before an audience the chance for the
second time never comes." In the shading of lines
of phrase he would tell you to look at pictures and
see how many shades there existed in one color.
He was perfectly certain, moreover, that half the
time of studying could be saved if one learned the
motion of phrases by walking freely around the
room. He often repeated, too, that "a crescendo
and diminuendo made a circle, so why not make a
picture in your mind of lines in circles, and in
this way have done with everlasting markings of
crescendos and diminuendos?"

Back in Vienna again, he began the first lessons
with pupils who had prepared for him during the
summer. His lessons began usually in November,
and Paul Goldschmidt was to have one of the first
on Leschetizky's return. He did not seem desirous
of having me present at his lesson, and for two or
three days I heard nothing about it. Finally Leschetizky sent for me, and as we were drinking tea
or coffee in the dining room, he began to talk about
the disappointments to be encountered in teaching; that among other things, every teacher, including himself, had to have the disagreeable experience of losing a good pupil. My heart sank—
Was he preparing me for some kind of a blow? At
last he explained that Paul Goldschmidt was disappointed with his first lesson and with his preparation for it, but did not want to tell me so himself.
His lesson had been a failure, he considered, and
Leschetizky could not understand his feeling at all.
At the same time he agreed with me that Gold-

schmidt should prepare further with Frau Breé or Fräulein Walle Hansen or Fräulein Prentner, if he cared to do so.

Very soon afterward Goldschmidt paid me a visit of apology. I assured him of my good will and told him I could understand his doubt of an assistant as inexperienced as I was. He stopped me, exclaiming that "he had at first thought exactly that, but he had since been to see Frau Breé, who said she could not help him either. I cannot understand at all," he said, "why I should not have had a brilliant lesson with Leschetizky, if my technique was good. How is it possible," he said, "that one cannot please him entirely and do exactly as he wants one to do if one has the technique to do it? I will not believe," he continued, "that I have not the greatest talent in the world, and yet my lesson was a failure. Nothing really made any impression upon him, and I cannot get the tones that he gets from the piano. I can't play at all as he played, and I don't know why." "Did you ever hear one who plays as he plays?" I asked. "I ought to be able to," he answered, "and if I cannot have success myself, then I must know the reason why."

Leschetizky did not live to know the unhappy ending of Paul Goldschmidt's career. After studying several years with Leschetizky he went to Berlin as a finished artist and played a great deal in public. He made a name for himself all over the Continent and many people loved to hear him play. There was great refinement in his playing and also great emotion and poetry, but much less of the quality by some called "temperament." Many people profited also by his instruction. He had inspiration and great talent and was a lovable and interesting young man, but he imagined himself to be a failure, and this tortured him. He fancied he had not met with deserved success in Frankfurt, his native town. Brooding upon this fancied slight unbalanced his mind, so his friends said, and on the way from Berlin to Frankfurt he took his own life by throwing himself from a moving train.

Since Goldschmidt's death I have often recalled the remark that Leschetizky made in Ischl, "Poor boy, what unhappiness such faith in his own talents may bring him!"

I think Leschetizky called it a mistake to wish for anything from the public that was not given spontaneously, and he felt rather sorry than otherwise for those people who could not accept with good grace whatever came to them. He considered the public as a whole a very good judge and thought that one could learn a great deal by putting oneself before the public.

He loved the public himself and liked to be a part of it. Some one remarked that although Leschetizky constituted the whole public at the classes at his own house, as a member of the real public he changed into a friend. Certain it is that in an audience he was the greatest inspiration to the performer.

An interesting little story was related by some Viennese gentlemen who had come across Leschetizky in the gallery of the Musikverein Saal where they had taken tickets for a concert at which one of Leschetizky's pupils was to appear in two numbers.

Young students were often asked to "assist" in this way at big concerts before they had actually made their first appearances as artists. The pupil was a young man whom Leschetizky had at first considered very talented, but as time went on this pupil did not develop his talent as the teacher had expected. He had been a keen disappointment to the master, but was just beginning to play in public. At this particular concert he was greeted with a great deal of applause and had to repeat two of his pieces. As the gentlemen in the gallery looked around they saw Leschetizky in the far corner with his face turned to the wall and weeping. There was no mistake, he was weeping. One of them who knew the master went quietly over to him and told him how proud he must be of his pupil's playing. "No," said Leschetizky, "he should have been far greater; he will never play better than he is playing just now. He is playing really too well to-night, but it will not last." Suddenly there was a break in the music, the player stopped and began again and still could not get himself out of the difficulty. Leschetizky's eyes were dried in an instant. "But that is not one of his faults," he exclaimed, "that is bad luck. I must try to save him now from being too miserable." While the player was striking more wrong chords and making a bad finish Leschetizky was on his way to the first floor and hurrying to the artists' room. Others in the audience, including the gentlemen in the gallery, also went back to speak to the concert giver after the concert and saw Leschetizky with his hand on the shoulder of his pupil, making light of his breakdown, cheerfully recalling similar instances in the careers of great artists and telling stories about them. "One of them," he said, "had had the resourcefulness to strike loudly on the piano and angrily leave the stage, calling for a tuner, saying he would not continue until that note had been tuned." The tuner came and the artist in the meantime took his notes and refreshed his memory. Another had risen from the piano and, after a wrathful speech charging some imaginary person in the audience with disturbing him, had abruptly left the stage for a sufficient period to bring back the lost notes. These and other stories Leschetizky told to the people who gathered in the artists' room where he had made an atmosphere of friendliness and success.

Leschetizky liked to be very near his pupil during a recital; between numbers he talked incessantly about the pieces to follow, making useful suggestions with regard to changes in tempo and tone. He might even propose a change in general interpretation to suit the temper of an audience, the acoustic conditions, etc. He would never advise changing the actual numbers on the program. This he considered bad taste, but he would often advise repetition of parts or omitting repetitions. He would make such suggestions as the following:

"Your last piece was rather too loud—play the next pianissimo. Don't declaim this next melody— make it more lyric and singing. Be as pompous as you like in that next—they need a little waking up."

As one came off the stage he would whisper, "Bow a little more the next time; you were not friendly enough when they were enthusiastic. Wait until the end to be so proud.

"There sits a critic over there to the right, who expects to see you obliged to play slower when you come to that difficult passage; take your time now with the phrases that come before, so that you will be rested—then let go—and disappoint him! I wouldn't pause after that first movement to-night; you will have applause if you do, and it may spoil your quiet mood for the second movement—it might break the thread; hold the pedal a little longer and then go straight on. You will have to put more tune into the scherzo because the piano is a dull one; make the runs more brilliant than you ever have before. Also throw in an extra top note at the end of the broken chords. Play the nocturne very slowly to-night; your program needs something dreamy that you haven't yet put into it."

There was often a steady fire of advice like this during a program. He thought the public should stimulate a performer to be daring and to introduce these variations according to his feeling. "You say one of two things as you stand before an audience: either, 'I love you all so much that I will enjoy myself and be free,' or, 'I despise you all so much that I don't care at all what I do.' There is no middle ground unless you are satisfied not to distinguish yourself."

Leschetizky was always delighted to discover adaptability in these things and had the greatest admiration for presence of mind under all circumstances. One of his American pupils was playing at a concert in Switzerland when the electric lights went out just as she was beginning the cadenza of her concerto. She was not in the least confused, and finished the concerto in total darkness. As the orchestra was about to play again the lights came on. This incident delighted Leschetizky, who often spoke enthusiastically of this pupil's self-control.

I once had the rare and curious experience of going shopping with Leschetizky. Early in the morning I received from him one of the little pink pneumatic cards of the Vienna postal service, asking me if I could spend the morning with him. At nine o'clock he was at my door. "You can't imagine the surprise I had yesterday," he said. "A letter came from Russia, from one of the teachers in a small place, asking me if I would hear his pupil play, the one who is giving the concert to-night. Of course I could hear her play and did. Such a surprise!" he repeated. "After all," he continued, "there is no reputation gained in anything that isn't deserved. This teacher one hears about from people who know but the joke is, here is a girl that no one knows who plays *well,* not to say, *beautifully.* We must do something for her. There will probably be only a handful of people to-night, and she is a real artist. She has something unusual in her playing. Perhaps it could be expressed this way: she brings her themes to a development that is like the unfolding or blossoming out of flowers. I can only think of big luscious roses when she plays. She is not handsome. She must have some good clothes—which now she has not. And we must get as many people to go to-night as we can. I am going to buy a dress for her. You can spend some money, too," he went on enthusiastically. "Buy some flowers and a few tickets that you can give away to people who wouldn't go otherwise, but we must all be there. Now let's go and see what we can buy her. Just think of that teacher," he said.

"If the pupil plays to-night half as well as she played for me, then he has had a great success. He is not known enough. There is one in Berlin, too, who is not known enough in this world, but it is his own fault. His pupils play well, consequently he is a good teacher, but he makes mistakes himself. He dislikes people and distrusts them and he shows it. He came out on the stage once in Berlin looking like a thief. This one in Russia makes mistakes. He hasn't any courage—he doesn't want to be famous."

And so Leschetizky went on as we made our way to a little shop in the center of the city. He decided I was about the same height and size as the girl who was going to play, so proposed that I should try on a certain pretty gray evening dress he had seen there. A nice woman came forward and instantly produced a dress that Leschetizky had examined the night before. The woman said it was too dark the evening before for the Professor to decide upon the dress, but she was sure that he would come back and she was glad that there was some one to try it on. Leschetizky took out his shabby old pocketbook and paid several large bills for this frock which he had chosen, and had it folded in a small parcel to take with him. "Now," said he, "let us get some more things. You can drop them all at her hotel, and she will never know who sent them, but they will make her happy, you may be sure, for she told me she had only the shabbiest clothes for the concert, as she had spent all her money coming here to play.

"Now what else can we buy? She should have some silk stockings, shouldn't she?" he asked.

After some trouble and many untyings of the parcel to match the color of the dress, we discovered some gray stockings; then, of course, there must be shoes. We found some quite beautiful gray satin shoes, but whether they were a good fit or not we never knew. Still Leschetizky thought the outfit incomplete without some ornament for the hair. This we bought, as well as concert tickets. I then took the parcels with some flowers and instructed the porter to deliver them as a present from an unknown admirer with a request that she should wear them at the concert. I was sure the porter told her they were brought by a smiling young lady. Leschetizky stood outside the hotel and was very glad to hear that this had all been accomplished so easily.

That night the weather became very stormy, but Leschetizky's pupils were in great evidence. Many of the conservatory pupils were there also, and several of the conservatory professors. Very promptly, a few minutes before the concert began, Leschetizky was seen walking down the middle aisle and taking his seat in a conspicuous part of the hall. A very smartly gowned girl appeared on the stage, her hair dressed beautifully with an ornament placed very becomingly at the side of her head. She glanced over the audience, smiling in rather amazed but grateful and dignified fashion, in acknowledgment of the warm reception. Leschetizky had dispersed his pupils to all parts of the room, where they organized themselves into *claquers* for the occasion.

However, there was too small an audience, owing partly to the bad weather, and Leschetizky thought this a great misfortune, as from first to last her playing was of a style remarkably beautiful and should have been heard by a crowded house and by the best critics of Vienna. We went to the artists' room to see her afterward. Leschetizky was the first to go forward and speak to her. He congratulated her on her splendid piano playing, and remarked that she looked very charming.

"Yes," she replied, "there has been a fairy godmother to me in Vienna. They told me that Vienna was an enchanted spot and I believe it is. If only I could find my fairy godmother," she said, looking around.

This incident Leschetizky loved, and he enjoyed asking people if they knew what she meant when she said she had found a fairy godmother in Vienna. "I think she meant that the dress she wore was given her," he remarked. "It would be very much like some of the charming Viennese or Polish or Russian ladies here to buy her that beautiful Viennese dress. They often do such things here," he declared. "Many of my pupils know this and know of their kindness and their interest in things artistic. No stranger suffers for lack of attention in Vienna if he really deserves it, and," he couldn't help adding, "especially when that stranger happens to be so good-looking and agreeable a young lady."

CHAPTER XI

IF Leschetizky had set the seal of his approval on a pupil either as pianist or teacher he did everything in his power to make that career a success. He never pretended that the road to success was simple or easy; on the contrary, he pointed out and emphasized the difficulties.

When accompanying a concerto, he himself often played as a poor orchestra would accompany. Then he would add, "But your orchestra may be a good one; then it would play this way, and you must be prepared for their good playing. It is a sadly noticeable thing when the orchestra plays better than the soloist."

He often referred to experiences of his own with orchestras. One director said to him, "Excuse me, Mr. Leschetizky, we have played that concerto a dozen times this year, and have never before taken such a tempo as this." "Am I your soloist or not?" asked he. "Where I have this melody, you are my accompanist." In another place he held the pedal over two different harmonies, which gave rise to controversy. "If surprises upset you," said Leschetizky, "it's far better for you to be surprised in this rehearsal than at the concert!" On another occasion his rehearsal was scheduled for five minutes past ten. "You are thinking of beginning on the minute?" asked Leschetizky. "We are supposed to do it," was the answer. "Well, let me have a seat near the piano, then," replied Leschetizky, "so that I can turn handspring to the piano stool, for that first tone of mine will take at least half a minute to prepare if I do it well!" He used to talk of Liszt's manner of going to the piano at his concerts. His appearance was electric, and his walk toward the piano, seating himself at the keyboard, and the first chord seemed simultaneous. However, when his improvisation was over, he brought about a very dramatic silence before the piece began.

His stories of the real and doubtful successes of Rubinstein, Wieniawski and others, as well as of their behavior behind the scenes, were most interesting and instructive. Vienna was not lacking in interesting episodes, and Leschetizky often witnessed them. A pupil was playing in a concert with a famous singer of the opera there and also a violinist. When the time came for the pianist, the famous singer preferred to sing herself, and intimated this to her accompanist. "You have the best place on the program, Madame," said Mr. Gutmann, the impresario, "and it is the number now for the pianist." "No matter," said the singer, "I am going to sing now." The accompanist took the singer, Mr. Gutmann took the pianist. Whether it was to be playing or singing seemed to depend upon who would be the first to reach the stage door of the platform. As it was, the pianist was sent out to the platform with a shove that nearly upset her. After the next number, which the famous singer had, there were naturally profuse apologies for bad behavior.

Mr. Gutmann was the important impresario of Vienna, and all the concerts of the Musikverein Saal and Bösendorfer Saal were under his management. He had connections with all the foreign

managements as well, and was nearly always present behind the scenes himself. He was very kind
and encouraging, and generally made a short, set
speech, as one was about to leave the artists' room
for the stage. He was a very busy man indeed, but
his heart and soul were in music and in the fulfill-
ment of successful concert appearances of artists.
He had many trials and tribulations, for the Viennese public was a difficult and somewhat capricious
one.

The real Viennese concert public, which made up
the Philharmonic audiences, could probably not be
duplicated by any other audience in the world for
its artistic and musical intelligence. They upheld
their own opinions against the whole world, and
had no consideration whatsoever for advertisement.
Advertisement implanted a suspicion in their minds
and rather kept them away from concerts.

There had been one supreme critic in Vienna, who
had never failed in directing the public mind with
honesty and without prejudice. They believed he
preserved the best traditions and was also sufficiently progressive. This was Edward Hanslick
who said that one should not take music as one swallowed a glass of champagne, for the sake of thrills
and sensations. The Viennese public certainly did
not go to hear music in this spirit. They went with
keen intelligence, making subtle comparisons, and,
above all, knowing and understanding the music
that was played. If they delighted in tradition and
good form and beauty of appearance, their innate
humor and intelligence saved them from ever becoming narrow-minded. They were on their feet
with enthusiasm for any unusually good perform-

ance, as well as for any really significant departure from old forms. They had courage enough to express themselves, even with hisses, when there was any fault or lack of taste in a performance, great or small.

For concerts by artists of great distinction the Viennese made themselves resplendent. Patti could never have been greeted by a more enthusiastic or distinguished audience than in Vienna in the Musikverein Saal, when she came there in her old age. All was well that evening for Mr. Gutmann. Not so at another time, when Sybil Sanderson failed to arrive in Vienna from St. Petersburg. She had made a mistake in the train schedule. Mr. Gutmann came before the brilliant audience to explain this. The audience expressed its understanding of the cause of its long waiting for the artist to appear by rising good-naturedly. They were told that Miss Sanderson would, however, arrive at midnight, and would sing the following evening. The next evening the same brilliant audience assembled with great expectancy and warmth of feeling. When Miss Sanderson appeared, she did not bow, but stood quietly, very beautiful and imposing. After a second's silence, the audience burst into rapturous applause, but waited and waited for the first tone. A few notes were sung, then she stopped and said to the audience, *"Je ne puis pas!"* This was in bad taste toward the indulgent Viennese. Of course, Mr. Gutmann could not explain this, and the hall resounded with hisses.

At another time the Musikverein Saal resounded with laughter for at least ten minutes. Two famous singers appeared on the program: one had been a favorite for four years, the other was making his first appearance. The new one came first and pleased the audience greatly. When the favorite appeared, she must have imagined there was less applause for herself than usual, for her bad grace on leaving the stage was apparent. The audience seemed to understand this rather as a reprimand to them, for, when her turn came again after the new singer, they did not fail in tremendous applause, though somewhat calculated and perfunctory. The singer's eyes filled with tears—tears rolled down her face, as she called out to the audience, "You can have the other singer all you want! I'll not come any more!" At this the audience burst into prolonged laughter. "No, indeed you shall not come again," said poor Mr. Gutmann, who was standing at the stage door. When Leschetizky heard of this his only comment was, "If one of my pupils ever behaves like that, he need never come to see me again!"

In one way Leschetizky was an autocrat. He demanded that his pupils confer with him before accepting engagements while they were inexperienced as public performers. I saw him many times positively angry when pupils accepted engagements that were either too important or too trivial to suit their capacities as artists.

I had had a very unpleasant experience with the patient Mr. Gutmann on this account. One evening, at the Musikverein Saal he spoke to me from his box and asked me to play the piano part of a new sonata for violin and piano. It was to have its first public performance there, and I should have to undertake to play it in a few days.

I had no time to confer with Leschetizky, and it did not occur to me to do so. But I asked him to hear me play it several days later, and the day appointed for my lesson was the same as that fixed for the rehearsal with Dr. Prill, the "Concert Meister" of the Vienna Philharmonic Orchestra. I noticed Leschetizky's bad mood the instant he greeted me, and in a few minutes his temper rose to the point of forbidding me to play in the concert. It was within two hours' time of the rehearsal. "You have not been well lately," he said. "You have just come back to Vienna and are not in a condition to play now. Besides, this is no sort of first public appearance for you, accompanying a violin sonata." All this I knew to be true, but I answered, "I know, but I must play. Think how angry every one will be with me if I give up two days before the concert!" Unmoved, Leschetizky repeated that he did not wish me to play. There was no appeal, but I persisted. "It would look so unreasonable if at this late hour I refused to play," I argued. "Tell Mr. Gutmann and Dr. Prill and the composer that I forbid you to play," was the answer. Again I demurred. The retort was final. "Well, you will have to chose between Mr. Gutmann and me!" I could only answer that, of course, there was no choice.

The interview that morning with Mr. Gutmann and Dr. Prill was too distressing to describe. In a crushing manner Mr. Gutmann dismissed me; I was a musical outcast. "Very well, Miss Newcomb," he said, "I shall see that you never appear in concert in Vienna again!"

But, autocratic as Leschetizky was, he was only

interested in pupils who intended to play in public, and to this end he always bent his energies.

One evening he came to see me. He sat down
and did not speak for some time. Then the conversation began with a hint that he always lost interest in pupils who did not prepare themselves for
concerts. "It is very wrong," he remarked, "to
sit down in Vienna and study without ambition."
He could not understand it at all.

"Do you think I can play now?" I asked him.
"Well, you belittle the criticism of the classes if
you think you can't! You've been playing there for
several years, and we do not play badly there! We
don't allow it! *I* don't allow it!" he said. "You
will not have to play better anywhere in the world
than you have to play there, but you must always
improve!" he added. I replied that I would go in
the morning to Mr. Gutmann and ask him to let
me "assist" at one of the concerts. At the same
moment it occurred to me that this might not be so
easy to arrange. I promised Leschetizky that I
would not put it off a day.

The next morning, as I waited my turn with several others at Mr. Gutmann's office, I met Madame
Frances Saville coming out. She had been to see
Mr. Gutmann in connection with her farewell concert in Vienna. She was greatly surprised to find
me there, and my surprise was of a different kind
when she told me that she had decided to ask me to
play in her concert, and had already told Mr. Gutmann so. He had not approved, she said, and she
had not understood this, but, after she insisted for
some time, the question had been settled. Her concert was to be with the Philharmonic Orchestra, and

I might play any concerto I liked. Madame Saville had just resigned from the Vienna Opera, after singing there with great success for several years. She and Mahler did not agree, and she preferred to leave. She was a great singer and a beautiful woman, and the Viennese admired her exceedingly. She used to sing the three characters of the "Tales of Hoffman," something which was rather a *tour de force,* but her clear voice remained beautiful to the end of the long opera, and she was always cheered to the last person in the audience.

I flew with this news to Leschetizky, who was delighted and agreed that I had had a great piece of luck. He spoke of concertos. When I told him my choice of the Schumann "A Minor," he took the announcement very seriously, and thought a long time before answering. It was a very dangerous thing to attempt for a first performance, he told me. "If you should play it badly, every one will say that you have attempted much too serious a piece for the first performance! If you play it very well, they will enjoy the music and may not appreciate your artistic playing! Why not play something more brilliant, the effect of which does not depend on your artistic powers and concentration of mind and feeling—'the Hungarian Fantasie, for instance?"

I at once felt that Leschetizky had made a different person of me and that I had grown ambitious to play in public, as I did indeed wish to please him. So, after further discussion, I determined upon the Schumann "Concerto," and determined also to stake my whole career on that concert. If I played it as an artist should play, I would go on.

If not, I would give up all thought of a professional career as pianist and teacher.

From that time until the concert, about two weeks later, not a day passed but Leschetizky sent for me to go over the "Concerto." One evening I played it in the class, and I shall never forget the warmth of the reception I got from the students. Their loyalty to any pupil whom Leschetizky thought ready for a public appearance was absolute, and their affectionate appreciation of my playing that evening is a beautiful memory.

As the day of the concert approached, Leschetizky seemed to think of every detail. His desire to have me play well and his foresight saved me many embarrassments and awkward positions which I should surely have got myself into, ignorant as I was of the purely practical details of a professional career. Leschetizky had great patience the first time with lack of attention to details, but never a second, and his thoughtfulness in looking after everything before that first concert made me so ashamed that I determined to profit by the experience.

The rehearsal was set for the day previous to the concert. At ten o'clock in the morning a servant came from Mr. Gutmann for the orchestral parts and the score, which, of course, I could not give him, as I did not even know it was customary for the soloist to supply them. Just as I was apologizing to the man, Leschetizky's servant appeared, laden with scores and orchestral parts, which his master had provided. Afterward he told me that he had awakened in the night and remembered that I had most probably not attended to the scores. My sense of triumph over Mr. Gutmann wavered when I caught a gleam of disdainful amusement in his servant's eye. He was well aware that I was a novice, I am certain, and must have reported, in his pompous manner, the whole occurrence to Mr. Gutmann.

When I arrived at the hall for rehearsal Leschetizky was already there. In fact, he had been there for some time, having put off all lessons for the day. As I came in, he was absorbed in examining the planks of the platform, remembering a performance of his own when part of the floor had given way. My master was not to rescue me from broken timbers that day, but he did come to my aid in a moment of another kind of danger.

We had reached the last movement of the concerto, and the place where the theme is brought in by the oboes. The conductor failed to give the oboes their entrance, and I, ignorant of orchestral etiquette, stopped and waited for him to repeat the part. He rapped on the desk, and, turning to me, remarked that I had failed to come in. At this Leschetizky came hurriedly toward the stage protesting, "Oh, no, Herr Direktor, the Fräulein has such a good ear that she could not play that part if you omitted the melody, to which she responds!"

The director smiled, signaled to repeat the part, and brought in the oboes. After the rehearsal we went to lunch. The first thing Leschetizky said was, "Of course, I said that to save you. I was not going to have all those musicians think that you did not know enough to come in, but, regardless of whether the oboes played or not, you should have gone on playing that part yourself in place of the orchestra, which you may have to do to-morrow night. I hope you have learned that part! The rehearsal has taught me something, too. In the future I shall try to make mistakes like that myself. That is the one point in preparation which we omitted!"

That night, at Leschetizky's house, we played the concerto nearly the whole night long. A dozen times I begged him to let me go, but he only sent for more tea, insisting that I repeat certain passages, and then not play them again, but only think them over, until the concert.

On the evening of the concert, I found Leschetizky in the artists' room waiting for me. I remember that I wore a very pretty soft white chiffon frock. Madame Saville was magnificent in a different kind of dress. Leschetizky took in every detail of my gown and coiffure, said he thought my hair too far over my eyes, and laughingly remarked that he did not admire long-haired affectations. Without further comment he took a penknife from his pocket, and cut off some small fluffy things from my sleeves, so that they could not possibly get in my way when I played. He very graciously expressed a regret for mutilating my beautiful dress.

In honor of Madame Saville's farewell a brilliant and distinguished audience had assembled. Leschetizky in the meantime went out into the hall and returned in about ten minutes, his face red and excited, saying that he had been up to the top seat in the gallery and had watched the house filling up, and that I must change the whole level of tone of that concerto to suit the acoustics of the house when filled. There was a piano in one of the side rooms, and he insisted that until my turn came to play we should practice playing the first phrase until I could play it with different tone, one that would be more penetrating. The quality which I had been accustomed to using in Leschetizky's rooms and in the empty hall the day before was not adequate for that packed house. So we went into the side room, and until time for me to go upon the stage, we practiced many phrases of the concerto with different tone, different touch, and slower tempos. Leschetizky did not appear in the concert hall until I was safely into the cadenza of the first movement. He then took his seat in one of the boxes, as if he had just arrived, and remarked quite casually to some one near by that it was interesting to see an American playing with the Philharmonic in the Musikverein Saal in Vienna. Madame Saville's audience gave me great applause, and the critics were generously disposed, so that Leschetizky told me afterward that he had no fears now for my whole career. The first thing he thought of was that I should go again to Mr. Gutmann, who would surely now receive me differently, and arrange for a recital in the autumn. I promptly obeyed him the next morning, and, assuming now the virtue of a desire to play in public, I soon found myself doing it a great deal, to his real delight.

Wherever I played I found a laurel wreath sent me by my master. At my recitals I was happy to receive many laurel wreaths, big and small, as is customary in Europe, but invariably a small one was there from Leschetizky. He sometimes hid himself behind the little doors of the artists' room in Vienna until I had come off the stage after the first number. Then he would emerge, either pleased or critical, and not allow me to speak of anything but the playing of the next numbers.

"You've got a fugue coming now. Good gracious!" he would say, "I am glad I haven't to play it myself. Be serene if you can, and do not let that lady sitting on the front seat confuse you by her whispers about the buckles on your shoes, as I heard her whispering way back here!"

"How could you hear it?" I asked him.

"There is a crack in the door behind the stage, and I watched her through it," he said.

After my concert with orchestra the next day, Leschetizky came in to see me, about tea time. He asked me what I had been doing. When I told him I had been practicing all day, he was quite beside himself with delight. "I've won a wager then!" he said. "I knew that you would study well after that!" he said gleefully. "I know exactly what would have happened if you had not played well, and had not succeeded. I should have had to do this all over again, or you would have gone home, or stayed here quite happily, enjoying yourself in Vienna. Everything is worth doing well, or not at all, and, if you are going to play, you must put yourself before the critics and great audiences! You will approach your next concert in an entirely different frame of mind. There is nothing so beneficial for some people as a success," he added. "And now I am hoping that you will play because you love to play, and not entirely to please me," he said, in his inimitable way.

Sometime during the following months I gave my first recital in the Bösendorfer Saal.

His prophecy was correct—I had grown very

fond of the memory of my first successful concert, and, if indeed my casual mood for the piano had disappeared forever, a great amount of nervousness had taken its place, and I was more than ever glad of the opportunity of trying my programs before the critical but friendly class that met every fortnight at the master's house. It was the class that it was difficult for me to play before, and not Leschetizky. I could always play better when he was near.

My mother was with me when I gave my first recital in Vienna, and when she saw me in such a state of nervous apprehension as we drove to the Bösendorfer Saal, she begged me never to play in public again. Leschetizky teased her a little afterward for her motherly solicitude. "Yes," she said to him, "we mothers must be a great trial to you, when we come with our daughters to Vienna! I am sure you would approve of it, if I gathered all the mothers together on a ship and we sailed for the South Sea Islands." "Yes, gather them all together, and put them on a ship," was the amused response, "but stay here yourself. You are the real 'concert mother,' with the 'concert' left out."

CHAPTER XII

LESCHETIZKY was no less brilliant as a pianist than as a teacher. This fact was unknown to the general public, for, after his marriage to Annette Essipoff, one of his pupils, he became so absorbed in her career that he was apparently willing to sacrifice his own, and gave up most of his concert engagements to her.

He made her a famous pianist, and when he spoke of her and her playing, he was all admiration and enthusiasm, and he always liked to tell of what a model of musicianship she was. He used to like to tell of her examination at the St. Petersburg Conservatory. She was given the piano part of the Schumann "Quintette" to transpose before a large audience. With such complete success did she proceed that the first movement was hardly finished when a prolonged storm of applause saved her the necessity of further convincing the audience of her ability to accomplish the feat.

When in later years Therese Leschetizka, her daughter, came to visit her father, as she often did, he always asked her lovingly how Madame Essipoff spent her day. Once the daughter answered, "The first thing in the morning she sews a little, then she reads a little, and then is ready for the real part of the day, which is devoted to music."

When Madame Essipoff came to Berlin, she and Leschetizky sometimes appeared at concerts together, when the whole audience would rise and applaud this famous artist couple.

While she was in Vienna, as Madame Lesche-tizka, one often heard of her playing duets, such as the Schumann "Variations," with the great artists who happened to be there, on some occasions with Rubinstein. She played all these duets from memory, and it did not matter to her which part she took, knowing both equally well. Leschetizky himself stood near by, always thoroughly enjoying the performance and the music. People who remembered them both at that time used to remark that he seemed perfectly happy when she played.

As late as 1900, Leschetizky promised Hermann Wolff, the well-known manager of Germany and a friend of his, to undertake a long concert tour in Russia and Germany. In speaking of this time he said that he had relaxed his continuous teaching a little, and had really practiced. This was noticeable in the enormous repertoire which he seemed suddenly to have acquired and in his willingness to play for people. He played, of course, a great deal in the lessons, and, as he sat at the second piano five or six hours a day giving lessons, he retained his technique and marvelous tone, so that no one seemed to compare with him. In lessons he invariably played the most difficult passages, never shirking the hard work imposed by any composition new or old, and indeed he would often learn the piece then and there. He once remarked that when the time came that he could not play better than the pupil before him, he would "shut up shop."

But this *tournée* came to nothing, for Hermann Wolff died, and Leschetizky's ambition was not a sufficient incentive for him to undertake the tour under other management, and his love for teaching made it easy for him to stay at home. Later he embarked on a "tiny concert tour," as he laughingly called it, to play for the Welte Mignon records. We went down to the station to see him off with his servant Johann. Indeed, he took very seriously his own playing, as well as that of all others, for this reproducing piano.

The time when Leschetizky was most willing to play was naturally after one of the classes. He might have accompanied two or three concertos during the class proper, but after the midnight supper and after having smoked strong cigars he was fresh again for hearing music or for dancing, in which he excelled, and often for playing himself.

Some of us knew a little trick which would usually succeed in persuading him to play. He often played for us to dance, always requiring us to dance perfectly according to his tempo changes, and when we had danced a while and he had become warmed to the beat of the music, some one would find the right moment to ask him to play one of his own pieces. "Oh, no, no!" he would say, "let some one else do it who can play it far better. Why not you, or why not you?" nodding to different ones. Finding nobody willing, "Really shall I play?" he would say quite diffidently and humbly. At once he became the inspired artist, sitting quietly and erectly, his head uplifted a little and his hands firmly down on the keys, his fingers showing almost no motion. With the first tone every one was spellbound. No one, I believe, ever succeeded in imitating the quality of his tone. Under his fingers a powerful and sonorous tone resounded and vibrated until every corner of the room was filled with beautiful sound. He spoke in tones, and every one felt himself directly spoken to. He played to all natures and all emotions, turning easily and simply from joy to sorrow. Then, as if seeing some one who needed to be stimulated or inspired, he played with a nobility and grandeur that was indescribable. Sometimes the volume of sound was really awe-inspiring, but never hard for a moment. There might be one crash, but only in momentary contrast, and to hear his pianissimo was to feel oneself dropped gently from a great height to listen to a beautiful voice somewhere in the shadows.

His interpretations were far above all calculation and intention, for of all desirable qualities in his playing, fantasy stood uppermost. His friends and pupils knew this. He learned to play a melody isolated from the harmonies around it, he said, by imitating singing—the beautiful singing of his first wife. One should learn to play all melodies by listening to them as to a voice, he thought.

Under the inspiration of his first marriage, early in his career, he had written a few songs. He loved singing and particularly a contralto voice. It was surprising to hear him say that he did not like the violin. The piano was the instrument of his choice, and he could never understand why its study should be considered drudgery, even under the most trying and difficult conditions. He told of a time in Russia when he had been obliged to remain in town through unbearably hot weather. The great heat made normal conditions of study impossible, but he was not daunted by this, and in some way managed to get his piano put into a small space surrounded by water. Here he could dispense with all clothing, lock his doors, and study in comfort all day.

If he had consented to play in his own house, after the classes, he would sometimes go on for an hour or two, and play a concerto, or even two. He could play at least twenty concertos, for his memory never failed him.

The time I best remember was when he gave us the "C Minor Concerto" of Beethoven, as the climax to many other small pieces. This was about four o'clock in the morning, when everybody but Leschetizky needed some stimulus to liveliness. This concerto was a great favorite with him, and in his opinion the second theme of the first movement could never be played simply and sublimely enough. No one would have thought from his playing that he had not been practicing this particular concerto for a special occasion; it was so surely and perfectly performed. Most likely he had gone over it lately with a pupil. Everybody felt revived after this performance. Leschetizky himself seemed so happy and in such excellent form that he turned and told Ignace Friedman, who was standing near, that if he would accompany the Litolff "Concerto," he would play that. Again he played as though he were playing in a concert.

We drank more tea, and about half past six walked into Vienna, Leschetizky being as usual the liveliest of the group.

Very few interpretations satisfied Leschetizky entirely. No one played with fantasy and freedom enough for him. "No *coulisses*" was one of his frequent phrases. "You are so worried over what you must do next," he used to say. "Throw all that away! It only hinders your free fantasy! Get down to the real meaning of the music and put warmth into every tone. Don't desecrate that music by trying to make it fit another story. The tones are the story, and the form the plot. What more do you need if the music is good?"

He brought out beauties in composition and tone relationships which were not produced by any rules or regulations of expression, and amazed the listener. Just once I heard him put words to a phrase, and on that occasion he was in despair because the pupil could not get any meaning or inflection in the phrasing. He himself had written one or two pieces upon a definite emotional idea, but he did not value them for this, regarding it as a thing extraneous to the music. The melody of the "Canzonetta Toscana" resembled a song he had heard from an old woman sitting on the steps of a church in Florence, mourning the loss of her daughter. When playing his "Mandolinata" he used to say, "This is where the tenors come in, sentimental, of course!" When he was asked why he did not write out the stories in connection with these pieces, he said, "Yes, I know, Liszt did that sort of thing, but it doesn't interest me." The farther away one kept from being influenced by words and stories in most works for the piano, the better one understood him in his teaching and playing.

He used to make the rather startling statement that music was a dramatic art. He saw direct connection between the expression of a piece and good acting. "Certain small pieces are all acting," he declared. To study rhythm, he thought, one should go where rhythm was. What could be more instructive than going out to the gypsies in the Prater and listening to their wild, free rhythms! He would often be found there sitting by himself in a corner, absorbed in their peculiar manner of playing.

On one occasion the presence of Leschetizky was greatly desired by some people in town, but he was nowhere to be found, and had left no word that offered a clew to his whereabouts. Servants were sent to one place and another, lastly to the theater, but still without finding him. Some one suggested the "Venice in Vienna" at the Prater. It was reported that he had been seen there earlier in the evening. But it was now too late to meet the people who wished to see him, and some friends, who had about given up the quest, strolled over to a café house on the other side of the Prater, where the peasants were amusing themselves. Hearing curious sounds issuing from the place, they went inside. A girl with bells on her wrists was playing the piano and making a great noise, to the utmost delight of her audience. Over at one side sat Leschetizky, watching every move of the player. "Hush," he said to his friends, who came up to him. "I shall sit here until she stops, for she has perfect rhythm! She has played twenty times, and every piece was with a different rhythm. You've never heard anything like it," he said enthusiastically, as if to forestall the banter of his friends. "I want to stay," he protested. "Don't try to take me away!"

Leschetizky attended many concerts in Vienna, not only the good ones, but poor ones as well. He liked to hear every new performer, and often, where one least expected it, he found something commendable in the performance.

He was annoyed if his pupils missed certain concerts, and often requested them to go to a certain one, which he himself could not attend, so that they could tell him about it afterward. But "telling him about it afterward" meant more than merely listening to the music. It meant remembering exactly how certain pieces were played—what tempos were taken, and even how certain tones were produced. He himself returned from a concert once, declaring that he would never again attempt certain single tones with the same hand. A young player had convinced him that they sounded better taken each time by a fresh hand, and he had also learned in this concert what not to do in some other respects. He followed the concerts of all cities in Europe and knew of every musical event in Paris and St. Petersburg. He read carefully the criticisms of all European newspapers, as well as those of the English papers.

"You have some good critics in America, too," he once said to me. "One especially—his criticisms are sound and give me great pleasure!" Of great interest to him were the first appearances of his pupils in Berlin, although the complacency of the Berlin critics was a perpetual irritation to him. He often spoke gratefully of that stipendium given him by Paderewski, which made it possible for pupils of his to appear with orchestra, who otherwise could not have afforded it. He was most attentive to the opinion of important critics, and it was a serious thing for a pupil of his to receive bad notices.

I once said to him quite casually before a concert, "What if I have no success with the critics?" His thoughtful, serious look made me realize the importance he attached to criticism.

"If your notices are not good," he said, "we will set to work to see what is the matter." Nevertheless, the German critics always annoyed him, and always had annoyed him. The Germans liked to pose as more dignified than the Viennese, and were most certainly jealous of the great distinction that belonged to Vienna by tradition and talent. Leschetizky studied the personality of critics as well as of artists, and did not speak without authority. He loved to relate his experiences in Germany, playing the "E Flat Concerto" of Beethoven, which he had learned with his master Czerny, a pupil of Beethoven. The copy he had used in studying had many marks on it in Beethoven's own handwriting. Over some heavy chords and some passages in the middle of the first movement, Beethoven had written the word "free." In one of the introductory passages there was a mordent written in also in Beethoven's own hand. He had many other interesting copies handed down to him by Czerny with marks by Beethoven. In several of them was advice to put in a cadenza *ad libitum*—notes which are never seen in any edition.

When the Germans, who thought they were authorities on the interpretation of Beethoven, noticed and commented critically upon these deviations, Leschetizky loved to remain silent and let them talk on. Whenever he was teaching a German to play Beethoven, or any one imbued with this German spirit, he knew where to lay his hands on these old copies easily. It utterly disgusted him to hear Beethoven played coldly, his idea being that if it was not played warmly it was played coldly. There was no middle ground. At the obviously intentional strictness of tempo that many affected in playing Beethoven he would mutter in contempt, "North German morality! Worse than the American machine! Father of twenty children! Relationship to Buxtehude, etc.!"

The pupils were told to search Vienna for certain old copies of Beethoven without the customary fingerings, comments, and explanations, and to study the sonatas as much as possible from those "unedited" editions.

Leschetizky was like a father to any pupil about to appear before distinguished critics, and often in the class paid glowing tribute to the one about to play. Just before an appearance of mine in Berlin he made a little speech in the class, expressing his pride in the pupils from many lands, who from time to time appeared before the greatest critics in Europe, and made touching reference to the little room in which all of this had been accomplished. While my own experience is clearer in my mind than any other, I know there were many instances of this sort.

On my return to him after the concert, I wondered what he would say about my newspaper notices, which he surely had seen. He met me at the door, flapping a newspaper in his hand, and calling out, "Aha, *you have no diatonic!* How is this? Come in and let's see what they mean. I don't know it, and I don't believe they know either." One of the critics said I had no diatonic in my play-

ing. Another said no American could play the
Beethoven "E Flat Concerto," anyway. "They
don't know how to play Beethoven themselves,"
said Leschetizky. "Haven't the Viennese heard
Czerny play Beethoven as Beethoven wanted him,
his pupil, to play?"

"Haven't they here all the best traditions? Now,
of course, they say the Russians can't play Beethoven, nor the French. Well, then, nobody can play
Beethoven. And they think they know so much
more than the critics of London, that great city
where all the news of the world comes in," and he
would speak respectfully of the London *Times.*

"Of course, here in Vienna," he went on, "there is
a whole world of dilettanteism; on the other hand,
there is no affectation." As a fact, Vienna was full
of dilettantes, who seemed almost artists. Dilettanteism there was of such a high order that only
really musical people could shine at all in its atmosphere. In the well-known family of Wittgenstein,
for instance, in whose home Brahms and Joachim
were constant guests, one would be asked perhaps
some evening to play the "Horn Trio" of Brahms,
or a quartet of Beethoven, or a sonata. If there
was any embarrassment, some member of the family would supply the part, perhaps not with technical perfection, but certainly with a fine sense of
musical values and knowledge of the composition.

Among Leschetizky's dear friends were the
Löwenbergs, living near him in the Währing
Cottage, who were immensely interested in all his
pupils. Paderewski used to visit them and play his
new compositions to them whenever he stopped in
Vienna on his way to Poland. Grandmother,

father, mother, sons, daughters, and grandchildren all played some instrument, and one heard the best chamber music in their house. And in many other households and places the performance of serious music was excellent. At the change of guards between twelve and one, in the courtyard of the Palace, one heard surprisingly good playing of overtures to operas, rendered by the military band. Indeed, one heard good music everywhere, as no poorly played music was tolerated.

Once Leschetizky counseled me to play more chamber music, and remarked that I should get one of my Viennese friends to practice the violin parts with me, as any one of them would be familiar with it.

Of course, in this atmosphere Leschetizky was regarded somewhat as an exotic. He had no more of a place in the world of dilettanteism than he had in the pedantic world. He wanted a new story told every time one sat down to the piano, but he stood for the perfection of piano playing and, in a sense, for the dramatization of it for the public. The most talented people in the world came to study with him and began there their famous careers, which the Viennese were quick to acknowledge as events in their traditionally artistic life. They accorded to Leschetizky their wondering appreciation, and loved also to believe that nowhere else could such a thing have been accomplished. In Vienna there was indeed every chance to become an artist, if there were only the capacity. There always seemed time for study and for the contemplation of beautiful things in this charming place, where talent so abounded and blossomed.

People were very simple here in their attitude toward music. There was hardly any such thing as a "best of all" artist. One artist played Beethoven better than another, they thought; one could not play Chopin well at all, but everything else beautifully. A look of amazement would come over a Viennese face at the words, "He is the best." When great artists and actors came together in Vienna, one heard these expressions in all simple seriousness, "I did that very badly, but I can do the other, I really believe, better than you can"; or, "Did you see how I changed the acting of that scene last night? Shall I continue it or not?" "No, by no means, no!"

Leschetizky told an amusing story of his old master of composition, Sechter, who once essayed writing an opera. He told his friends to come to supper afterward if the opera should be a success. It was a flat failure, and no one came to supper. After Sechter had gone to bed, a small voice called him from below.

"Who's there?" asked Sechter.

"I am," said the man below; "you invited me to supper!"

"But on condition that the opera was a success!"

"Well, I liked it," replied the friend.

But Sechter was not a *poseur,* and the next day went around quite simply telling every one that he didn't like his opera himself when it came to a performance on the stage.

There were always many in Vienna who composed. They did not always publish their compositions, and Leschetizky made it his duty to examine manuscripts as he heard of them, for fear of missing something first-rate. There was an American in the class, who wrote music—a young man from Virginia. He had been a pupil of Leschetizky's for more than a year when he brought to his lesson one day a theme and variations which he had written the previous summer in America. Leschetizky heard him play, then he left the room in great excitement, calling for Edouard Schütt, who was in the house at the time.

"Schütt," he shouted, "come down and see what we have here!" It was learned for the first time that day that the young man had studied composition in America, but was now more concerned with becoming an artist. "You must go on with composition too," Leschetizky advised him. Of course, he meant to compose, he said, but he wanted also to develop his own style; he did not see why any further lessons were necessary. Leschetizky thought differently—it was just as necessary for him to study how to compose as to study how to play. Still they disagreed, but in the end Leschetizky had his way. "To-morrow you will go to Nawratil for composition," he said, "or you need never come to me for another lesson!"

When this young composer's "Sonata Virginanesque" for piano and violin was performed in Vienna, it had a good reception by a most austere body of critics and musicians. They smiled broadly at some of the mistakes, grunted approvingly at some of the moments of inspiration, and on the whole treated the composition with great respect.

It did not take many years to confirm Leschetizky's estimate of John Powell's splendid talent as a composer. Leschetizky was very proud of the distinctions won by his pupil in Vienna.

Margaret Melville also had several large compositions performed in Vienna by the foremost musicians. Frank La Forge was pleasing everybody by his beautiful tone and sympathy in playing. Paula Szalit delighted large audiences, and, as Leschetizky expressed it, she played everything well. She had absolute poise and confidence. At ten years of age, at which time she came to Leschetizky, she had composed many small pieces and the musical papers of the Continent spoke highly of her sense of form. At her age this puzzled her very much, and one day I found Leschetizky laughing heartily over her curiosity as to what the critics meant by this opinion of her compositions. She played with great freedom, and several times amused her audiences by making an improvisation at the place in her piece where she had struck a wrong note. On one occasion at the end of a run she struck a wrong note and took the note as motive, improvising for several minutes upon the theme. This was done so artistically that it excited the greatest wonder, and the audience of the Bösendorfer Saal stood up to watch her.

These were interesting events in Leschetizky's life, and an observer of his manner might easily believe that his own career as pianist could never have been so interesting to him as those of his pupils. He was tireless in his efforts to make artists of us all. Nothing was too difficult for him to undertake, and formidable obstacles were many times overcome. By the greatest patience in trying to cure fundamental faults he succeeded in almost eradicating them. One of his best pupils had no memory, and he was determined that she should be able to memorize her pieces. He set himself the enormous task of dictating every note of the Schumann "Concerto." When they had at last finished this process and were ready to play from the beginning again, she had forgotten every note. This did not discourage him in the least, and when, in the third attempt, she showed signs of improvement, he was overjoyed and exclaimed that there was a way to learn everything if one could only find the way. "No, not everything," he added, "for there was one thing impossible to learn, and no amount of effort would accomplish it!" What he referred to was the playing of one tone with expression. Then he mentioned the case of an actor who by the pronunciation of a single word could move audiences to tears. In playing one might feel and know how the tone should sound, but it could not be learned. This was easy, or else it was impossible.

CHAPTER XIII

ONE often heard from Leschetizky that all arts were related, that the knowledge of one gave an understanding of the others. To him, however, the most interesting part lay in the study of their differences. He saw a great similarity between acting and piano playing, and so it concerned him greatly to find the differences between them. He compared the movements of an actor on the stage to tempos and rhythms, expressions of faces to interpretations. Tones and shading in music should be studied as an actor studied his words, with the same endeavor to suit the acoustics. An actor who could not be intense in his interpretations was a poor actor, and so was a pianist a poor one who could not be dramatic. In form and dimensions he often likened compositions to pictures, and traced the lines in a picture to illustrate phrasing, but he thought the whole art of piano playing most akin to the art of acting.

A frequent guest at his house, in my earliest recollection, was the great actor Livinski. On my introduction to this aged man, he greeted me with the words, "Well, are you learning to act at the piano? You can learn it here, in this house, if you can understand your master!" Leschetizky passed us at the moment, and remarked that the great actor was invaluable to him, and Livinski replied that Leschetizky's playing was the best acting he had ever known. "No paint, or powder, either," he said.

Later, in speaking of Livinski, Leschetizky remarked that he could have been a good actor with his own great variety of emotions and intensity, whether he had scenes and plays to put himself into or not. He could recite you the alphabet in such a way that it would be an emotional story. "Mediocrity could not achieve this," Leschetizky said.

One time another great actor at his house did give an exhibition of this kind. He spoke for fifteen minutes in unintelligible words of no special language and of no meaning in relation to each other. He began in a mysterious tone of voice, becoming pathetic as he went on, then rising to a great climax of indignation that overawed his listeners. He finished with great tenderness in melodious tones and sank, as though exhausted, into a chair. Leschetizky wanted him to repeat this, if possible, but he thought he could hardly do it a second time, and so gave us another exhibition of the kind, but with entirely different emotions.

"We only need some Chopin music now," said Leschetizky, "and we will have it! But nothing with titles. What's that name I heard you giving one of the Chopin études?" he asked. "How can you ever do it? 'Butterfly Etude,' for instance! It's such a pity to do those things, and you may be far away from the composer's idea of the piece. Probably he never meant the butterflies to come into it. It is as wrong," he went on, on this occasion, "as if you tried to name a picture according to your feeling, and tell people what they should feel in looking at it. Why not let them alone, and let each one have his own feeling? It's bad music if you need to help it along by words or stories!"

Artists of all kinds liked to confer with Leschetizky. "Please try to bring Leschetizky to us sometime!" said Alexander Goltz, one of the well-known artists of Vienna. "His criticism of the portrait I am painting would be valuable!"

Leschetizky had not met this artist, but was delighted to go out to his house at Nussdorf. He stepped quickly into the studio and took one glance at the picture. Goltz asked him what he thought of it. "The thumb is too long, I think," said Leschetizky. "It looks useless; as the picture is of a pianist, that would be a fault." "Her thumb is long!" said Goltz astonished. "Yes," replied Leschetizky, "but a long thumb is better when playing than when looked at in a picture!"

After a while Leschetizky and Goltz walked away together and did not return for a long time— too long for the other guests that the charming Madame Goltz had invited. They returned finally, deep in conversation about the differences and similarities of painting and piano playing, and far into the night the conversation lasted, marked by excited disagreements, but always carried on in a most friendly and deferential manner.

Leschetizky was only stimulated by disagreements with his friends, or with people that he admired, and whose temperaments were congenial to him. He used to quote the Austrian proverb, "Only men of the same mind can argue."

At supper that evening Leschetizky made one of his most humorous speeches. There were one or two Americans present. He began by a lively description of Christopher Columbus, in some way connecting him with painters and pianists and making him an artist, and then went on, "I have not often had the experience of being introduced to an artist in Vienna by a foreigner, especially by an American. Oceans sometimes separate, but again they bring you together. Columbus could never have known the momentous consequences of his voyage." And he went on in this humorous fashion a long time, to the delight of the guests.

Pauline Lucca was one of Leschetizky's great friends. They had sometimes found each other in foreign countries where both were on concert tours. She loved to tell stories about Leschetizky, that showed him a romantic figure against a background of conventionality and dullness. She was an adept at telling a story herself. She emphasized everything by acting, and was a very witty and inspiring person as well as a great singer.

"Has he never told you," she said to me once, "of our bad behavior at the house of an English nobleman? It was a terribly formal dinner party—terribly! Not a word had been spoken at the table for a long time—not a word, my dear! It was too much for us. We tried bad table manners to enliven things, but this did not succeed at all! Oh, not at all! We were becoming shocking—I could not bear it any longer—I ran around to your dear master with a glass of wine, and he left his seat at table smiling broadly, and we drank *Bruderschaft* before them all. We linked our arms, and kissed each other on both cheeks, and, oh, these people were so glad, *so glad* to have something happen! We all enjoyed ourselves from that time on. His grace found himself in a mood to talk politics with Leschetizky, and after that everything was lively. We didn't have to play or sing either, to make ourselves understood."

Dullness was probably the only thing that made a wide gulf of isolation around Leschetizky. He became tired and depressed among people who did not interest him. And as for stupidity, he showed his impatience and disapproval by quickly excusing himself. Alone he was never bored. He would sometimes leave the room during lessons and go off by himself to be quite alone. In the class it was most serious and embarrassing when the master disappeared. Less trying perhaps would have been his sarcasm, but he himself took the easiest way and left. He would sometimes pace the floor outside, or look for a book to read, as an antidote to a bad mood that might become troublesome. Reading refreshed him, and was to him a great recreation. He once said, "I think I will go and read to rest myself; I feel empty and as if everything I knew were gone. I need some new thoughts."

He found no virtue in suffering of any kind, and very little in patience. Something, he thought, was radically wrong if one needed patience, and his patience only lasted so long as it took to right a wrong. He once remarked that he thought he could bear any amount of suffering if it were short, and have enough fortitude for any degree of physical pain if it were brief, but he was sure his courage would fail for any protracted troubles. Slowly increasing dangers and anxieties were a terror to him, and I think he suffered greatly in his lifetime from a prediction made in his youth by a fortune teller, that he would die in the year five.[1] Consequently, he did not like to look forward to the year 1905, and said he had felt much relieved when the clock struck twelve on New Year's morning, 1906.

A well-ordered and peaceful house was essential to him for a profitable and successful day—the contrary, most infuriating. "I go into furnished rooms to-morrow with my valet if that matter of housekeeping isn't instantly corrected," he used to threaten. "You can all putter and do as you like, but I warn you, I hold myself free to go!" He himself observed great order and regularity in his affairs, and he wanted order in the background, he said, so as to be free in the foreground. His servants were devoted to him and never wanted to leave him. He was polite and kind to them. A lack of politeness to those serving one was truly undignified in his opinion. He expressed himself in no uncertain terms on one occasion to some very rich people who always had trouble with their domestics and were never polite to them. He had observed this opulent gentleman one day at the post office, where he was in so much of a hurry that he shoved a poor man out of the way. I am afraid that on that occasion Leschetizky assumed one of the notorious privileges often imputed to artists, for he suddenly found himself in a great hurry and shoved the very rich gentleman out of the way in the same manner as he had pushed aside the servant.

One of Leschetizky's moments of delight was on hearing that this same millionaire mistook for a

[1] This prophecy was in part fulfilled when he died ten years later, in 1915.

servant a very charming and brilliant countess
whom he had never seen but desired very much to
meet. As she was dressed in plain, old clothes, he
pushed her aside from the counter at the market,
where she was buying oranges.

As Leschetizky wanted order, so he expected
propriety, and his temper rose to the boiling point
at a lack of either. One did not like to make mistakes of propriety before his observing eyes, as he
was quick to impose correction.

A young Polish girl once allowed herself a moment's hesitation on being beckoned by Leschetizky to come to him to be introduced to a nobleman at his house. He stepped over to her, and
brought her quickly forward, telling her he hoped
he would not be obliged to teach her good manners,
as well as music, for at the piano, at least, she had
shown some talent.

He was present at a five o'clock reception one
time when an American girl, one of his new pupils,
entered the room, and, after shaking hands with her
Viennese hostess in very hearty fashion, seated herself comfortably on the sofa. As the hostess walked
across the room with one of her most distinguished
guests, a Princess, she thought of presenting to her
the young American girl. Firmly seated on the
sofa, the girl extended her hand, but did not rise.
Leschetizky could not endure this, and walked as
inconspicuously as possible over to them, and took
the girl by the arm, saying, "In Vienna one stands
on being introduced to a lady, and certainly to a
Princess. Let me see you on your feet, and making
a curtsy too!"

One of his most delightful impromptu speeches

was partly the outcome of the apparent neglect
of a certain guest at one of these five o'clock receptions where brilliant artists and poets had come
together. Off in the corner stood a rather awk-
ward-looking and diffident person whom Leschetizky had been for some time observing curiously.
After listening to the good conversation of other
people for a long time, Leschetizky was seen going
over to his hostess and putting a question to her.
She nodded enthusiastically, and seated herself with
ceremony in the middle of the room, asking her
guests to be silent for a moment.

"My dear friends," said Leschetizky, "I want to
speak a few words about modesty, and also to tell a
little story. Modesty is a quality innate in some
people. It is so natural to them that it becomes
almost a fault. It is not one of my faults. I am
more envious than modest, and wish that I might
have done some one brave act in my lifetime that I
could brag about—for I surely should brag about
it. But there are people who seem to be almost
ashamed of having distinguished themselves. I
think it is nothing to be ashamed of to have saved
lives, for instance. Goethe was not right when he
said that only blackguards and idiots are modest.
There are no such characters in this room, for instance, and yet there is one here supremely modest,
and we are all deprived by this modesty of the benefit of his great spirit and philosophy of life. Discretion, of course, is a part of modesty, but we take
issue with discretion and modesty, and being self-
ish human beings, and artists, we like to be amused,
we like to hear the daring deeds, and we like to

think we might have done likewise. We are rascals *not* to be modest!

"A few years ago there were terrible storms in the North Sea. One of our number here to-day sailed across the channel in one of the worst of these storms. Boats were tossed about like chips on the rough seas, engines were disabled, and all along the Dutch coast were the wrecks of small boats.

"But this was only the beginning of the bad storms. A week later one of the channel boats was split on a rock in plain sight of people on shore. Half of the boat sank with most of the passengers. The other half was supported on this rock for three days. There were six people left. Brave sailors lost their lives trying to save these people. There was little hope unless the storm abated. Then it was that Prince Henry arrived, having traveled as fast as he could to reach the spot. At the same time came—wonder of wonders—an artist and modest, one of those blackguards and idiots that Goethe speaks about. The sailors found among themselves, however, a powerful helper, and cheered by Prince Henry, they made still another heroic attempt to save the exhausted people. The stranger threw himself into the waves—he had no fear for himself—and performed marvels of heroism until these people were saved.

"I heard, on coming into this room to-day, that this man was here. Are we right or wrong?" he inquired, turning slowly toward the silent and awkward guest. His eyes rested on the guest for a moment, then turned back to the audience. "This is my little speech about modesty," he concluded.

On Leschetizky's birthday his pupils and friends liked to make a celebration for him. These were often very large affairs arranged by committees, and Leschetizky seemed to enjoy them, but not whole-heartedly. They were rather too formal to make him altogether happy. There was no music, and in the midst of the long speeches Leschetizky was embarrassed and bewildered. The well-known signs of boredom were on his face, and instead of being the life of the party and becoming more and more cheerful as time went on, he made pathetic excuses that he had not slept well the night before, and left at an early hour. If the truth were known, one might have found him at five in the morning walking about the streets, or sitting on a bench in one of the beautiful Vienna parks.

Leschetizky was very fond of excursions to the country, and on one occasion, when he had really been feeling ill, he suggested making his birthday celebration himself. Six of us were invited for a two or three days' trip down the Danube as far as Pressburg.

We had to start early in the morning, and Leschetizky, who was never late, was the first one to arrive at the boat. He was happy and contented, except for the fear that some one might be late, and looked forward to a long, quiet day. His attitude of mind was of peaceful and affectionate meditation on the past and present. He had made the journey there before with Liszt and Rubinstein. He wondered if we could not find the hotel, and stop at the place where they had been together.

He wanted also to find certain gypsies that would perhaps be in Pressburg still. The Prater was the

nearest place to go to hear the gypsies play in
Vienna, but he reminded us that the wildest gypsies did not come near big places, and if people
wanted to hear them play, they had to search for
them. He thought one hardly knew how to play
an Hungarian rhapsody until one had heard and
appreciated the playing of the wildest band of
gypsies.

The boat glided noiselessly along, and Leschetizky talked about his colleagues, then of the pupils
he had had in the years since he had first made this
journey. From how many corners of the earth they
had come! He called himself a fortunate man.

We had been so entertained all day that by the
time we landed in Pressburg, about five o'clock, we
suddenly discovered for the first time that we were
tired. We were led around many corners and down
many streets, until Leschetizky was sure we had
found the small hotel where he and his friends had
stopped. Now Leschetizky was just beginning to
live and enjoy himself. He asked us reproachfully
if we really must take a rest. Frau Breé thought
we really ought to do so, but we all appeared again
after a short time to start what was in reality
another day with Leschetizky.

As we sat at the dinner table, Leschetizky called
for the proprietor, and asked him if he happened
to have the old registry books. Search was made
for them in the cellar, where they were finally
found. Leschetizky turned page after page in
great excitement until he discovered the three sig-
natures of Liszt, Rubinstein, and his own.

After dinner we sat in one of the parks of Pressburg—a rather dense park with enormous trees.

One tiny incident came very near marring the perfect happiness of our excursion, but, as usual, Leschetizky knew how to make good situations out of bad ones, and harmony was restored through his prompt action. He seemed suddenly nervous and irritable, and remarked to me that he had overheard a conversation that annoyed him. He described it as absurd and conceited, on one side, and altogether too resigned and passive, on the other. "I can't wait to relieve my mind," he said, "so let's find the gypsies and get settled in the room where we can be together and where we can talk."

Leschetizky led us again down many streets to the outskirts of Pressburg, where we found a special type of gypsies. It might have been that they were the same ones whom he knew years before and who remembered him. At any rate, they must have recognized in Leschetizky a man after their own hearts, for, as he walked down the path toward them, they fairly swarmed about him, danced around him, and began to play close to his ear. "Don't play too well," he said to one of them, "we shall be jealous. We have much to learn from you, even if we know a little bit ourselves." They asked him what he wanted to hear. "I want to hear you," he replied. "Don't worry about what you play."

They became very animated. They waved to us, and the whole band bowed from time to time. The leader walked round and round our table as he played, then back, nearer his band, and they all leaned toward us as they made great crashes of crescendos or passionate diminuendos. But Leschetizky was still uneasy. After a while came a pause in the music, when people could talk and move about.

"The gypsies have a dynamic quality and rhythm that very few people have," Leschetizky began.

"But the Germans have it also!" said one of our number.

"The Germans least of all," said Leschetizky. "They have their own qualities: sentiment, sweetness, and poetry, but the real fire, and certainly the abandon of these gypsies, you seldom find among the Germans."

"Oh, Professor," protested the one addressed. "You forget D'Albert."

"Is he a German? You forget," said Leschetizky. "The Viennese have what I mean. The Poles, the Russians, and the English and Americans are not lacking in this quality. No, indeed!" He grew more severe and masterful with every word. "The Germans would like to think they possess the qualities I am speaking about. They often pretend to have them, but their eloquence more often degenerates into declamation, and their abandon into affectation. It is almost racial. These qualities women often have, and play with great fire. Carreño, for instance. Fannie Bloomfield Zeisler, an Austrian-born, Katherine Goodson, an English girl. These qualities often amount to grandeur," he said with emphasis. At that at least two of our party flushed with excitement, and one with embarrassment. "Take every good quality where you find it, and be glad, and give it all the respect it deserves. If such things have been given you, you can always allow yourself to say so, and you can be as proud of them as you like. If you don't recognize them where they do exist, it is because you are envious. But don't let us theorize any more in this place," said Leschetizky. "We came down here to forget our troubles and to enjoy each other, to forget ourselves, didn't we?" he asked, very much relieved and smiling.

"Look at those gypsies. They have forgotten everything but the pleasure of playing. They are magnificent!" Leschetizky gave them more money, and they played on. He was happy, and none of us would have offended him by appearing sleepy or tired, though we stayed until broad daylight.

We made another excursion one time to the beautiful Semmering, which is a favorite resort of the Viennese, on the edge of the mountains one crosses on the road to Italy.

Mark Twain and his family were in Vienna at that time, and during the two years that they were there, he and Leschetizky often came together. They became great friends and seemed to understand each other perfectly, in spite of the fact that the English of the one was as limited as the German of the other. Leschetizky was full of admiration for Mark Twain, as were all the Viennese. As he walked through the streets of Vienna, people made way for him, and his white head and distinguished bearing made him a conspicuous figure.

Once, as Clara Clemens, his daughter, was going through the narrow Kärnthnerstrasse with a friend, she saw her father far ahead, and tried to overtake him. Coming up to him, she reached out with her parasol to stop him, when a policeman instantly threw himself between them to protect the distinguished visitor! Mr. Clemens laughed heartily on turning around and seeing the two abashed girls.

While in Vienna he gave one evening of story telling in the Bösendorfer Saal, and this was a matter of pleasant recollection for years afterward among the Viennese.

A party consisting of Mr. and Mrs. Clemens, their daughters, Clara and Jean, Leschetizky, Madame Leschetizka, Jane Olmsted, two American doctors, my sister, and me, went together to the Semmering for several days. The mountain sides there are covered with thick pine woods, and in winter there are sports rivaling those of Switzerland. Further on is Mürzzuschlag, a mountain place where the peasants have inherited curious traditions of winter sports.

Their tobogganing is famous. The toboggans are large and look like sleighs. There is a wide seat in front, where the driver sits and with his legs propels the sleigh. You arrive at nine, are driven, or nearly dragged, for four hours to the top of the highest mountain. There a luncheon is prepared for you, and during the interval of lunching, the horses are driven home down the mountain, so that there is no danger of their being in the way when the toboggans follow. We had six of these sleighs, and a stalwart man sitting on the wide seat in front. The sleighs came down the mountain regular distances apart, steered by the strong men in front with a sureness that was almost incredible. We covered in ten minutes the distance which it had taken four hours to climb. The occupants of one belated sleigh had been rather terrified at the speed, and persuaded their reluctant driver to stop for a few minutes.

In the winter there was the best skiing in the Semmering, and in the spring and autumn wonderful walks through the pine woods, and over the mountains on splendid roads. On one of these roads I found a Gemsbart, which Leschetizky stuck in his hat, and wore all the time we were at the Semmering.

Our evening suppers at the Semmering were real events, when Mark Twain and Leschetizky vied with each other as after dinner speakers. Mr. Clemens used jokingly to complain that Leschetizky made the best speeches he had ever heard. Once or twice after dinner we resorted to old-fashioned games, in which Leschetizky joined with amused curiosity.

On reaching Vienna again after this excursion, some of us sat down with him in the station restaurant for a little supper. We were tired from the mountain air and the late festivities, and heads were drooping. Some one remarked that the only person who did not seem tired was Leschetizky. "When I was your age," he said, "I was not only studying music but preparing myself for the university as well, and had to satisfy myself with two or three hours' sleep. There could be no sagging like that during waking hours, or in the presence of people. I learned then how to keep myself lively!"

CHAPTER XIV

LESCHETIZKY liked to stroll alone at night. He loved the poetry and mystery of night, and rarely went to bed before morning. When signs of the practical and sordid began to appear, such as street sweepers, and shopkeepers dusting off their wares and taking to their brooms, he was ready to go home. He never kept regular hours, and used to exclaim, "Oh, what misery it must be to be obliged to lead a regular life!" If he felt like staying up all night he would do so. Some one asked him once if he ever saw the sun rise. "Probably just as often as you do," he answered, "but if I really want to see the sun rise I shall get up one morning for this purpose. I shall appreciate it the more, not being obliged to look at it often."

"You cannot have everything all the time," he went on. "Regularity is one of the worst of habits if you want your days to be interesting."

He had amazing physical strength and endurance, which he attributed for the most part to common sense and will power. When he was tired he rested, no matter what the hour. He used to laugh at the expenditure of energy it required to take physical exercise by flinging one's arms and legs about. He thought that no intelligent person would do this and that one should conserve one's energy for something worth while, like riding, for instance, or dancing, or for study.

"Study should not be timed and regulated by the

clock. You are always at it more or less," he said,
"if you take pleasure in your profession," and he
had no patience with those who were so carried
away with Viennese life that they could find no
time or energy for a few hours' study out of every
twenty-four. He went to the limit of his strength
in five or six hours of teaching, and fairly staggered
to the dining room, incapable of speech until he had
dined.

His dinner usually began with a special kind of
caviar which was hardly ever missing from the
table. It pleased him when he sometimes had a
present of a small box of caviar, but he preferred
his own brand, which he had specially sent from
Russia. A certain kind of sweet champagne was
another important part of his meal. He loved
champagne, but not especially the dry quality.
After a long, well-served dinner he was himself
again, and it seemed as if his physical resources
were unlimited. He was ready then to play again,
if necessary, or even to play the whole night long
with some pupil preparing for a concert, if he
wanted to do so or thought it essential to that pupil's success, or he was ready for the opera or the
theater, which always put new life into him. After
the theater he was usually in very high spirits, and
wanted to go and sit in some café to talk and to
watch people, or for dinner he would like to go to
"Venice in Vienna" in the Prater, where one could
order the best dinner that a Viennese or Parisian
chef could prepare. After that he liked the gondo-
las or the *allées* where they threw confetti.

It was in this park that the famous flower fêtes
of Vienna were annually held, and Leschetizky

liked very much to take part in these exciting and interesting spectacles.

Late at night again he drank liqueurs or the good Hungarian Tokay. A famous wine in Austria was that made at Klosterneuburg, near Vienna. Leschetizky tasted his wines with the critical interest of a connoisseur, smiling and rolling his eyes about, and seemed to enjoy a process of slow sipping rather than actual drinking. He thought that no real artist could be oblivious of the pleasures of wine. He thought that, besides being judges of wine, artists should know how to cook, and if they were women should know how to make a dress; seasoning of food was an art, and in making a dress there were form, composition, embellishment, and color to be studied.

Leschetizky practiced economy and did not spend his money foolishly. He carefully studied the quality of everything he intended to buy and use, and knew usually where materials and objects of art were manufactured. If he had had time and money for it he would have made an intelligent and shrewd collector, for he had the keenest sense of intrinsic values, and was willing to take great pains in studying these values.

"But there are times," he said, "when one spends money not wisely but well. I used to be more foolish about that when I was younger, and spent money sometimes when it was to be my last penny. Now I haven't the pleasure any longer of being so stupid, for I have more money."

He well remembered a youthful time when he was one of a convivial company of young men who were spending a great deal of money. He felt a strong desire to contribute his share, but the money in his pocket was all he would have for several days. If it was spent he would not only have to walk home, go dinnerless for a day or two, but probably would have to pawn some of his clothes; but it was impossible to sit there without paying for something. With perfect *sang-froid* he ordered several bottles of the best champagne, and took the consequences.

He liked to make the most of every situation and enjoyed himself. Consequently, he made no rules of conduct for himself, trusting to intuition and good taste to bring romance and poetry into daily living. He was entirely without creeds and doctrines of any sort, and relied upon his own will power and common sense to keep him fit and in good health. He smoked a great deal, but evidently with certain restrictions, for sometimes he would take a cigar and after a moment's hesitation put it aside for another occasion.

He had a few small prejudices and aversions. Cut flowers were distasteful to him. When he took a walk into the country he had a positive dislike of returning by the same road. His walk was an event to him, and he delighted in making it as circuitous as possible. A straight approach to a point and a direct return gave him no pleasure. Rather than be bored by retracing his steps, he would order a carriage to take him home.

Cards were a favorite form of diversion with him, but he was not an agreeable person at the card table. He played with an intense absorption in the game, and gave way to extravagant expressions of disgust if the others did not show the same interest and skill. Those who submitted to the agonies of playing with him were frequently humiliated by his amazement and scorn at any misplay, which he always attributed to stupidity. He would shout at the player and call him a stupid fool, and sometimes became so angry that he would not speak to the unfortunate person for days afterward.

At the billiard table, however, he was cool and self-possessed and a most excellent player.

He rode very well, too, and maintained that one should sit at the piano as one sat in the saddle.

He had an aversion to clubs and societies, and as for becoming a member of a church, this was something which he could not take seriously. For pagan philosophy he had great respect, but he had a theory that the Christian religion had done more harm than good in this world and that theology was a futile subject which might best be left alone altogether. Religion was for the few, he thought, not for the many. The idea of a missionary's imparting spiritual ideas and emotions to a savage always roused his wrath to the highest pitch of protest and ridicule. "How much better it would be," he said, "for them to have soothing and happy music played to them—music with no words.

"Left to themselves, the savages of Borneo exhibit a high sense of honor," he went on. "I was told this by an explorer whom I met. After all, the explorer is the true missionary. He learns from the savage. But we must not be Hottentots and be without ideals. To go on one's knees and look up (not down) is a helpful act. It distracts us from the miseries of this world, as music does, and the more you can appreciate this benefit, the

more you will gain by it. That earthbound ignorant man who goes into church and makes the sign
of the cross comes out with a poor spiritual equipment. The things of the spirit are beyond his grasp,
and his interpretation of the spiritual is on a level
with his intelligence. Better far to make him superstitious and turn the evil eye upon him, or to
appeal to his pride. This will content him and
often save him from disgrace. You try to make
him feel humble and he will show you that he is
not. Then you have but one recourse—to make
him a slave."

Leschetizky could not find sufficient idealism in
Christian doctrines. How often I heard him say,
"Be ideal, think ideally. We can all afford to cultivate that quality. We can learn from the pagans.
Read the works of the great French critics, and see
with how much of the old Greek philosophy they
are imbued. Whether it makes you happier or not,
it is worth the trouble to try to live ideally. If you
think yourself a poor specimen, you will probably
always remain one, or most likely become one, but
if you think of yourself as having possibilities of
greatness in you, there is a chance for you.

"I learn useful things at night," he once said.
"I learn how mistaken we are in thinking we know
so much. You can learn much from peace and
quiet—and from music. And music begins where
thought leaves off.

"I study for hours," he went on, "when I am
walking alone in the night. I look far down the
street and imagine a beautiful voice, and I learn
that far-away pianissimo quality—that means at-

tention. I look up to the sky and it teaches me
pride and grandeur. When I see that poor man
lying on the ground, I know how to play a loving
phrase. But the next moment there comes a theorist or a moralist and spoils it all. He tells you
what should be, not what is, and then I ask, 'Where
is the music?' "

Many pupils remember those mornings when
Leschetizky walked with us into Vienna from the
Währing Cottage after the classes. If it was
toward six o'clock, we would sometimes wait until
the doors of a coffee house were opened and could
have coffee. More often we stopped to talk with
sleepy peasant women who had just driven in and
were spreading their wares at the corner markets.
Their wagons formed a long procession. The men
drove with their heads nodding, the women asleep
on straw or blankets spread on top of their boxes,
or on heaps of vegetables or fruit. On reaching
the places where they would improvise their count-
ers for the day, they would crawl lazily to their
allotted places amid a concert of sighs and groans.
In a few minutes, however, they were chattering
like magpies or busy quarreling. It was a joy to
see how Leschetizky could bring out their good
nature.

"The devil take you!" called one.

"There he comes," shouted another, as we approached.

"Good-morning," said Leschetizky, "how is your
business?"

"Good," she said, "and we earn a little."

"Then have a good time," he replied. "When

you get older you might forget how to enjoy yourself."

"Have an apple," said she, handing him one of the handsomest.

"Thank you," said Leschetizky, "these are worth looking at and eating, too."

"Good appetite to you," called out another. (*He answered many of them in their own dialect.*)

"Aren't you going to buy?" asked another. (*General laughter.*)

"Yes, indeed," said Leschetizky, "but not from you. There are better-looking fruits elsewhere. I try never to waste my money."

"They told her that her fruits were poor," said her neighbor, "but she would not believe them."

"You seem to have fairly good eyes," said Leschetizky, "perhaps they are looking too far away." (*Great laughter this time.*)

"Now he will like you all the better," said Leschetizky, "if you attend properly to your business. Why don't you try to outdo the others, and have the best-looking counter here? My advice isn't bad, I am sure."

"Why are you here at this time?" asked another. "Are you dancers?" (*Much sudden curiosity among them.*)

"No," said Leschetizky, "but we can dance. We are a band of poets and are up to see the sun rise."

"You are not so tired as we are," spoke up one of the market women; "*we* danced all night."

"Can you dance well?" asked Leschetizky. "That is the question. That takes practice. It is your duty to dance. Dance a little the first thing in the morning when you have slept all night, and your faces won't grow any longer."

"Buy of me," whispered another.

"Buy here, beautiful gentleman," called another.

They were all ready now for the market and looked strong and healthy and happy.

"This is scandalous for us," said Leschetizky, addressing our little party. "It is well enough for me who can stay in bed until one o'clock, but what have you to do this morning? It is dreadful of me to keep you up so late, but still it is better than staying up all night for a ball. Think of the playing we have heard to-night, such as Friedman's, for instance."

Then Leschetizky would hail a rumbling one-horse conveyance and be driven home for a few hours of sleep before the lessons of the day.

There were, of course, no morning appointments with him. The first lesson was fixed for twelve or one o'clock, and it was always somewhat difficult for him to get started. His mood, when he appeared, was determined by the list of pupils waiting for him. His expression was peaceful if good names were on the list, and businesslike if they were new to him. If there was one among them who had become an artist, his attitude was one of delight and expectancy, even of deference.

He was the keenest of observers and had an æsthetic sense that made him notice every detail of one's dress and appearance and conduct. If one dressed elaborately he expected the playing to have some resemblance to the dress. If one was shabby in appearance he generally found some shabbiness in the playing, and of such appearance he was particularly critical. "I am sometimes ashamed of myself," he once said. "I am afraid I judge too much like the French and Italians. They want good looks on the stage. They cannot help it, and they treat bad looks with no consideration at all. A public performer need not be a man of the world, but he or she ought to look distinguished in some way or else stay away from the stage."

He told a story of one of Madame Marchesi's pupils, a beautiful singer and a great artist, but very ungraceful and disappointing in looks, who was discourteously hissed as she stood before an audience at her first concert. The kind Madame Marchesi had evidently prepared her for what might happen, for she had advised her not to make her first public appearance in Paris. When the singer saw the mood of her audience, she stepped forward courageously and said, "Ladies and gentlemen, I have come here to sing, not to be looked at." This speech at once turned the tide in her favor and she proceeded to sing, arousing the greatest enthusiasm.

It was not safe to go to Leschetizky with a button off one's glove or embroidery even slightly frayed. These things he observed at once. He remarked to one girl, "You have the same fault in your person that is in your playing. You have a button off your shoe every time I have seen you.

"You have improved in your dress as well as in your playing," he said to another. "Your clothes used to look fussy. The first time I saw you you had your dress covered with bows."

Once he was indignant when two or three American girls appeared in middy blouses at their lessons, and thereafter made a point of asking any girl who came to a lesson so attired if her father were a sailor.

A really serious incident occurred when a young Viennese friend of his began suddenly to affect an English sportsman style of clothes, which was conspicuous in Vienna. Leschetizky took every occasion to make fun of his thin legs. It is probable that other and more serious affectations were developing in the character of this youth, else Leschetizky would never have resented so bitterly the knee breeches and the checkered waistcoat, nor have mortified this good friend by drawing attention to his clothes before a crowd of English friends.

Colors which did not harmonize were an annoyance to him, but more annoying still was an ungraceful and awkward bearing. This he noticed instantly and put down to lack of rhythm. Rhythm was of the greatest importance to Leschetizky. He defined it as balance and had a keener sense of it than most people.

He used frequently to say that if there were any rhythm in the waves of the ocean, one could walk so as never to be seasick. Faulty rhythm in playing literally made him sick, and I remember seeing him hurriedly leave the room on more than one occasion when there was real unbalance and lack of rhythm in a performance.

He was critical, naturally, of quality in a voice and of enunciation. "The Pole speaks with a great rise and fall of voice; a characteristic almost Oriental, whence comes," he said, "the great variety

and inflection that is natural to them in playing."
He criticized the rough tones of the Germans, while
admitting that their language had force and accent. From the French, on the other hand, he
expected great clearness in playing, but some monotony of expression. Of the English and American manner of speaking he had really nothing good
to say. The English had soft voices but mouthed
their words, and he thought we English-speaking
people ought all to study Italian to learn to move
our lips, and he always wondered why we did not
smile when we spoke.

"Here comes the Rule Britannia," he once exclaimed, "the best person in the world, but you
would never think it from the way he speaks."
And in speaking German, we English and Americans were the same. We didn't open our mouths,
and therefore spoke indistinctly.

One girl was greatly mystified as to why Leschetizky always tiptoed around the room during
her lessons, at the same time speaking to her so indistinctly that she always had to ask him to repeat
his words. At last she realized that this was to be
an object lesson for her, and she finally cured herself of her almost inaudible speech.

Every little detail of personality interested him.
Sometimes a pupil's whole career was changed
when the master became aware of some particular
charm or grace he had at first overlooked. Arthur
Shattuck was one who did not interest Leschetizky instantly. One evening he saw the young
man dancing. He watched him intently and
seemed utterly bewildered on discovering his
rhythm and grace. "Tell him to come out to-mor-

row for a lesson," he said. "If he can dance as well as that he is not so stiff and cold as I thought."

Clarence Bird was another to whom Leschetizky made amends for a hasty judgment. To quote Mr. Bird's own words, "it was difficult for one unacquainted with Leschetizky's mode of teaching to fall into it easily, for his energetic, often passionate, manner and highly concentrated intensity were likely to intimidate a new arrival. Thus it was that I at first failed sadly to follow his biddings. He attributed this to the shape of my head. It showed obstinacy, stubbornness, he said. Heaven knows that my gifts are few, but a desire to learn is and was one of them. Of this Leschetizky later convinced himself, and though my unhappy head was before him all the while to remind him of his mistaken judgment, he nevertheless took great pains to show his change of opinion of me, until finally nothing could exceed the kind and fatherly intimacy of the lessons. I think he appreciated willingness and good intentions for all they were worth, and his sense of justice as illustrated in my case was very acute."

There was a certain æsthetic sensitiveness in Leschetizky which made any physical deformity or peculiarity, however slight, repugnant to him. There was a very well-known blind musician who wished to visit one of the classes. "I have often tried to think I could have him here," Leschetizky said, "but it is not possible. I could not bear to see those eyes."

If he lost his temper sometimes and there was an avalanche of wrath, the result was the entire smoothing out of all his troubles and he was ready to give his whole attention to improvement. He could not rest during the few hours he took for deep sleep if he thought he had really injured any one. A pitiful expression on the face was a torment to him, as was also a disappointed tone of voice. This might easily spoil his day, and he could never rest until he had made more than the fullest amends.

He had one thoroughly talented and interesting pupil who had disturbed him for several months by various little negligences. Leschetizky seemed, indeed, to be very critical of him. He was first dissatisfied with his clothes, his collars were either too low or too high; then with his manner at lessons, sometimes, and, it was reported, with the length of his hair. "There are plenty of others who affect long hair," Leschetizky told him; "yours is too short. Long hair would be becoming to you."

The master had a reputation among some pupils of being very pointed in his remarks and of being witty at the expense of the exact truth, but one did, nevertheless, do well to take more or less seriously every word that he spoke in lessons, whether emphatic or casual. Some students made the mistake of not doing so, to their ultimate sorrow and regret. Many will remember that painful scene in the class when the situation came to a climax. There was a particularly festive atmosphere that evening. Several distinguished American guests were present, among them Miss Inness, the daughter of George Inness, the famous painter. This evening Leschetizky seemed more than usually critical of everything. He sent me to ask the guests to remove their hats. Some one had appeared in real evening dress and had brought several uninvited people with her, which greatly disturbed him. The atmosphere was not serious or definite enough for him. He went to the piano and struck a few chords impatiently, and it was very obvious that something was wrong. When it came this pupil's turn to play, either his low collar or his short hair or his manner affected Leschetizky too disagreeably and his repressed wrath burst forth.

"Before you play," he said, "you should turn and apologize to this assembly. We do not like your looks. We do not like the looks of others here, either. We come here for one purpose and we should come thoughtfully and considerately. This is not a social function. Neither is it a peasants' brawl. Until you have learned to be more correct and proper in your manner and in your dress, you need not come here."

There was an awful moment, when several of the class rose. Miss Inness and her friends silently left the room. Other strangers followed, remarking that they would not care to stay in a house where such a thing could occur. The pupil left the room humiliated, but with an expression on his face of patience and forbearance that irritated Leschetizky the more. His wife, Madame Eugenie, came into the room, earnestly protesting that it was really too much. Leschetizky answered wrathfully, "No, it was not. Any one may leave who pleases."

Martinus Sieveking, with great kindness of heart, went out into the hall where the poor boy was standing, thoroughly crushed and miserable, not knowing which way to turn. Sieveking advised him to do nothing at the moment, but for the sake of his music to forgive Leschetizky. "Yes," he answered Sieveking and the other sympathetic pupils who had gathered round him, "Leschetizky told me never to come to his house again, but he is right. He has criticized me for nearly a year and I have never listened to him seriously. I shall stay here and try to change and come back to him again."

My lesson happened to fall on the day after this trying scene in the class. I found Leschetizky greatly agitated. He put off my lesson and gave the time to pacing up and down the room and talking. "I have tried to be kind for months," he said, "because he is talented and a dear boy. How could one speak plainer than I have spoken all this time? And still there is no sign of a change in him. He is not dull, and so I have hoped that he would not need a shock to wake him up. It would not have been so bad last night but for that haunting, injured look on his face. Now I have heard that he is trying to save his money, and does not care about clothes, and so if money will help, he has some that I have sent him anonymously. Perhaps it does require money to be always presentable, but I did not realize that before. Why didn't some of you relieve me of this duty? People think I am harsh. That beautiful Miss Inness does evidently, and two or three others. Madame Eugenie also!

"Well, let us be more cheerful," he concluded. "There are things we can do. I shall send for him first and apologize. I can at least make amends and give him all the lessons he wants. Why even the newspapers might write about this, and I should appear as a monster!"

Leschetizky was miserable and uneasy until an hour or two later, when he found an opportunity to apologize to his pupil. It was a matter of rather secret delight to the rest of us to watch the improvement and success of this pupil in Vienna. He told us afterward that Leschetizky's kindness at the lessons, in an attempt to make up for what had happened, was really pitiful and always made him weep.

Those pupils of Leschetizky who have heard with shame of a girl who struck Leschetizky in the face because of some reprimand, will always regard this other pupil with affectionate appreciation for his resignation and fortitude.

One evening about midnight my bell rang and the *Hausfrau* came in with a horrified expression, saying that I must come to the door at once. Leschetizky had been brought to my house by a *fiacre* driver, who explained to us that he had found him in a half-conscious state by the roadside in one of the suburbs of Vienna. He happened to be one who had often driven Leschetizky and had recognized him at once. Leschetizky, it appeared, had just strength enough to give him the address of my house, which he knew they must pass on the way home, and then collapsed. We at once gave him stimulants and sent for the doctor. After he revived, Leschetizky related to me how since four o'clock that afternoon he had been searching the suburbs for one of his pupils, about whom he had been worried. The day before the pupil had taken his lesson. He had asked Leschetizky if he thought he could become a great artist. Leschetizky had replied very emphatically that it was impossible. He was a temperamental and visionary young Slav, and his pitiful expression when he left the house had haunted Leschetizky all that night. His anxiety increased the next day, and at four o'clock he found himself unable to go on with the lesson in hand, excused himself abruptly, and started out in quest of the boy's lodgings in one of the suburbs. The housekeeper told him that after hours of wretchedness her lodger had left the house about half an hour before. She said that all the night before he had raved. She thought the Professor must be a terrible man if he could do such things to any one. Of course, he had a dreadful reputation anyway. She shook her fist in his face. She called him a bear and a devil and all sorts of horrible names. She wanted to shut the door in his face and said it would be a great deal better if no one ever came to Vienna to study with him. Leschetizky asked if the boy needed money, and she told him that he had not been able to pay his last board bill. After giving her the proper amount and a few more gulden to buy something comfortable for his room, he hurried off in the direction the young man was supposed to have taken. He walked far into the country, and about ten o'clock he found the boy sitting in a swamp, a revolver in his hand, apparently about to end his life. Leschetizky got him home, but for once his strength failed him and he sank down exhausted in the road where he was fortunately seen and recognized by the coachman.

There were many instances where he tried to avert scandal and tragedy in his class, but did not always succeed. To many who came to Vienna to study success was a matter of life and death. He knew this, and the responsibility bore heavily upon him. His face often wore a troubled look for the things he felt himself obliged to say. I once heard him remark with an expression almost of anguish, "What I want to be in this world is an honest man."

He looked after the desperate pupil who had attempted suicide with great tenderness; during the next year the young man appeared at the class with a conspicuously pale and tragic face, and I am sure Leschetizky gave him every chance to develop what talent he had.

It may be truthfully said that the moral tone of Leschetizky's class in Vienna was far higher than that in most musical centers, and Leschetizky himself was the reason for this. He was poetic and romantic, but hated sordid scandals. Serious experience of any description he considered not only valuable, but necessary to the life of an artist, but if these experiences were not tinged with romance and poetry, he would not hear of them. He loved freedom in words, in actions, but it must always be artistic freedom.

Leschetizky was perhaps too much an idealist, and in consequence he suffered many disappointments. Practical as he was in his teaching, he said nothing so often as he said, "Play ideally," and in every relationship he hoped for perfection.

One evening he took Jane Olmsted, my sister, and me, to see the first production of "Old Heidelberg." As the curtain rose on the first act, one heard a gasp from him, and in a minute or two he turned to us and said, "You will have to excuse me, I cannot see this play." We were amazed at his sudden departure. Later on he came back with very red eyes, much agitated and just managed to control himself throughout the rest of the performance. After that, instead of going somewhere to have coffee, as we generally did, he excused himself again and went home. He explained to us the reason for his trouble. As the curtain rose on the opening scene, he saw the picture of the sunny hillsides and peaceful valleys where he and Essipoff had walked and the same shady trees under which they had been accustomed to sit when they spent their honeymoon in Heidelberg. It was there, he said, he had dreamed of being a happy man.

CHAPTER XV

It was not difficult to get access to Leschetizky. No introduction or influence was necessary, for he would listen to any one play who came and knocked at his door. Strange indeed were some of the letters he received, letters from all parts of the world, oftentimes containing nothing about the applicant's talent for the piano, but chiefly taken up with a report of his or her good looks, amiability, and the vague desire to get out into the world and achieve something.

A letter from a Bohemian girl was brought by four gentlemen, who made an appointment with Leschetizky and took up a great deal of his time telling him how this young woman had strange fantasies all her life, how the birds singing in the trees had affected her, and that since childhood the sound of a brook had inspired her to write poems. She had been blessed with many love affairs, and each had contributed something to her ability to interpret the emotional heights and depths of music. Schumann, she said, made her melancholy; Chopin, sentimental; and when she played Beethoven, she felt herself translated to the skies. Leschetizky would be the very one, they thought, to recognize her sublime talent. They dwelt upon her marvelous endowments, including her poetic temperament, and were greatly astonished that he did not respond, as they had expected, and promise to receive her with open arms.

Some were not at all daunted when he told them, on hearing them play, that they had no talent. Oftentimes there was absolutely nothing at all to justify their ambitions. Many of these applicants were as blissfully ignorant of their own incapacity as they were confident of Leschetizky's power to make musicians of them.

America, too, contributed its share of freaks to the hosts of would-be pianists that went to him for lessons. One entirely misguided young man came boldly forward with the utmost confidence in himself. He and his mother had first appeared at one of the Thanksgiving receptions at the American Embassy, where Mrs. Samuel Clemens was among those who received. They were humble, ignorant people, and sympathizing with their embarrassment in such surroundings, Mrs. Clemens went out of her way to be kind to them. They appeared to expect much from the influence of the Clemens family, who were living in Vienna at the time. The young man went to see Miss Clemens, who did not spare him a very frank and discouraging opinion of his talent. To be told by Clara Clemens that he had better not even try to see Leschetizky, made little impression upon him. At Mr. Clemens' suggestion, he sought encouragement from the younger daughter, Jean, who received him with her usual gentleness. Then he went to Leschetizky with a little speech carefully prepared. First he asked the price of lessons, and then went on to say that he had sold his cigar store in America to come to Vienna to devote his life to becoming an artist. His mother had come with him to help. "How does she propose to do that?" Leschetizky asked.

"By making paper flowers until I can earn a living by the piano," he replied. Leschetizky was appalled by the young man's ignorance and egotism. "You are not even educated," Leschetizky began. "I don't suppose you can read, to say nothing of knowing music. What do you expect to do?" "I am going to do my best," was the answer. "But, my dear boy," said Leschetizky, "what do you think your best can be? You must remember that you are here in Vienna among clever and gifted people." "Oh, yes," he answered, "I have met a number of them." He said that the Clemenses had been kind to him, and that he and his mother had been invited to the home of Mrs. Krause. Mrs. Krause had asked them to come again, and had said she would do all she could to help them. He had met one of Leschetizky's pupils also, Miss Newcomb, who had likewise encouraged him, and had called Leschetizky one of the kindest people in the world.

Leschetizky assured him that the kindest thing he could say to him was that his playing showed neither talent nor knowledge. But the youth protested that he was quite sure the master was wrong. Hadn't Paderewski begun at the foot of the ladder; why couldn't he? He refused to be discouraged. No one could discourage him. He would go to some one else and study and return in exactly one year to show Leschetizky how mistaken he had been. The young man did stay on in Vienna, and in time rose to a high position, not as a pianist, but as the Princess Metternich's coachman.

Even where there was little excuse for seeking

his advice, Leschetizky rarely hesitated to give it. He laughed heartily when he told of one instance when he yielded too readily. Two American women once came to play for him. After he had heard them, he asked, with subtle politeness, why they did not study singing instead of the piano. They answered that if that was his advice, they would do exactly as he said. A year or two afterward, when Leschetizky was playing in some city in Germany, two ladies announced themselves, and asked to sing for him.

He listened to them, and then, to their utter amazement, asked why they did not study the piano, which was so much easier in some respects than singing. When they replied that it was he who had advised them to take up singing, Leschetizky was completely at a loss to know how to get himself out of the embarrassing situation.

He once asked why it was that so many young American women came to study in Vienna just after they had been married. Sometimes, when a young woman played very badly at her lesson, he would ask her why she didn't marry instead of trying to learn the piano. Very often the reply was, "Why, Professor, I *am* married." "Well, then," he would reply, "you should go home and present your husband with a baby."

One day he showed a letter from a gentleman in America, thanking him for urging his wife to give up music and go home. She was one pupil, he said, who had evidently taken his advice; and this was the first husband who had ever written to thank him.

Sometimes he was able to rid himself very

quickly of the hopelessly untalented. Upon entering the music room one morning, he found two ladies sitting there, dressed in deep black, as solemn as crows. When he came in, neither rose nor spoke. Leschetizky waited. At no word or sign from them, he waved his hand and exclaimed: *"Auf!"* They rose to their feet, but still failed to express themselves in any way. Leschetizky then pointed to the piano. *"Spiel!"* he commanded. One of them played, whereupon Leschetizky pointed to the door. *"Weg!"* he said. With three words the visitors were received, heard, and dismissed. Needless to say, they were never seen again.

Spectacular entrances were sometimes made by people who afterward claimed Leschetizky's most serious consideration. Laughing a little at his own part in the affair, he once related the story of his introduction to a certain pupil, now a musician of excellent reputation. This pupil appeared in the music room one day, demanding a hearing with Leschetizky in a most unusual and erratic manner. After playing, he wanted to know at once about beginning his lessons. Leschetizky was not at all sure he wanted to teach him, and said so. The man was not young; his style was muscular and heavy-fisted.

"You are Jewish," Leschetizky began, "and for that reason I have a certain faith in your talent."

He protested, but Leschetizky went on, "You needn't conceal that from me. If you are to study with me, we must understand each other."

The man continued to look about the room with a rather wild-eyed expression, and then deliberately began to roll up his sleeves. Leschetizky slipped quickly through the side door of the music room. When he came in again, he was prepared for any emergency; there was a revolver in his pocket. It appeared, however, that no pugilistic assault had been intended. The pianist had merely wished to exhibit a portion of his technical equipment—a pair of powerfully developed forearms.

One day a charming Londoner asked permission for an interview. His interview became a pleasant conversation with Leschetizky, who rather prolonged it than otherwise, fearing to break the spell by approaching the subject of music. But the excuse for the visit being music, he was invited to play. What was Leschetizky's astonishment to hear him play faultlessly and with expression his own piece "The Two Larks." On being asked to play further, the visitor announced that it was the only piece he had ever played. He said he had improvised all his life, but wanted a real accomplishment for the London season. "This is something new to me," said Leschetizky. Students who cannot play at all by ear I advise most earnestly to cultivate the quality. Many pianists deplorably lack it, and should try playing simple tunes entirely by ear, training themselves to the habit of improvising also—especially when the memory fails, as it sometimes does in pieces. These students study too much from the theoretical side. But you know nothing of the theory of music, and do not intend to study it, and have been taught one piece entirely by ear. I will give you a few lessons myself," said the master all curiosity and interest. "You asked for permission to study with an assist-

ant; I shall take great interest in learning myself
what can be done by the ear alone."

These lessons were a pleasant diversion to
Leschetizky, who taught him a Chopin nocturne entirely without notes, and the pupil returned to
London, playing very beautifully this addition to
his repertoire.

One winter four child prodigies came to Leschetizky; the youngest was six and the oldest nine.
They were assigned to the assistants, and I was
given the one of nine. Leschetizky considered her
the hardest to teach because she was the oldest. A
lovely-looking little creature she was, a Russian,
slender and tall for her age. Her mother came
with her. They had fled from Kiev during a rev-
olution, and lived in Vienna in a nearly penniless
condition. There was no question of paying for
the lessons, but talent was never sent away from
Leschetizky for lack of funds. Of course, every
one was kindly interested in the development of
these prodigies, who soon became prominent in the
class because of their remarkable talent.

I quickly discovered my pupil to be as difficult
as Leschetizky had said. She played a great deal
by ear. She could transpose without trouble, and
playing from memory in any key was as easy as
possible for her, but she could not concentrate her
mind. Her tone was beautiful, but she had no
memory for phrasing. It was almost impossible
for her to change the inflection of the phrase. She
might accomplish it once, but it was forgotten as
soon as it was done. Catching sight of my beautiful Russian wolfhound in the corner, she would
break off in the middle of a piece, jump up from

the piano, and exclaim, "Oh, what a beautiful dog!"
As the weeks went by and she was still unprepared
to go to Leschetizky, he used to ask me what was
the matter, and seemed disappointed that she was
not ready for a lesson. Her mother was much concerned over her slow progress, and I was in despair of finding a way to get hold of her flighty little mind. The six-year-old child had already
played in the class; and the other two were amazing
every one with the simple and beautiful expression
in their playing. They all had to use the raised
pedals, and because of their short arms, to sit on a
bench, so that they could slide from one side of the
keyboard to the other.

At last this prodigy came to a lesson with Leschetizky, to which I accompanied her, anxious to
see what his genius for accomplishing wonders
would do for her. A Czerny study went perfectly.
She was asked to play it in another key, which gave
her no trouble. The Schütt "Canzonetta," which
she played next, seemed to please him, and he asked
her to transpose that, too. This she did also without any difficulty. All went well at first, but when
he told the little girl that he wished her to copy a
phrase, as he played it, I foresaw difficulties. With
the utmost patience he played it for her again and
again, speaking in a very calm and kind tone.
There was no apparent change whatsoever. Then
he tried a more emphatic tone of voice, and it was
only then that she made any real attempt to follow him. Under the influence of fright, she seemed
to bring some expression into the phrasing. Even
then she showed herself too slow at changing anything. The six-year-old child, he told us, played

her little pieces musically and transposed them as well. Moreover, he found he could influence her in her playing in any way he liked. He thought she showed a certain gift, but it was not the sort he cared to bother with. Only a plastic talent interested him. This he explained to the mother, and advised her to take her child to another teacher. He was sure she had to be prodded to study, and he advised me also to discontinue teaching her. The mother's distress was so touching that I promised to go on with her child. She went on her knees to the master, begging for another chance. Their only hope of a decent living was to prepare the little girl for teaching as soon as possible. I tried having her come every morning, hoping to hold her attention more easily in this way, before the day brought too much to distract her. When I told this to Leschetizky, I found that he had given the matter a great deal of consideration. He was very fond of teaching prodigies. He thought that I was probably not enough the master with her. "There is a way to make her learn," he said, "and if you try what I recommend, there may be a chance for her. The only time that she really listened or paid real attention was when I frightened her. Some people are like horses, when they are nervous a calm voice will calm them; others have to be touched with a whip. Now, if you are going to continue with her, I advise you to take your riding whip, and every time she does not pay attention, touch her with it."

Privately I determined to do no such thing, but as the days and weeks went on, and I found no way of getting hold of her easily distracted mind, I told the mother what Leschetizky had said. She confided to me that the only way she had of making the girl obey, was to give her a whipping, and was delighted that Leschetizky had shown enough interest to make any suggestion at all. "Not only touch her, but whip her soundly," she advised. So I began the terrible career of the whip. It took all my courage to touch that beautiful child ever so lightly, but every time her mind wandered to the dog or to some other distraction, I took the whip in my hand. She actually did begin to improve, and in a few months had a long Haydn piece ready to play for Leschetizky, who asked her how many years it would take her to prepare another lesson. The child progressed very slowly, but Leschetizky continued to take interest in her, partly for the sake of her mother, whose gratitude was touching.

In my experience of teaching in Vienna, one pupil came to me already possessing what Leschetizky called a "splendid technique." It was very unusual for him to speak of a technique as splendid, and he naturally remembered this pupil. And certainly it was a most unusual occurrence for an assistant to be able to start at a stage so advanced.

Leschetizky was quick to note any individuality and to foster it in the lessons, and was only too thankful to find no limitations in the technique. But he preferred a preparation of correctness and good style to a studied interpretation, so that nothing should hinder the quick application of his ideas. It was not long before I realized that this young man had fixed ideas of interpretation and a rigidity of expression that would not please Leschetizky. It seemed, also, that it would take a long time to eradicate these faults.

Leschetizky recommended the "G Minor Ballade" of Chopin to prepare for his first lesson, and often inquired if he could play the first phrase well. As time went on, my pupil showed no inclination to accept my suggestions as to the way Leschetizky wanted that first phrase played. I told him Leschetizky would never listen to such an interpretation of it, and I should have to postpone his lesson until he had changed it. He replied that D'Albert's interpretation was more to his liking, but for the sake of a lesson with Leschetizky he would try to conform.

When he appeared, Leschetizky said, greeting him, "You are the one with such an excellent technique. I have been expecting you for a long time. I congratulate you upon your good fingers. To have acquired at your age the degree of technique you have, is an achievement in itself. It shows intelligence and industry. But you mustn't think technique is everything. Now you can really forget your technique, and concentrate your whole mind on the artistic use of it. A very good choice— this Chopin ballade." After the first phrase Leschetizky stopped him.

"That is not Chopin!" he exclaimed. "Have you ever read the life of Chopin? His music must not be declaimed," he said; "you must sing, it must be lyric. Remember your heart is broken, you want to find a little happiness in this world, and so you sing. Play it this way," Leschetizky said. The pupil tried, but in vain. "Did not my assistant show you how I like to hear it played?" he asked. The pupil admitted that she had, but said that D'Albert had played it more to his liking, and that he had tried to copy him. "So you think that is the way D'Albert plays it, do you? Well, if you can play as he plays it, why come to me?"

D'Albert had played the ballade in Vienna some months before, and Leschetizky had heard him. Going to his piano, he sat down and gave an exact imitation of D'Albert's beautiful rendering of it. Every phrase, almost every note, it seemed, was as D'Albert had played it. He got up again and turned to the pupil, who for the moment appeared rather ashamed of himself.

"You should show my assistant more respect," said Leschetizky. "What do you suppose I care about your technique? Anybody can get technique. But I did expect more of you. What a disappointment," he went on, "here's a technique, a real one. What would some people not make out of it! And here it is of no use. You are a man set in his ways, a block of wood with no ability beyond this. Quick, out of here!" he shouted to him. "I've no time to waste, not a moment. I am growing old, but I shall never be so old that I'll have to teach such as you." The young man made an impertinent reply and started to go. The exit was not speedy enough for Leschetizky, who ran after him and literally pushed him out of the room.

"Oh, oh!" he exclaimed to me. "How can you bring such a pupil? That man is not teachable, but you will see he'll try to come again. See that he never does. What was his name? I want to remember, so that there will never be a repetition of this."

I cannot vouch for the story, but I heard that the unfortunate young man found courage to return to Vienna a year or two later disguised by a beard and by another name. Through one of the other assistants a lesson was arranged, but Leschetizky recognized his hands, and the second exit was as speedy as the first.

A pupil who had the misfortune to come for a lesson after any such trying experiences as these was to be pitied, unless he had good playing at his instant command, and would preserve a cheerful demeanor under all circumstances.

Leschetizky liked to be treated with confidence and freedom. He understood perfectly the nervousness of a pupil, and when it did not affect the pupil to the extent of making him incapable of learning, the master grew patient and good-humored.

An English girl, Marie Novello Williams, a pupil preparing with me for Leschetizky, always kept him good-humored under all circumstances. It was refreshing to witness these lessons, not only for her facility and her quickness in copying Leschetizky's playing, but also for her ready answers, which were a source of enjoyment to him. When I took her to her first lesson, she smiled so affably that Leschetizky was at once encouraged. At the first note, however, she put down the pedal, and kept it there for several bars. Very much surprised, Leschetizky asked her why she had not changed the pedal. "Because I am so scared of you," she answered. "You are really scared of no one," said Leschetizky. "And it is a relief for me to find some one who smiles as you smile. Let us see now if you can smile in your playing. You must smile in your heart, too, and not only wear smiles on your face!"

At another lesson she appeared very rosy and happy. "Another love affair?" remarked Leschetizky. "Yes," she answered, "I have just made the acquaintance of the chord of the ninth." "Don't let that set you too free," replied Leschetizky.

He often related to friends that he had one pupil who was better than a doctor for the nerves. Leschetizky had the misfortune of being nervous during thunderstorms, and, as during a most violent one she had been perfectly placid and had played her pieces with the usual concentration of mind, he called her "a model of British self-possession." "The English make it a point of honor not to be nervous," he said. "What a splendid trait!"

There were not many students who succeeded as well as she in having an easy and agreeable time during lessons.

I had another pupil with many good qualities, but the road for him was long and rough. He was over six feet tall, unusually slender, and had very long hands. There were many mannerisms in his playing, and his way of sitting at the piano was conspicuous, to say the least. He had, however, the ability to study thoroughly, and was a good musician. His good qualities were rather far beneath the surface, and it was always difficult for him to do anything naturally. During his months of preparation the young man and Leschetizky met at my house at tea time. Leschetizky asked him how he was getting on, and advised him not to hurry, as the more thorough the preparation, the better he would fare in the lesson. "It is no great pleasure taking lessons of me," he said. "You must first get order in your playing. You get the order, then I put in the disorder."

As I handed my pupil a cup of tea, I noticed that Leschetizky could scarcely suppress his amusement. "Did you see him?" he said to me afterward. "He does nothing naturally. If you hand him a cup of tea he goes through the motions of a contortionist in reaching for it. And did you see him shake all over when I came into the room? I am afraid I am the ogre of Vienna," said Leschetizky.

By the time this pupil was ready for his first lesson I was still at a loss to know how to warn him of the effect that his mannerisms and whole conduct at the piano would be likely to have upon Leschetizky's sense of humor. At last I brought myself to say that if he got himself into such ridiculous positions, Leschetizky would surely think that he did it deliberately. He surprised me by replying that his legs were too long to go straight under the piano, and that he had to twist them around in order to sit near enough to the keyboard to play.

I took pains to accompany this pupil to his lesson, and happened to leave the room while he and Leschetizky exchanged a few words before the lesson began. When I returned, I saw at one piano my pupil sitting in his usual position, while Leschetizky was lounging back in his chair at his, with his feet resting on the keyboard. There was perfect silence in the room, and not a word was said until I laughed.

Leschetizky asked me solemnly the reason for my mirth.

"I am laughing at you," I said.

"Your pupil is not," he answered. "He sees nothing queer about this at all. Every one may sit at the piano as he pleases. He is sitting as he likes, and I am doing the same." Then turning to him, he continued, "This is the only thing you have not done to-day."

When the young man explained the reason for his awkward position, it was Leschetizky's turn to laugh.

As he went on with the lesson the master tried hard to be serious. He had not failed to perceive some talent, in spite of these ungraceful attitudes, and in his kindest manner told this pupil to study well, and come again after due preparation. This was not so quickly accomplished, for he spent much of his time in trying to rid himself of his eccentricities of manner.

Later on, he told me how he had once irritated Leschetizky by failing to use a little judgment. The master, wishing to test his endurance, told him to play repeated notes in a quick tempo with one finger until that finger was tired. Just then Leschetizky turned to speak to some one in the room, and a moment or two passed before he could give his attention again to the piano. He found him still repeating the note in a slow tempo by a finger so stiff with fatigue that he could scarcely lift it from the key. To be taken so literally exasperated

Leschetizky. He burst out, "You needn't be a fool, even for me!"

That music room was a place of many dramatic surprises, strange entrances and exits, but Leschetizky was equal to all the situations which arose. They were real events to him, and he never ignored them. Individuality always held his attention, and to be mistaken in his judgment of a personality, he considered a great failure.

Only such an intensely youthful and courageous spirit as his could have coped with the great variety of temperaments which his reputation as a teacher attracted to Vienna.

CHAPTER XVI

LESCHETIZKY's pupils came from all over the world. Many were very quiet and unassuming, others quite the reverse. They came to him recommended in all sorts of ways, by all kinds of people, by artists, whether strangers or friends, by people of prominence, by committees, or by managers. He never seemed to forget his first impressions.

"I want to recommend to you most warmly," ran a letter from a beautiful and distinguished woman then in a far country, "this dear boy, who is going to Vienna to study with the greatest master we know. Allow me to tell you something about his character, great master! His parents have refused their support, because he is determined to be an artist. He refuses now the money and support of his friends, and did not ask for this letter, which I am writing entirely on my own responsibility."

"Hm," remarked Leschetizky, "a good trait."

"He writes very well, and has traveled a great deal," the letter went on. "Through his visits to all parts of the world he has become a many-sided and interesting person. But he has given more of his time to writing than to anything else; consequently he is beginning rather late to concentrate his mind on playing the instrument of his choice."

"Hm," said Leschetizky again, but in another tone.

"However, he is still young, and we trust to the

genius and kind attention of the great master, to
show him the way to achieve his heart's desire. We
firmly believe our young friend will not disappoint
his host of friends in this part of the world," etc.

"There you have it!" exclaimed Leschetizky.
"These beautiful and well-meaning ladies put upon
me the responsibility of making an artist of a man
already grown up, who has never really played or
studied music seriously at all. What falderal!—
But I like one thing about him! He doesn't want
to live on other people. That is rather unusual
these days. Well, when he comes we shall see. It
is better to have an interesting dilettante than some
of those that are here now. They make my blood
boil! They come to me recommended over and
over again and they are really worse than the untalented, just showy and conceited and stupid!"

Leschetizky was constantly bombarded by the
untalented, whom he always discouraged and sent
away, telling them never to come to him again.
Some of these discarded pupils went quietly away
to study elsewhere, and would perhaps return later,
better equipped. Others tried their luck at the
good Vienna Conservatory, but there were always
many persistent ones who remained and sought an
occasional lesson with him. There were times
when Vienna was filled with these noisy, self-styled
pupils of Leschetizky, who made a great show with
their big technique. The Viennese, with their innate musical sense, hardly knew how to accept this
class of students, whose limitations, in the opinion
of the Viennese critics, reflected somewhat upon
Leschetizky's reputation as a teacher.

Often his friends thought they saw a miracle

being performed, but as soon as his influence was removed from their studies, their careers were apt to end in failure.

He wanted his pupils to become musicians, if they were not already such, "as well as mere pianists," and to have his full approval required the utmost seriousness in the cultivation of chamber music, the study of composition and, among other things, the ability to accompany singers.

"To play the piano," he contended, "one must understand composition, be a singer and accompanist all together." It was a long time, indeed fully a year, before the "dear boy" recommended by "the beautiful lady" was ready for a lesson with the master. He had sent him to me for his preparation, and he was now as fit as I could make him for his first lesson. He had studied with great intelligence and determination, had acquired a technique, but I could not see that he had made any improvement beyond that point. I had asked Leschetizky if he thought my pupil had better go to study with some other assistant, and he had only replied that he dreaded the time when he should have to hear this pupil play, for his troubles, he said, were most likely incurable.

"If the fault in him is purely technical," he said, "he might possibly try another assistant, for you all have your different ways of getting at the same thing. But I have a real premonition of difficulty with this young man, interesting as his personality seems to be in other respects, besides music."

As the time approached for this pupil to go to Leschetizky, he seemed to look forward to his first lesson as a most interesting adventure, and had presented me with a written imaginary account of it, which I found most amusing. This gay attitude might please Leschetizky, and it might not, and so, with some misgivings on my part, we went out together to Leschetizky's house in plenty of time to compose ourselves, remembering one of his frequent admonitions never to begin the new thing badly. We waited in the room called by the students "the torture chamber."

Another lesson was going on that had evidently begun badly. Leschetizky was occasionally prevailed upon to give one or two lessons to some persistent student who remained in Vienna in spite of his advice to give up trying to play. Great pressure was often brought to bear upon him to give such a lesson, and it was much to his credit that he often complied, in the belief that he might have erred in his quickly formed judgment of his pupil's capabilities.

But some lessons went badly in spite of every concession on the part of Leschetizky, and from these failures grew the unfair criticism that he was a cruel and impossible person to study with.

He appeared suddenly at the door, looking very dejected and annoyed, and asked me to come into the music room to interpret for him.

"Here is a terrible specimen," he said. "One of those who either refuse to speak or do not know how. I cannot find out what language he speaks, if he speaks any at all; whether he is English, or American, or Australian—I don't know. You must tell me where to place him. You will have to wait anyway," he said, consulting his watch, "that is, thirty minutes more, and you might as well come in and enjoy yourself. Dreadful it is! I have already spent thirty minutes and more! Your pupil may come in, too, if he likes," he said, looking witheringly at him.

We followed him into the music room and the lesson proceeded.

"Ask him if he knows what I am saying," said Leschetizky to me.

"Certainly," replied a raw and trumpetlike voice in English. "But I do not believe in being talked to this way! I've done nothing."

"He understands you," I translated to Leschetizky, "but he says you confuse him."

"If he understands, it's all the worse!" growled Leschetizky. "I don't get along with people who won't speak."

"Do you want me to speak louder?" suddenly shouted Leschetizky at the top of his voice. "You see I can do it," cried he. No response came from the pupil at the piano. The other one was bursting with suppressed laughter, and clutching his chair for support.

"There are all kinds of men," continued Leschetizky. "The little ones talk more. It takes a big one to be surly and silent. I can't make him say a word, no matter what I do! He would not speak if a bomb exploded at his feet. One day a little one came to see me in Berlin, a nice little talkative one, and forgot to take his hat off. 'Take your hat off,' I said, 'you are in a civilized country.' He removed his hat with an apology, and flung it the whole length of the room. 'Pick your hat up,' I said, 'this isn't my house, and, even if it were, there's a place to put things.' But the little one went on talking so fast, it was hard to stop him. Give me the little ones! I understand them better, because they'll talk!"

"Play," commanded Leschetizky suddenly. "We've got to go through this ordeal." The pupil was the kind with a heavy, hard technique. He pounded fearfully, so that Leschetizky had to shout to stop him.

"Do you think this is a circus?" he asked. "Am I obliged to listen to such playing? It hurts my ears, and if you had any ears it would hurt yours. I tell you, my dear sir, it would be better if you did not come to me. I cannot bear it. I have too much respect for the piano to see it struck that way.—He says nothing, you see!" said Leschetizky to me, after a pause.

"You cannot say 'bo' to a goose, can you?" he resumed, turning to the wretched pupil. "You can just pound the poor piano. Why did you come alone?" asked Leschetizky. "Where is your teacher?"

"I asked her not to come," said the pupil in fairly intelligible German.

"Ah!" exclaimed the master, "a word at last! Perhaps you would like to tell me that she is to blame for some of your bad playing."

"Perhaps she is," retorted the pupil.

"There, you see," said Leschetizky, "you are that kind of man. I would like to inform you that I feel I owe her an apology for asking her to teach you. But she knew how to manage you. She understands you! Did she forget to remind you to speak respectfully of her? I heard of a very impertinent remark you made of her on one occasion. You are the kind to say such things! Do you understand me?"

No reply.

"I'll hear one more thing on her account, the poor creature. What else have you brought me? A piece of mine. Well, where are the notes? You haven't brought them? Now what do you expect me to do? Search twenty minutes for the notes? It's so kind of you to have brought me one of my own pieces! Thank you very much. We will not hear it to-day. We can perhaps get over a bar or two of the other. I think I know where to find the notes of that. Of course, you have not brought them either? No!—Now, let me ask you what you think you are playing? It is a nocturne, I believe, and you are playing at the piano. You certainly are not in a bowling alley here! You do not have to take any such postures at the piano! Why do you hate everything so?" asked Leschetizky. "Hatred makes people play as you play. It is not entirely that you do not know how to play! You have a little mind—I can see that by your technique. But you must lie awake nights hating people, hating the piano! Couldn't you lie awake for something better than that?

"Oh, can't you smile? Can't you say something —something to give me some notion of what you are thinking? Perhaps you are thinking of a beef-steak?"

"No, I came here to play," said the youth finally.

"Well, I wish you would play then, and not pound," pursued Leschetizky. "Yes, you will never want oysters and champagne. You'll never buy them either with money you earn by playing the piano."

"I suppose I am here to learn to play and not to talk," said the pupil to me.

"What did he say?" asked Leschetizky.

"He says he supposed you wanted him to play only, and not to talk," I translated.

"You are not telling me the truth," said Leschetizky. "I saw in his face what he meant. If you had wanted to play to-day," said the master, trying to keep his temper, "you have had the chance. We have been waiting for it a long time, and have been ready to listen with attention, but does it never occur to you that you were not born to play? It is not playing! Don't you understand? There is no modulation in your tone, because there is none in your mind, or heart, either. This organ here," continued Leschetizky, putting his hand to his heart, "is an important factor in all art. The only excuse you have for playing any instrument is that you have a heart, and that your heart inspires you to express yourself in beautiful tones. You won't put anything into your music until your nature changes, and that, believe me, is the hardest thing in the world to change. I don't like such natures as yours! Do you understand?"

A wiggle only from the pupil.

"I prefer my man here in the house, who can speak when he is expected to. He does exactly as he is told. He walks softly across the room, is respectful, really respectful, is not conceited, and is intelligent! Oh, yes, he is intelligent! You don't believe it, but he is! What do you think I can change in your nature in this one hour?" he went on, waxing more intense with every word. "Strong fingers are easy enough to get, and even technique. I don't see that you are any too intelligent in that even. Now, we will take a few notes at a time."

The pupil began. "Bang," said Leschetizky. "Hit it again, that's right! Hit it a little harder; perhaps you'll break a string and then I'll have the pleasure of mending it," said Leschetizky. "But why that crescendo there?"

"At one of the classes," replied the pupil, "I heard you say 'Good,' when Friedman played it that way."

"You don't mean that you actually heard that?" said Leschetizky. "Then you are not deaf at any rate! Perhaps I did say it, but Friedman can do these things where you cannot! Tell me," said Leschetizky, "did you ever hear of the inch more on a man's nose? Well, that changes the whole expression of his face, and so does this crescendo also change the whole expression of that phrase. If you knew how to place that crescendo it would be all right, but you do not, and you never will! Never! Never! I tell you!

"Take this one note. No, no, just one! I didn't ask for any others. One note, you see is too much for you! You don't know how to strike it! You do not know how to hear it, to say nothing of giving it any relation to the notes around it, as Friedman does."

Leschetizky rose and walked down the room trying to be patient.

"And they told me that some people considered him talented," we heard him say. "They have written no end of letters about him. What then is talent, I ask you?

"Johann!" he calls to the butler, who is passing down the hall, "Johann, come here! Now I want to show these people that it is perfectly easy to play one note exactly as I say. I believe you can do it." Johann appeared very timid, but interested and bright-eyed. "Now," said the master of us all, to Johann, "sit back in the chair as comfortably as if you were sitting in one of those rocking-chairs that you saw once. Put your hands over these keys," he said, showing him three keys in the bass, "make this one finger a little longer than the others, so that it will strike with a different sound. Don't look at them any more now. You don't need to, do you, if you have your hand over them? But look up here at this group," showing him a group of keys some distance up the keyboard. "Now," said Leschetizky, "I want you to strike the ones under your hand, but keep your eyes upon the others, and, as you strike move up to the ones you have your eyes upon."

"Shall I strike them, too?" asked the butler.

"No," replied the master, "that's just it, we are trying to do only one."

The butler, who knew not one note of music, took the chord under his shaped hand, throwing his arm around with a graceful, sweeping motion to the other chord that he had religiously kept his eyes upon, and waited, without playing further.

"Is that difficult?" asked Leschetizky.

"No, sir," said the butler.

"Well, you see," continued Leschetizky, "you

have grace of motion. Not every one can do that as well as you did. Thank you. I will now go on with the lesson.

"You cannot do that to save your life!" he said, turning to the pupil. "That was a far better tone than any of yours. And why?" he said. "Because his motions are graceful and smooth and easy. He doesn't even know the kind of tone he wants, as you ought to know, if you call yourself a student of music. But you, you don't know what a beautiful tone is.

"My dear sir," said Leschetizky with sudden emphasis, "to play the piano one must have all kinds of qualifications that you have not—grace of motion, a quick eye, a good ear, but, above all, intelligence, and a little tiny bit of feeling. Ever so little of that will keep you from pounding the piano, as you do. I have now spent over an hour of my time, that I consider valuable, trying to make you do what the butler can do in five minutes. I have had enough of this. You and I may possibly meet again in our lifetime, but, if we do," said Leschetizky, "it will not be at the piano."

This occasion was embarrassing, to say the least. I looked at my pupil, but happily, I believed, I detected spirit in his eye rather than fear. "Splendid," he said to me in a whisper.

"A Czerny étude," said Leschetizky to my pupil. "No, not this one or the next two in the book. I have heard them enough to-day. Play one of the others. The one in double notes," he said, flinging himself into his chair.

"Bad!" he exclaimed at the end. "Two fast, and you lost two notes of it; that must not occur in a good technique. Why are you studying the piano?" asked Leschetizky, wheeling around at him.

"Because I would like to be able to do something well," said my pupil.

Leschetizky looked at him with impatience. "That is not enough for me," he said. "If you haven't talent, you'd better not come here."

"I think I have some talent," said the pupil.

"You don't look it," replied Leschetizky. "You are not artistic-looking in the least. Perhaps you would be a little ashamed of looking artistic, would you not? Probably, I am right. Be thankful in these days if you can look like anything. It isn't easy to distinguish oneself in anything in this world. There are too many good ones now. You imagine you are far above that awful person that we've just got rid of, but I am not so certain of it. You have at least some things in common, I tell you— letters of recommendation from foolish women, for instance. I know all about him; his people are poor people, and he takes every penny they can earn, sisters and all, to live his own self-centered, conceited life. He lets them think he is a genius—his sealskin coats some one else provides. He has apartments! Mind you, apartments! He is not a modest student, oh, no! He's full of conceit. So are you, probably. And he is hard, hard in his playing, hard in his character. He'll never get anywhere, believe me, nor will any man who hides behind petticoats. Doting, silly women are not discriminating—they help you along for a while, and then, where are you? Worse off than ever! I tell you, they are the first to go back

on you, as soon as you do not obey them and flatter
them! I don't like the type," said Leschetizky,
growling. He stopped talking suddenly, and took
a look at the pupil, who had just risen from his
piano and appeared to be staring simply at the keyboard.

"You are a great master," said the young man
with great dignity, and in perfect French, "you
may be right in regard to some people, but are
entirely mistaken in my case. I do not intend to
be spoken to as you are speaking now." With
this he started to go, but Leschetizky slipped
around the piano, and stood with his back to the
door, barring the way.

"You are angry," said Leschetizky. "I was
angry too, but I shall forget it now, as you have
given me the real pleasure of being treated like a
human being. Won't you come back? You had a
right to be angry, and ought to have told me that
if I were younger, you would have known better
how to treat me. That is exactly what you were
thinking a moment ago. But I thank you for
speaking a sensible word to me and convincing me
that I was wrong. To-day has been too much for
me. Some people think I am a machine to be
turned on here from one o'clock until five. They
think it makes no difference to me who comes to
me. To-day I have heard nothing but noises. I
could even bear the wrong notes and the inaccura-
cies, but the ear is outraged. The ear becomes
tired quicker than the mind. My ear revolts
against the hard tones. I come here to the piano
to hear it played, and to find intelligence, as an aid
to arriving at a common understanding, but I do

not hear the one nor find the other. And this is such a waste of time when there are so many who deserve to be heard.

"Why, even the little diffident Viennese girl is beginning to play with expression. Give me the modest ones! Think of those who are here, those who are sympathetic and distinguished people! They are here for study and learning, and they enjoy themselves, too, but not too much, you understand. Neither do they advertise themselves in any way; they are too good for that. Do you know the charming Ada Thomas, for instance? No advertising," he repeated. "And what does she not know? The whole piano literature. She transposes everything at sight, and in tempo. Would she presume to come to me, playing as that man played? People play as they are—she has sympathy in her playing, he has none. There are too many conceited idlers here at present. Conceit! Conceit!" he said, throwing his hands in the air, and becoming angry again. "Not one who can put one bar rhythmically together. But I shall have done with them all sometime.

"I'd rather hear Erich Wolff for twenty hours at a stretch. He is more of an accompanist, you understand, but sympathetic, and plays softly. He's a lover. It's not bad to be a lover in this world. Love people, love nature! But if you hate people and hate nature, then go and be a woodchopper! But why do these woodchoppers come to me?" said he, more calmly and thoughtfully. "It's a mystery. They can learn more in the gymnasium, can't they? And these putterers and blubberers who cannot say a word for themselves——"

"Would you not prefer to postpone my lesson?" interrupted the pupil.

"No," said Leschetizky. "Let's sit down and talk it over. Have a cigar? I want to apologize to you and to the charming lady who wrote me on your behalf."

My pupil looked so surprised that Leschetizky laughed.

"I was entirely wrong, I know," said he, "and I want to show you that I am not such a savage as you may think. You played those Czerny études very well indeed, but let me ask you now to think as profoundly as you possibly know how to think, of what you are undertaking if you intend to study to be a real artist. Think of what that means. I take it that you would not be satisfied to be third-rate, or even second-rate; you have something first-rate in your personality, and I am convinced that you can do something well, but it is not playing the piano. I want to hear your Beethoven sonata, but I shall be very much surprised if I can honestly change my mind. Are you a good musician?" asked the master.

"Not yet," answered the pupil.

"An honest word," said Leschetizky.

After the pupil had played a Beethoven sonata, Leschetizky sat silent for a long time.

"Do you suppose that I have not had my disappointments?" he said. "I wrote an opera once, called 'Die Erste Falte.' I wanted to write music, but after the first performance of my opera I was convinced that I was not born to be a composer. When I came home, I took the manuscript of my piano concerto, that had not yet gone to the publishers, and threw it into the fire. I wished afterward that I had not done so, but I said to myself, 'Theodor, do not deceive yourself, your talent lies in another direction!' "

Turning to the young man, he said, "What are you going to do?"

Leschetizky looked pale and tired, and so did his pupil.

"I have decided already," he answered, "and shall not study the piano any further."

"I am sure you are right," said Leschetizky, "but you can do something else better, I believe. I understand that you will not let other people help you and that you have no special income yourself. How do you live here?"

"I just manage it," he replied, "by a little writing."

"Bravo!" said Leschetizky. "That means that you have your audiences so to speak, already. Be happy then," he went on, "and put all that personality of yours into it, and if you do, I am sure you will succeed.

"I have a son," he said, "and he is an officer in the army. I always say to him, 'What is the use of being a soldier if you do not take the greatest examples of history as your model and try to attain their greatness?' What is the use of doing something if you do not do it well, or even of living if you do not live well?

"But, to be happy or even successful, you must judge well what it is possible for you to achieve, and not spend your lifetime in striving to do what the other can easily do better."

CHAPTER XVII

THE word "work" in connection with learning to play the piano, Leschetizky called an Americanism. This word impressed him as being often too significant of the way we studied and felt about studying, and he felt that if many "worked" less and thought more, they could play better. The American student often tried to accomplish by hours of hard work what he thought could be done in half the time by relaxation and vision. Many of the Americans, and of course those from other countries, were adventurers in art, who had perhaps just finished college and had never studied music, as a result rather expected Leschetizky to perform some miracle over them. There were others of the hardworking type who minimized the necessary quality of talent and personality. Of the two I think Leschetizky preferred the former.

He used to say to the overconscientious, nervous, strained type of pupil, "Believe me, my dear, the time you learn the most is when you take your cigarette and go to the window to think it over, not when you are plodding at the piano,"—a remark that some found musically as well as morally incomprehensible.

From the tense and hurried American students, Leschetizky suffered much misrepresentation in this country. Every summer steamers used to carry their little groups of pilgrims—pianists bound for Vienna. Often their time and funds were lim-

ited and their local reputations depended upon
their returning in a year or two with everything
learned. From the steamer chair one watched with
curiosity these bands of aspirants, proclaiming
loudly their different ideas, and shouting that they
were on the way to Vienna and fame. As a rule,
they knew nothing of the tests to which they would
be put in the artistic atmosphere of a European
capital, and of study with a great master and its
possibilities they had no notion at all.

Once in Vienna, they had without exception to
go and study with one of his assistants there before
being allowed to take a lesson from Leschetizky.
Madame Wienezkowska, one of his very successful
assistants, might be in America; Madame Stepanoff, another highly respected assistant, in Berlin.
But even their pupils coming to Vienna were advised by Leschetizky to take a few lessons of the
preparatory teachers there, as hardly a year passed
that he did not receive and incorporate into his
teaching some new impressions and ideas. "My assistants have methods," he used to say, "but methods
are bound to change, especially if they are good
ones."

Some objected to being sent to an assistant, but
Leschetizky was so impatient of teaching technique,
and also so impatient of one who did not have a
technique, that real study with him was entirely a
question of being prepared for it. The pupils
themselves were generally satisfied with this system and were often only too glad to return to an
assistant after lessons with him, to prepare themselves still better. It was generally outsiders who
could not appreciate these advantages. "He won't

have to send my daughter to be prepared for him,"
said the mother of a girl about fourteen, whom she
considered already a great player. "When he
hears her," she said, "he will take her at once, and
we want him to come twice a week!" "I want to
get two lessons," said another newcomer, "so that
I can say I have had lessons, and I'll pay him any
price he asks, to get them. I have got to say I have
studied with Leschetizky."

Others had apparently resigned themselves to
any treatment that might be accorded them, and
hardly listened in the lessons to his clear and simple
illustrations and explanations. There was sometimes a very baffling lack of attention to the real
matter in hand, due to nervousness or to lack of
comprehension of what a lesson with Leschetizky
meant. He said to one pupil, "In this serious little
piece of formal manners that run should not be
fluffy like that—it is like a string of real pearls—
every note must be a tone." "What a great teacher
you are!" replied the pupil, clasping her hands, and
tears coming to her eyes, while Leschetizky only
smiled and sighed. "There are no great teachers
without great pupils," he quoted.

There was only one goal with him, and that was
good piano playing, and he did not believe a teacher
could be a good teacher who could not play himself.

Only the very talented ones studied directly with
him the first year or two. Many were lucky if they
were able to be prepared for even one lesson from
him during the first year, and when the day came
for the great ordeal, it seemed a terrible one to face.
One pupil told how he prepared himself for this
event. First he went to a Turkish bath, then had

his hair cut in a new way that he hoped would please Leschetizky; finger nails had to be short, of course, so they would not make a noise against the keys. The money for the lesson had long been put aside in the envelope to be deposited on the master's piano, but he made a visit to the bank all the same for the sake of his peace of mind. For fear of getting tired he drove to the Währing Cottage. He could walk enough afterward, he said. Alas! the *Einspänner* broke down, and so he ran a few blocks. Then, seeing a *fiacre,* he hailed it, but the driver insisted on going toward the park. Finally he jumped out without paying and both arrived at Leschetizky's door in a state of agitation. "How could I play well?" he said, "and Leschetizky asked me first of all, 'Are you a European or are you a cannibal?' 'I am an American,' I said. But why did Leschetizky laugh so? Anyway, I am glad I am alive to tell the tale," he said. "I learned nothing in that lesson, except that I had no talent. Oh, yes, I did learn that I might be good-looking if I had cut my hair differently. I don't see where Leschetizky gets his great reputation. I cannot remember that he said a word about music."

The conversation in the little room where pupils waited their turn for lessons was sometimes interesting and illuminating. It was often bad-tempered and ludicrous, but frequently friendly and instructive enough. One might hear something like the following:

"You are not nervous, are you?"

"Nervous? Of course, one is always nervous in trying to play well."

"But you are not afraid of the Professor?"

"Oh, yes, that, too. One must play well for him."
Or again,

"How are you getting on?"

"I cannot seem to change the phrases as quickly as he wants me to."

"Ah! That is the main thing with him. If you are talented he expects you to be able to do it."

"But I know the piece and played it a dozen different ways before I came here. I have studied the piece well, but I cannot get his tone."

"Well, if you could get his tone you would be a Leschetizky."

"I am playing this for the second time and the last time he was angry with me at this place."

"Angry with you?"

"Yes, of course. He said it was not rhythmical. I will show you what I did, and he called it affectation and not correct besides."

"You cannot be affected or unnatural with him in playing one tone. He knows it at once, as will see as you go on."

"Now I have these Brahms-Handel 'Variations' for to-day and I am afraid he will find another place that is affected. I have been off playing and have not had much time for study, and he expects me to have studied even then. He says, 'If you are playing in public, there is no excuse for not being prepared.' Down there in Graz I played these 'Variations' for people three or four times. There were some critics there. One of them said he liked it. The others thought it was too Brahms, a little too monotonous. But Leschetizky holds you down in Brahms. He says Brahms does not want too much emphasis. He wants serenity, but not much expression. I love these motives and phrases and I cannot help playing them as if I did, but Leschetizky seems to think that you should be a little above showing your feelings when you play Brahms. At least that is the way he talked in the last lesson."

"How are your lessons?"

"Well, I have never yet had a bad one."

"Never? Then he must like you if you have frequent lessons. He is only lenient with those he never expects to see again. Where do you come from?"

"A little town in the United States. I never thought much of myself and nobody else did, to tell the truth. If I could come back home a pianist, every one would be surprised, but Leschetizky encourages me. He says I have everything to make a good player. I want to be more than a good player."

"Good! Come and see me sometime. Perhaps I can help you."

"Oh, would you? Tell me how on earth to please Leschetizky, because I would rather do that than anything else."

"He likes good stories and I tell him a lot of stuff. I tell him about foreigners coming to America, or about Americans coming back after a long time being Continental in their ways. He loves these stories. Yes, and he will listen all night if you play him American tunes and ragtime."

"Yes, I know that too. Last night we played awhile."

"He is giving a long lesson now, isn't he—one of the quiet lessons?"

"I thought it was finished long ago. I've waited here an hour and a half and he is still going on."

"Yes, he loves good stories, but he wants you to tell them well, too. He was awfully amused with my story of the American who had not been in his own country for years, and after his arrival in New York ordered six club sandwiches for tea at the Waldorf, expecting to be served with little diamond-shaped sandwiches such as they have in Europe. He could not stop asking me questions about the expression on the boy's face when he saw what he had ordered; then the expression on the faces of the people around him, and how he had to sit there under the gaze of a roomful of staring people, with a pyramid of club sandwiches before him on the table. I tell him all these funny stories, but I *must* please him at the piano."

"Where did you study?"

"Here at the Vienna Conservatory. They are splendidly thorough. But we all hope to come to Leschetizky if we intend to be artists, real artists."

"But you are one?"

"Well, they all say so but Leschetizky. But there is something yet he is not satisfied with. He says I am not free enough, too rigid in everything, and yet when he plays it is so simply done. You don't see how it is done. You don't know at all how it is done. It is as if the piano were speaking to him. I wish I could get that quality."

"Couldn't I come in to your lesson to-day?"

"Wait out here if you will. For I want him to

feel free to-day to say the things he might not say
before another person."

"Well, here you are," said Leschetizky, who had
just come into the hall with the departing pupil.
"I thought you two would get together sometime.
Look out for this young one. He is going to do
something. He is the kind that has to know everything, and that is why he is thorough. A good head,
but everything must go through that brain first,
you understand. Look at his wide forehead, and
that jaw, too; brain first, but that is not bad. But
if he will ever play as well as he holds himself, then
all honor to him. His bearing is perfect. You two
should cultivate each other. You can help each
other. He is too modest. A little more conceit
would not hurt him. He has not got that immense
poise that you have [Leschetizky pronounced the
word "immense" with much affected pomposity as
he lovingly laid a hand on his advanced pupil's
shoulder]. So much dignity that it scares me.
You will make your audiences sit up and say, 'Now
we have to behave ourselves.' "

"Brahm's 'Variations' to-day?

"Not quite enough dignity of yours in Brahms
yet. A little more John Bull perhaps than you
have.

"Were you ever in England?" asked Leschetizky.

"This is a John Bull theme and you still play it
too expressively. It is not *ex*pressive; it is *im*pressive. And it must be confident and straightfor-
ward. No straining after effects, no special
rhythm.

"I was in England," said Leschetizky. "Those

people are splendid—not self-conscious. They speak simply, are not theatrical. Those are great qualities. An Englishman says weighty things with a simple manner, and says simple things with —art. You Americans have not so much of that quality. I have heard some of your public speakers too, from time to time. They are a little too orator-ical, too emphatic, and don't always lay aside those manners when they should. One should speak as the occasion requires: in ordinary conversation, with simple words, and simple tones of voice; in public, more distinctly, but still naturally and simply. Theatrics are not much. One must not be theatri-cal in playing, either. Yes, you can learn by play-ing the piano well many things for your conduct in life.

"You are going home to study, aren't you?" he said to the modest young pupil.

"I will tell you about the opium dens in London when we meet again."

"I saw them," said Leschetizky. "You must play me some negro tunes and ragtime. That is not an easy rhythm to get, but there is no dignity in it. Come let us hear the Brahms-Handel 'Variations.'

"That boy is very likable," said Leschetizky. "He has a soul, too. You should have heard him play this morning, and you should see him go to the piano. He has all the instincts of a player. He tells a story, children have that instinct. They sit down; they look round; they get absolute quiet, a nice background of silence for the first tone, then they are going to tell me something, and they do, too. They tell me delicious things; with the first tone I feel warmed and exhilarated. How beauti-

fully and simply they play! Oh, there are two or
three here that will be famous pianists—one boy,
anyway, and one of the girls surely. They have
begun their careers already. They say things, and
they are not afraid to say them before an audience.
There is that little one, for instance. How she
flushes when she begins to play; her eyes brighten,
and everything is done with intelligence, and when
I say, 'Good!' she toddles over here to my piano and
asks me why it was good. I say, 'Go back to your
piano and do it over again and find out for yourself why it was good.' And she has a trill. Well,
that trill of hers is just as beautiful as Carreño's
trill, and that is saying everything. Patti had a
trill. Once upon a time (probably more than
once), she made the orchestra wait a minute and
held up the whole performance with a long trill.
The audience was in raptures.

"You have a trill you need not be ashamed of,"
he said to his pupil. "You really improve all the
time, and you study in a talented way.

"My pupils do not excel in smooth-passage playing," said Leschetizky. "I am going to attend to
that from now on. Pay attention now, I shall be
after you. There are some who come from France
and Italy who are better in this respect; some
Americans are not bad. Goodness knows what the
Americans 'work' at, as they call it. Is it work to
listen to a smooth scale?

"But from now on I shall have a duty," said
Leschetizky. "Take Josef Hofmann as a model.
You can. His passages are as smooth as oil.

"Well, let us begin now. Brahms' 'Variations.'
"Too *rubato*, I tell you. What do the critics of

Graz say to your playing? There is one good one down there."

"He said it was not free enough," answered the pupil. "I played it specially for him."

"He said that, did he?" said Leschetızky. "He must be prejudiced against Brahms, then. It is not Brahms' way to be free. You don't have the Brahms spirit if you play it with any sentiment that is not there. He is simple and broad and placid.

"Well, it is not my idea, that is all," said Leschetizky, "and in Vienna they know what Brahms is like, too. You remember how that great artist was hissed here for playing that theme sentimentally and too *rubato?* Vienna knows pretty well how to judge for itself. Think of Ysaye here—no one at his first concert but the critics—fifty people in the Musikverein Saal—all more or less skeptical. But how he played to those fifty people! He went straight to their hearts, and the critics had to give in; they were overwhelmed. Perhaps they learned something, too—they learned a little more respect for the opinion of the rest of the world. You know what happened. Gutmann canceled the concert for the next night, and advertised Ysaye a second time, and the house was sold out. He plays simply, too.

"More like this," said Leschetizky, going to the piano and playing the theme of Handel.

"Sing more," said Leschetizky, "you know how—it is in you to do it. You did some beautiful things the other night in your concert, really beautiful," Leschetizky went on very seriously, "natural things —the things that no one can learn and no one can tell you. Yes, you can be proud of these things. You can always be proud of the qualities that are

natural to you—that have been given to you. Any
one can learn to study, and so no one can be too
proud of himself for doing that well. But you
underestimate your best qualities. You slight
them. You do them injustice, for you don't use
them enough. Play this with simplicity and dignity. Don't descend to searching after expression.

"But," continued Leschetizky, "it is your own
affair after all. You must not think that there is
only one way to play this, either. I play it one way,
but you may hear some one play it to suit you better
—it *may be better,* I mean," said Leschetizky.

"By the way, I heard these 'Variations' very well
played by a new pupil the other day, one that you
don't know. She has not enough technique or
strength, but it had continuity throughout. This
is the way she did it." Leschetizky sat down again
and played the whole set of "Variations."

"The fugue is easy," he said. "Every one can
play that except me. I get nervous in fugues. I
always did, always shall. Come, let us see the
'Variations' as you have finished them."

After eight or ten Leschetizky stopped the
playing.

"Do you honestly like them that way?" he inquired. "Now let me show you exactly how you
played them. Go off to the end of the room and
listen.

"I exaggerate a trifle perhaps," said Leschetizky.
"But I tell you you would not dare to go to Berlin
and play those 'Variations' that way. They won't
care about your beautiful tone so much, either.
They will want a better interpretation. They will
call you too Viennese or too Parisian. One gets

sentimental in Paris. No, you must change the tone of your theme. You are going to play some other pieces on your program, that will show you have humor. Humor we must forego in the Brahms-Handel, to be sure.

"Between us," said Leschetizky, "Brahms had not much humor himself, and how he could have lived in the house he chose in Ischl, I cannot understand. You might have called him a Stoic, if he had been obliged to live there. You and I are foolish perhaps. We want beautiful things around us, and not empty rooms to live in.

"Well, put a touch of humor into the playing of the 'Variations,' and let the critics say what they like. It is written for the piano, and the piano plays music if you will only let it.

"Brahms always troubles me," said Leschetizky. "He had no regard for the piano as an instrument, and he thought anybody could play the piano.

"We know better, don't we?" he said to his pupil. "When you study five years to get one tone as you want it, and still cannot always be sure of playing it that way, then you know how difficult it is to be a pianist."

CHAPTER XVIII

Leschetizky was sometimes heard to remark that orchestra leaders knew nothing, an opinion which could be traced more or less to his resentment against certain actions of Gustav Mahler. When Mahler came to Vienna he superseded Hans Richter who was a great friend of Leschetizky, but Leschetizky admired and respected Mahler greatly. At the same time he was shocked at Mahler's too autocratic and revolutionary methods. There was also the element of a personal grievance in their relationship, as Mahler announced that there would be no more soloists in the Philharmonic concerts. Hans Richter had been very willing to bring out Leschetizky's pupils in these concerts.

On one occasion Leschetizky went to Mahler to ask for an engagement for a celebrated artist who was one of his pupils, and Mahler did not refuse him.

Leschetizky tried to be friendly whenever they met, but only half succeeded, because Leschetizky was as free as Mahler himself, and the sparks usually flew.

A reported quarrel between the two once furnished Vienna with much amusing gossip. It was really not a quarrel at all, Leschetizky said, but others told that it had threatened to become nothing short of a personal encounter before both men got control of themselves. Paderewski had just played in Vienna for the first time in many years, and there was a small supper given for him at the house of two distinguished American gentlemen, to which Leschetizky and Mahler were invited. Mahler had arrived, and Paderewski was late. Mahler fidgeted and fumed. "Great men never come late," he remarked to Leschetizky, who glared and retorted, "For once you are mistaken, Herr Direktor." Mahler was very silent the rest of the evening, and Leschetizky more brilliant than ever.

From the box which he occupied at the concerts of the Philharmonic when he was not conducting, Mahler would hiss any one who came into the hall during the performance. At one concert he was hissing loudly when the Emperor Francis Joseph came in. The people around were indignant, but the Emperor quieted every one, remarking, "No matter, it is only Mahler."

Mahler himself was treated almost like a king in Vienna, and received the greatest recognition and acclaim. Nevertheless, his bad manners were notorious, and there was sometimes public resentment of them.

His actions toward Winkelmann, the famous tenor of the opera, was an instance of egotistical high-handedness which earned him a great deal of wrathful comment and criticism. Winkelmann was old at the time, his art scarcely more than an echo of its earlier glory, but he was still received with that hero-worship and touching loyalty which distinguishes the Viennese public. There was a clash between him and Mahler, and his resignation was requested. As Winkelmann came out into the little square back of the opera house, he was greeted by the shouts of hundreds of people who had gathered

there protesting against his resignation. They
hoisted him to their shoulders and carried him
through the streets. They demanded the with-
drawal of his resignation, and Mahler finally permitted him to continue, but he never relaxed in his
search for an opportunity to humiliate this great
artist, and one day he took advantage of some trivial
circumstance to send him a curt note of dismissal.

Madame Frances Saville was another who suffered from Mahler's imperious and unjust temper.
At a rehearsal she had the temerity to disagree with
him over a point of phrasing, and before several
others of the company was requested by him to
resign. Her hosts of admirers were incensed at this.
When Alfred Grünfeld heard of the affair, he
started for the opera house with a horsewhip in
hand to avenge the insult, but changed his mind on
the way.

When Mahler's engagement to be married was
announced in Vienna, it was reported that one of
the men in the orchestra came forward to offer his
congratulations. "This is a place of rehearsal for
the concerts and nothing else," said Mahler, and
knocked him down on the spot.

But Leschetizky himself was as quick-tempered
and impulsive as any one, although many of Mahler's traits seemed brutal and inhuman to him. I
myself once witnessed a scene between him and a
Royal Highness which took my breath away.
When the Royal carriage drew up at his door,
Leschetizky held up a hand as though to say,
"Here is something interesting." This visit was
for the purpose of interviewing Leschetizky about
engaging one of his pupils to teach at the Castle in

the country during the summer. I went into the next room. For a time there was steady talking, then a crescendo of excitement in the voices, followed by a long silence. The door opened and the two walked out from the hall. Just as His Imperial and Royal Highness turned to say good-by, Leschetizky looked him squarely in the eyes, and made the "long nose" at him. "What do you think," said Leschetizky afterward, "I set a moderate price for the lessons and suggested Martha Schmidt, who would be brilliantly capable of that work, if she would accept. But he thought it too much and tried to bargain with me for the smallest possible price."

Stiffness and lack of humor or spontaneity provoked in him a spirit of mischief which was the cause of more than one hilarious situation. Those who were present at the class one evening will never forget his antics with a titled lady, whose formality and dullness irritated him to the point of making her a most ridiculous figure. The classes were really private musicales and not open to the public, but artists who visited Vienna were always welcome, and were usually invited by Leschetizky to stay for supper afterward. One of the pupils asked to bring this lady, and after the class also requested Leschetizky to invite her to supper. I am sure he never would have asked her of his own accord, for he had been amused and bored the whole evening by her intensely prim, unbending manner. She stood rigidly and bowed stiffly at everything Leschetizky said, without making any reply. As he escorted her out into the hall after the class was over, the pupils were already on their way up the

broad staircase to the room above, where Leschetizky smoked and talked after the class until the
supper table was prepared. At the other end of the
hall there was a spiral staircase which led perpen-
dicularly to the floor above. Leschetizky walked
with the countess passed the first stairway to the
second. "Come, Madame, our pupils are going
upstairs," taking her by the hand. "Let us go up.
This is the way to do it." With astonishing agility
he sprang up the spiral stairs, calling to the countess
to come along. Panting and purple with exertion
and confusion, she scrambled after him. At last
she was obliged to unbend and say something intelligible. At the supper table afterward we were
so amused at the pointed remarks that Leschetizky
made, and his witty shafts directed against stupidity and stiffness and lack of expression, that we
all had great difficulty in remembering our manners.

A pretentious manner was disturbing to Leschetizky, and he used to tell amusing stories about
Madame Clara Schumann, whose rather pompous
personality was antagonistic to him. He told about
her stage appearance, and felt that she had not
always been thoughtful enough about how it would
appear to others. She rather affected no manner at
all, and used to sit knitting in the audience until
her time came to play. And sometimes as she
walked to the stage she was so deeply lost in
thought, that she forgot to look where she was
going. Once, unfortunately, she missed the step
to the stage and fell sprawling forward, to the con-
sternation of the audience.

Once, when she was giving a concert in Russia,
he met her at a small reception, and she asked to

hear one of his pupils play. He sent for the young lady whom he always referred to then and afterward as the best pupil he had ever had. Her repertoire was literally unlimited. Madame Schumann inquired of her in a very grand manner what she played. Leschetizky managed to whisper to her to say that she played everything. "Well, I suppose that is not true, my child," Madame Schumann smilingly replied. But the girl repeated that she would play anything Madame Schumann asked for. The Henselt "Concerto," she suggested. Her challenge was immediately accepted.

Leschetizky always enjoyed telling of a little episode that occurred between Chopin and Madame Schumann, who was very proud of her solid German interpretation of his compositions. Chopin remarked to her, "I see no reason why such a great artist as yourself should not play my compositions exactly as you feel like playing them." Then in an aside he went on, "Even without any feeling at all."

Leschetizky's talked-of aversion to Brahms' music is not authentic. It was he who gave the Brahms "Concerto in D Minor" one of its first public performances—its first in Russia. Brahms and Leschetizky conferred upon the orchestration, and Leschetizky wanted some changes made. They always disagreed, but Leschetizky was happily surprised to find his suggestions accepted in the printed score. The songs and orchestral works, everything but the piano pieces, he admired very much. He contended that Brahms had not written one original melody for the piano, and he would grow visibly nervous over whole pages which were given up, as he said, to tweedledee and tweedledum. I once brought to him the "Rhapsody in E Flat," with which he was not familiar, when he seemed surprised at the opening bars and exclaimed, "Well, at last there is an original melody."

As I went on playing I saw him tiptoe to the back of the room to a shelf of old music. "Stop playing," he said, "I have an idea." For a long time he searched and then triumphantly produced a certain old Russian march, which was the exact theme of the opening bars of the rhapsody. His theory was vindicated. Brahms had written no original melody for the piano.

When they were together, Brahms always made fun of Leschetizky's compositions and Leschetizky made fun of Brahms' piano pieces. If any one else spoke disparagingly of Brahms, Leschetizky was the first to correct him, and insisted that his pupils learn not only the great variations, but the smaller pieces as well.

When I asked him one time if I should study one of the concertos, he looked at me in the greatest astonishment, saying, "What do you mean by that? You must learn every note he has written for the piano."

It was the Brahms fad to which Leschetizky objected. The affectation of profundity among a certain group in Vienna when speaking of Brahms irritated him. These people adopted a pose of great intellectuality, spurning any grace of musical or personal expression. They worshiped Brahms in plain garments, and played his music as tastelessly as they dressed. Of a certain pianist, noted for her dry performances of Brahms' music, Leschetizky used to say, "Of course, to be really deep enough to play Brahms, one must be middle-aged, wear spectacles, and adopt dress reform."

At one time it was popular to give entire programs of Brahms' piano pieces. In England the cult was particularly strong; many people appearing awe-struck on repeating his name.

When English girls came to Ischl, where Brahms spent his summers, Leschetizky would sarcastically ask them if they had come to live in the same street with Brahms, and assure them that there were far more romantic spots in the Salzkammergut.

In reality, Brahms and Leschetizky were the best of friends. Every summer they met in Ischl and always started together for Carlsbad in the autumn to take the cure; according to all reports, quarreling all the way about their different ideas of composition, interpretation, and technique.

Some of us stood under Brahms' window one night, listening to his playing of the "F Major Romanza." It sounded as though he were striking every note with a raised hand, and there was no quality to the tone nor shading to the phrases. One realized how different were his ideas from Leschetizky's about the art of piano playing.

On one occasion Brahms told Leschetizky that his pieces were only fit for sweet-sixteen and for young men in love. "Well," retorted Leschetizky, "yours are only fit for the years after ninety."

For a long time I lived in a house in Vienna near the Houses of Parliament, past which Brahms used to walk twice a day. He walked very rapidly, and one never saw him with a hat on his head, even in winter. Swinging it in his hand, he always hurried along, looking very much agitated, his gentle face a dark red from the illness which afflicted him the last years of his life.

At the Philharmonic concerts, whenever his works were performed, he would be greeted by a tremendous ovation. Toward the end of his life, when he was too ill to walk or stand without support, he was still brought to the concerts, and lifted from his seat in the artists' box to acknowledge the storms of applause. It was a glorious sight to see a living composer so rapturously acclaimed. No sooner would the applause die down, than it began again, Richter joining in by beating loudly on the desk with his baton. Richter seemed only too happy to allow himself to be carried away by these ovations for Brahms. He smiled up at the artists' box, and waved his hands to his great contemporary, Brahms sometimes bowing in acknowledgment to Richter. Only Vienna could furnish such a public, immoderate, almost, in its expression of delight.

A familiar sight in the audience was Leschetizky, steadily applauding until the end.

After Brahms' death we sat one evening with Leschetizky at a performance of one of his symphonies. We looked up at the box where Brahms had so often sat. Leschetizky's eyes filled with tears, as he said, "It will be a long time before there is another as great as Brahms. This audience misses seeing him up there in that box, but they will never cease to applaud in Vienna these great symphonies. Yes, I envy him this great tribute,

and he used to envy me some of the talented ones
who came to study with me, some who will one day
be great composers too."

The death of Brahms was a sad event to Leschetizky. I recall that it was my day to play for him,
and accordingly I went to his house. Madame
Leschetizka stated that he had sat all night beside
Brahms' coffin, and could not give any lessons or
see any one.

One of the strongest affections of Leschetizky's
life was for Rubinstein, whose playing he also
adored. They had been intimately associated in
St. Petersburg, and were also rivals for the affections of the lady who afterward became Leschetizky's wife. Leschetizky related many stories of their
years of association at the conservatory at St.
Petersburg. There were stories of examinations
and rehearsals, and the humor of some of them
could only be appreciated if one knew how Leschetizky loved Rubinstein and admired his art.
They used to direct the orchestra for each other's
performances of works for orchestra and piano.
According to Leschetizky, Rubinstein could rarely
pass over without mishap certain passages in the
last movement of the Schumann "Concerto."
Leschetizky begged him once, before one of these
concerts, not to throw his hands so high in the air
when he broke down, for no one cared whether or
not he made a mistake, so wonderfully inspiring was
his playing in other ways. The music was probably
too beautiful to Rubinstein, thought Leschetizky,
for him to study it long enough to be technically
perfect, and he played so much according to his

feelings at the moment, that if he cared at all what the effect was upon his audience, he was entirely unaware of it.

Once, at the conservatory, Rubinstein burst into Leschetizky's room, tearing his hair over his efforts to make one of his good pupils play a rhapsody of Liszt as he wanted it played. The pupil was in tears, and Rubinstein was in despair. He finally brought his shattered pupil to the piano where she made another vain attempt to imitate Rubinstein's interpretation. "She tries to play it too fast," said Rubinstein. "It should go slower, this way," and going to the piano he played it with such amazing rapidity that when he had finished he turned to find both Leschetizky and his pupil holding their sides with laughter. "Was that really fast?" humbly inquired Rubinstein.

He had intended to dedicate one of his larger works to Leschetizky, but on one occasion seemed to take offense at some observation that Leschetizky made about his manner of repeating several single notes in his compositions. Leschetizky had good-naturedly played G's and D's from one end of the keyboard to the other, and then walked on in the room, still trying to repeat these notes in the air. Rubinstein showed no signs of annoyance at the time, but the next day scratched out the dedication on the manuscript and the printed editions bore the name of some one else.

Shortly before his death, Rubinstein came to Vienna to visit Leschetizky. He took the greatest interest in Leschetizky's pupils, and his visit happened to coincide with one of the Wednesday evening classes. Accordingly, this was to be a gala performance, and Rubinstein promised to play for the students afterward. Leschetizky's trusted and tried butler was instructed to watch at the door for the prettiest and best dressed girls, and to be sure to seat them only in the front rows. "Rubinstein is æsthetic," said Leschetizky (speaking this word also to the butler, who yearly became more intelligent and wise, as well as fonder of his master). "Little things sometimes disturb Rubinstein. We must have flowers also."

Rubinstein listened with the greatest interest to the playing of the pupils, but at eleven o'clock had disappeared entirely. Leschetizky went upstairs in search of him, and found him in one of the back rooms, pacing the floor, pale and agitated. "What can be the matter?" asked Leschetizky. "The matter? It is very simple," said Rubinstein. "I am nervous. I am too nervous to play before those pupils." But they walked downstairs, arm in arm, to the piano. A few wrong notes at first acted like balm to the expectant and overjoyed class, and Rubinstein played himself into one of his grandest and most sublime moods.

They loved each other like brothers, and when Rubinstein died Leschetizky was unable to give any lessons for many days. Some one brought the Rubinstein "Concerto" to play in the class, and Leschetizky tried to accompany it. At the opening chords his hands trembled and faltered, and it was with great difficulty that he finished the first movement. In the second movement his eyes were blinded by tears. He was unable to proceed and left the room weeping. Pupils were very timid about bringing Rubinstein's compositions to him for study for a long time. Later, when he was calmer, nothing pleased him more than to hear his music either at his own house or in concerts. At such times his behavior was often as if one had made him a present. He felt it a personal favor to him to play a piece of Rubinstein. No night was too stormy, and no effort too great to prevent his being present at concerts where Rubinstein's pieces were played in a whole program as by Paul de Conne, or in part by other artists. Leschetizky himself played everything that Rubinstein had written, and showed his pupils as nearly as possible the way that Rubinstein had played them. He wanted his pieces to be interpreted according to Rubinstein's idea of them, and often he would ask his pupil to wait a moment, to give him time to think and to remember. He would sit with his head in his hands for some time, then walk around the room, then come back to the piano, and play the piece not once but many times, explaining that at one time Rubinstein had interpreted it so, at another time so, and again quite differently, and always with an atmosphere of free fantasy. There was one great crescendo after another as if he were sorry to stop, and if one could understand this intense personal quality of emotion that he had in playing, then one could play—Rubinstein.

CHAPTER XIX

VIENNA was a democratic world in its relation to art. Distinction without affectation was the password for enjoyment in its society. There were people living there of international fame, meeting together at all hours, apparently entirely unaware of their distinction. A duchess would climb many flights of stairs if necessary to visit a cheerful, struggling sculptor, who had no thought of fame or of himself. One of the archdukes played the violin most beautifully and was always humbly respectful to one who could play this instrument better than himself. Arthur Schnitzler seemed only too glad to return fresh from great acclaim in foreign land to his friends in Vienna who, he declared, cared too much for him to make a great "fuss."

The public balls of Vienna were great events, and Leschetizky took part in many of them. Several of them were annual functions held for the pleasant purpose of bringing together the famous intellects and artists of the capital. They lasted until three or four o'clock in the morning, always shorter, however, than the smaller dances which went on all night. Indeed, it was only a rather unsuccessful ball that broke up before daylight. Leschetizky greeted me once with congratulations upon my good sense in returning early from a ball. He had heard that I came home at two o'clock instead of dancing with the others until seven or eight o'clock. Of course, Vienna was not moderate in its dissipations, although it looked like a deserted city after ten o'clock at night, at which hour the porters promptly locked the doors.

The first great public ball opened the season of the Carnival in Vienna. Then there were Hungarian balls, where Hungarian national dances prevailed and the Czardas danced in the wildest manner. There were Polish balls, where the "Mazur" was the event of the evening. It was a beautiful dance, but very difficult, and required the greatest freedom of movement and sense of rhythm.

The most important ball was the one called the "Ball of the City of Vienna," when the Emperor graced the occasion with his presence. At a signal the crowd separated, the orchestra and bands played the national anthem, and down the long line walked His Imperial Majesty with a simple but incomparable dignity. Edward VII had the same admirable poise, and when on one of his visits to Vienna a gala performance was given at the opera in his honor, the Viennese remarked the resemblance of the two rulers and long remembered it. As soon as the national hymn was played, the orchestra broke into the beautiful "Blue Danube" and Edward Strauss outdid himself to please the hundreds of Viennese assembled there to enjoy themselves. This ball was given in the great hall of the Palace of Justice, a handsome Gothic structure facing the park along the Ringstrasse. From the Palace of Justice stretched away as far as the eye could reach a succession of noble and beautiful buildings. The Ringstrasse itself looked like a beautiful park, particularly at night when the shadows were blended and only a few lights were

visible. There were four or five rows of trees separating the bridle paths and walks along the side.
Where parks were, still another row of trees and
magnificent statues might be seen, such as the
Grillparzer Monument, with scenes from his plays
carved in large pictures. A Greek temple could
be seen between the trees. Ruskin criticized the
character of the Viennese for putting that Greek
temple down in a swamp.

There was the big Equestrian Statue in the
Palace grounds, and Maria Theresa looked down
upon one from the other side of the street. Beyond the Ring the streets took erratic courses, wind-
ing in and out among parks, large and small,
swerving deferentially at the foot of statues and
monuments in which Vienna abounds.

They are an interesting study, apart from the
dignity and beauty they lend to the streets and
parks. The Viennese love statues and put them in
the oddest places; not only in parks and museums,
but in nooks and corners around and near the city.
It is delightful to come suddenly and unexpectedly
upon one of these groups, perhaps a little company
of poets, musicians, or sovereigns—expressing so
much and yet forever silent. For those who wish
to sit among them in friendly fashion, marble
benches are provided and glorious trees make pri-
vacy and shade.

There used to be a ball given at the opera house
in Vienna called the "Redoubt." The seats of the
parquet were covered with a floor so that the boxes
were on a level with it. This was a masked ball of
intrigue. The men had to submit to appearing in
ordinary clothes and unmasked, while the opposite

sex could disguise itself in any way it pleased. At about one o'clock, at a given signal, off came the masks.

Leschetizky was particularly fond of this ball, which was like a game to him, and his pupils often made a real study of ways and means to mystify and intrigue him. They would even hold meetings, secretly, long before the day for this purpose. "You may think you can deceive me," he said, "but I believe not. I shall remember the quality of your voices and there will be some inflection that I can recognize." He agreed to make a wager with us. The one who succeeded in "taking him in" was to receive a present from him; if he won, we were to give him something. We well knew that our hands would be surely recognized, and that even under gloves it would be dangerous to show them. For several days we practiced different tones of voice, cultivated a strange and novel gait, and tried strange ways of holding our heads. Leschetizky, we heard afterward, had been pressed to accept a dinner engagement and had done so on condition that he could be excused early in the evening on the score of having three or four determined young pupils to cope with at the Redoubt.

This ball was a magnificent spectacle. The boxes were for those who liked them, but most of the people preferred to wander about on the main floor. This place was occupied by gorgeous imitations of gardens alternating with thick groves of trees where deep shades made capital trysting places, leaving brilliant lights in the open spaces to show off the glittering costumes of the dancers. Vienna, of all places in Europe, knew how to give a ball of this kind. The imagination and fantasy of the Viennese were inexhaustible. It was said that some of the stage setting of *A Midsummer Night's Dream* had been brought from the Court Theater for this particular occasion, for the famous directors never spared themselves trouble in making this ball a quite superlative affair.

Leschetizky found his match at this ball, for one of his pupils completely "took him in." She walked boldly toward him, under a great blaze of light and greeted him in Viennese dialect.

"I see some of your pupils are here," she said; "they are waiting for you, and you look as if you were waiting for them."

"Yes," replied Leschetizky, "and I am all excitement, for they are clever girls and I must keep my head. They all have their young beaus here and I am jealous, I suppose."

"Is your wife here?" she asked. "I have never seen her. They say she is beautiful. But beautiful wives do not usually have such handsome, elegant husbands as Master Leschetizky."

"Only a Viennese knows how to flatter like that," said Leschetizky. "We have plenty of time, let us walk through the garden."

"With the greatest pleasure," she replied. "I have so often wanted to meet the great Leschetizky. You have the reputation of being very hard on women sometimes.

"How do you like the English?" she added.

"If only they and the Americans could take on one or two of the charming qualities that Viennese ladies have!"

"You are a flatterer," she said.

"Well, Vienna is good enough for me, although I should not speak, for I have never been outside it except once to Venice for a fortnight."

Here followed a long monologue by Leschetizky about Venice and Italy.

"Your Italian pupils are here to-night, too," she resumed. "I think I saw Mr. Sinigaglia over there."

"Yes," he said, "possibly he is here.

"He is versatile and interesting, isn't he?" said Leschetizky. "His latest amusement is forming a quartet to sing in imitation of bagpipes. I could listen to it by the hour. It makes me laugh as I have not laughed in a long time."

"There comes one of your pupils who has a real claim on you," she said. "I recognize the English gait."

"Yes, I know her," said Leschetizky. "I have just caught sight of her hand. Let me see yours."

"Mine are big and ugly," she protested.

"No, not ugly at all, but your gloves are too thick. Will you take them off?" he asked, growing suddenly suspicious.

"Not until afterward," she said, "and then if you do not recognize me I will say these words to you, 'We met once in Italy.'"

"I shall remember," said Leschetizky.

After many hours of great enjoyment and various attempts to intrigue Leschetizky, and sometimes for a moment successful, the signal was given to unmask. We went to one of the rooms behind the boxes together and of course one of our little party was in high spirits. "I succeeded," she said, "until at the end when he looked at my hand and almost recognized it. He saw the thick glove and became suspicious, but I will still try when we go down separately."

As this quiet girl came into the ballroom unmasked and in usual evening gown, Leschetizky, who stood scanning the appearance of every one who descended the staircase, stepped forward and asked, "Haven't we met in Italy?" She looked straight at him with a blank, bewildered expression, and passed on. Leschetizky still continued to examine the returning people and exclaimed to one of us who was near by, "The witch! I was so sure I had her at last." This was too much for our gravity, and he had to admit that he had been well intrigued.

We started home together with several Viennese friends, and on separating at the park back of the Houses of Parliament, a girl called softly to him, "We did meet in Italy, Professor."

"Was that really my English Rose?" asked Leschetizky gayly. "Italy was a pleasant place, wasn't it? I should like to have stayed longer."

Another famous ball of Vienna was the Concordia, organized by writers and journalists. Artists of all kinds attended, while composers contributed new music dedicated to the Concordia. Strauss, Franz Lehar, and others composed new waltzes and polkas for the ball of February 4, 1904, given as usual in the Sophiens Saal, one of the largest in Vienna. This year the ball was an exceptionally brilliant one, it was said, as so many celebrated strangers were present. The souvenirs presented to each guest were in the form of small white leather hand bags, the two sides resembling the covers of a book, beautifully impressed in green and yellow, with a copy of a famous painting in medallion; inside this book, with a gilt handle, was a collection of sixty or more leaflets entitled "Letters that reached"—little letters written and dedicated to the Viennese ladies from poets, actors, and critics all over the Continent. There were several from Italy and many from France, and with few exceptions, they were accompanied by a photograph of the author.

One exception was Catulle Mendes, the famous French poet and critic, who had answered the request for his photograph by replying that he preferred to have his likeness conspicuous by its absence, and would attend the ball himself, trusting rather to his own efforts in person to make some impression, if that were possible. His letter was as follows:

"Little Letter for the Ladies of Vienna
"LADIES: So far away it is easy to be brave, but I am beginning already to tremble at the thought that in a few days I shall have the honor and the temerity to speak to you, humble poet that I am and doubtless ignored by you. They tell so many precious things of that charm, entirely original, that distinguishes you from all the other women of Europe. May it be that your perfect and finished grace and your exquisite taste will not judge me too harshly!
"In admiration,
"CATULLE MENDES."

Gerhard Hauptmann wrote a beautiful poem that many of the guests pored over and committed to memory, while Adolf Wilbrandt, Ludwig

Fulda and Otto Brahm (the great director of the Lessing Theater in Berlin), wrote charming long letters in verse. Eugène Brieux contributed also, and George Ohnet wrote from Paris:

"DEAR LADIES: Our writers, our composers, and our artists are so cordially received in Vienna, that your beautiful city seems to be another Paris to us, and we have heard played so often the beautiful 'Blue Danube,' that this river seems to flow by us at the same time as our Seine. This is why, dear ladies, we can never refuse anything to the Viennese."

Arthur Schnitzler, the Viennese, wrote a characteristic letter, saying (freely translated), "When one who is not good himself but only good-hearted has the fortune to achieve something really worth while, that his negligent heart has hardly intended, there is still seldom a rose without a thorn, for as much as the memory of an undertaking that was not worthy of us troubles us, still harder to bear is the remembrance of an act toward us of which we ourselves were not perfectly worthy."

At the end of the room was a large stage where the most notable guests congregated and talked. Great actors from the theater were there; Goltz and Rauchinger, the well-known portrait painters; Philip de Laszlo, taking artistic delight in the surroundings; Madame Wiesinger, the celebrated painter of flowers; many composers of Vienna, of Italy, and of France; Leschetizky and other famous musicians. Catulle Mendes was talking with evident great enjoyment and many ladies were hovering about him.

The spirit of Vienna was in the truest sense of the word artistic. Writers, actors, musicians, royalty, came together there for art's sake. It was the Emperor's delight to be present at rehearsals at the theater and opera, and he would lend historical costumes when he thought it necessary to enhance the beauty of the scene or enliven the imagination of the audience. The great libraries of Vienna were searched for chronological details. The Emperor contributed largely to the preservation of traditions in Vienna, both artistic and religious. People marveled at his energy in his old age, as for example, on Corpus Christi Day when he walked for miles through the city in the famous pageant. It required three or four hours for this slow procession to pass the different stations where his Apostolic Majesty knelt and prayed and so preserved this ancient tradition for his people. This celebration was instituted by Papal decree in the year 1264. It was appointed for the first Thursday after the festival of the Trinity, and has been famous from that day to this as one of the most magnificent pageants in Europe. All the offices of the Court and of civil life were represented. The official representatives of all the provinces of Austria and Hungary, mounted soldiers in magnificent gray uniforms led a procession of companies from all the charitable institutions of the church, including priests of different orders—Dominican, Franciscan and hooded Capuchins, and bishops and archbishops in their robes of office. Finally there came the gorgeous white-and-gold embroidered canopy, supported at its corners on staffs borne by officials, beneath which walked the Cardinal in his red robes, carrying the Host upon a golden salver. Following this on foot and bare-headed, humbly passed an erect and kingly figure—the Emperor. Behind him came members of the Imperial family, princes and nobles.

Another tradition that the Emperor upheld was the pious *"Fusswaschung."* Only a few people were allowed to witness this commemoration which took place in the Imperial Palace. Through their ambassadors foreigners could obtain cards of admission, with instructions to appear dressed in black. The Emperor passed down through a long line of people on both sides to the place where twelve of the oldest and poorest men that were to be found in Vienna were waiting to view their Emperor face to face, as he imitated the humility of Christ in washing the feet of his disciples. These twelve old men could be seen trembling with emotion, or weeping, as the Emperor approached and distributed to each one of them a bag of gold. One might write for hours about the life and traditions of this beautiful city and still leave much to be told.

At the Court Chapel on Sundays and at the Votive Church, old Palestrina masses were given. Very beautiful organ playing was to be heard at the Cathedral where old Sechter had played in former years. In all this, it was said, the Emperor had a hand, and his influence upon the artistic atmosphere of Vienna was of the best and of his many kind and considerate actions there is abundant record.

One American girl felt herself amply compensated for a bad fall in a blinding snowstorm and a narrow escape from being run over by swiftly driven horses, when she saw bending over her the anxious face of the Emperor who had sprung from his seat and would have helped her to her feet had it been necessary.

On a few occasions American ladies were presented to him, who always paid most glowing tribute to his sincere and interesting conversation, which was indeed not always abbreviated. To one he remarked that it made him proud of his Vienna to think that so many strangers found it profitable to study there. Another one had prepared herself for every possible question that might be asked her in French or German, and was naturally somewhat confused when His Majesty addressed her in perfect English.

In the brilliant society of Vienna, Leschetizky was a great magnet and therefore always a much sought-for and welcome guest. People seemed exhilarated by his presence. He drew them around him and in some curious way stimulated them to talk, become animated, tell stories, and express their opinions. There was never a trace of self-consciousness about him. I think he saw everything in pictures, and the picture itself interested him. He listened intently to every word that was spoken to him, and lost himself in the conversation of any one who had something interesting to say. He never, by any chance, went anywhere he did not want to go, but he loved people and, next to music, found humanity the most interesting thing in the world. He liked best those semiformal assemblages where he could hold real conversations with those he chose, meet people he had already met and meet them often enough so that the threads of previous conversations were not broken or lost. If he had to drive long distances or to take the train even to spend a few hours at friends' houses, he thought little of the inconvenience, and was apparently happy all the way in the contemplation of the pleasure that lay before him.

There were pleasant places in the neighborhood of Vienna where Leschetizky spent many hours with congenial friends. One of these was Kaltenleutgeben, where Madame von Dutschka, one of his greatest friends, spent the summer. Among the many who frequented her house were Alice Barbi, the great singer; Countess Wydenbruch-Esterhazy, a most accomplished and beautiful woman; the Baron Berger, for some years the director of the Court Theater in Vienna; Adolf Wilbrandt, the poet, who had for a long time been director of the theater; Count Coudenhove, princes and princesses; and last, but not least, Mark Twain and his family.

It was here that Alice Barbi discovered the beautiful voice of Clara Clemens, and persuaded her to give up the study of piano for the sake of her voice. Clara, who played really beautifully, had come to Vienna to study with Leschetizky. She played at one of the classes, and Leschetizky thought we would all remember it as most poetical and charming.

One of the brothers of the Count Coudenhove was a naturalist and philanthropist. He had a large farm in South Africa, but instead of going to the north to kill wild animals, he collected them in their wild state and domesticated them on his farm, where they could be safe from danger. He was

known to be a man incapable of killing any living
thing.

The poet Wilbrandt, who now spent much time
in Rostock, came back frequently to his beloved
Vienna. His son and daughter-in-law lived in Germany, while his wife, Madame Wilbrandt-Baudius,
was one of the great actresses of the Court Theater
in Vienna, and Wilbrandt divided his time between
them and relatives in Rostock. He was a real poet
and a man of exalted idealism. He often came to
Vienna to be present at the first performance of one
of his dramatic pieces. His play *The Master of
Palmyra,* now considered a German classic, was
much admired by Mark Twain.

Of Madame von Dutschka's salon in Vienna
Wilbrandt wrote a long account in the *Neue Freie
Presse.* He called it a salon of the best traditions,
and so indeed it was. Statesmen, clergymen,
artists, and actors from all over Europe met there
on the most familiar and easy terms. A member of
the House of Parliament remarked that he could
not live without half an hour's conversation every
day with Madame von Dutschka. Directors of
museums liked to talk with her. Mr. de Scala, the
artistic director of the Industrial Museum, sought
her opinion on laces and other special matters. The
well-known opera singer Marianna Brandt was
usually at her house, and Alice Barbi was a welcome
guest whenever she was in Vienna.

Madame von Dutschka's Friday afternoons were
devoted to music, and Leschetizky rarely missed
looking in on these occasions. The charming hostess turned easily from one language to another,
and conscientiously spoke to each guest in his own.

Leschetizky loved her brilliant conversation. He thought it a great privilege and a compliment to him for one of his pupils to play at her house, and he called himself her "Court pianist."

One day Marianna Brandt consented to sing if he would play one of his mazurkas. She sang some Schumann songs, especially the "Nussbaum," with a depth of feeling that moved the guests to tears. Leschetizky then played not only a mazurka of his own, but other things as well for nearly an hour.

Whenever a pupil of Leschetizky played at one of these musicales, he advised him to improvise for a while until he had overcome all nervousness, for it was not the easiest place in the world to play. The guests stood or sat rather near the piano, and had a way of listening rather curiously and critically to amateurs. Leschetizky would tell us to play small and appropriate pieces, but to play them beautifully. One afternoon when I was asked to play Leschetizky came quickly forward. "No waltzes and no humorous pieces to-day," he said. "Lenbach has just died, and his friend Wilbrandt is here."

Madame von Dutschka loved her friends and they were all devoted to her. She very seldom appeared in public, and almost never visited other people, either alone or among other guests. Her life was most methodical. She rose early and devoted some time to reading. Then she walked for two or three hours, taking a light second breakfast out of doors. After that she composed and prepared herself for receiving her guests, who began to arrive at about three o'clock. She sat at the head of a long table, except on Fridays, which had become famous as afternoons of good music. At her table she gave herself to the entertainment of her guests and talked brilliantly on any subject that seemed to be uppermost in their minds. At least a dozen people came to her house every day, and went away refreshed in spirit and looking forward to the next day when they might hear and see her again. Her rooms were simply furnished, but extremely comfortable. There were six or eight large sofas with large comfortable chairs around them. When there were few people, she shut off a room or two so that there should be no empty or lonely spaces.

Another famous salon was that of the Princess Lubomirska, who was one of the cleverest and most beautiful women I have ever known. Besides being an accomplished person, she was a woman of large and varied affairs and an indefatigable participator in works of charity. She rose at five o'clock in the morning and had her household affairs mapped out in perfect order before any of her household had begun the day. She taught her children the classics and music, and after her husband's death she continued to carry on his extensive interests in the Galician oil fields. She paid visits to the poor during part of the day, was at Madame von Dutschka's for tea at five o'clock, and could be found dancing the "mazur" in the evening at Polish balls.

Her father, the Count Xaver Zamoyski, was a man of the highest culture. He was a patron of art, an excellent judge of pictures and wrote some charming songs. He was clever, a delightful *raconteur,* and a great favorite in the Viennese society. Artists loved to have him with them, and

Leschetizky, too, felt greatly pleased and honored whenever he came out to his house to one of the classes. In these pages I salute with reverence his lofty idealism and his high attainments as scholar and artist. He was a great Polish gentleman, and, as Wilbrandt once said, "there are no better in the world."

The Princess Lubomirska's Saturday evenings were like Madame von Dutschka's Friday afternoons, devoted especially to music. One met there the distinguished Hungarian portrait painter, Philip de Laszlo, who was also very musical. He often sang delightful Hungarian melodies at his own house. They were always very free and weird. If one could accompany him at all at the piano while he chanted or sang these wild songs, he was delighted, but this was very difficult, as he had no notes and sang very freely and emotionally. Mrs. de Laszlo, who was an Irish lady, played the violin very beautifully, but could never be persuaded to appear in public.

The Flonzaleys also played one evening at the Princess Lubomirska's and Frank La Forge pleased every one there several times with his beautiful phrasing and exquisite tone. Royalty sometimes appeared there. The Japanese Ambassador was often present, and also the Chinese Ambassador in his Oriental dress. It was a rendezvous of famous Polish and Hungarian statesmen who could be heard conversing in Latin.

A very vivid picture in my memory is that of Leschetizky coming quietly into the room one evening looking rather white and old. His brilliant eyes glanced about the suddenly hushed room, and peo-

ple whispered, "Leschetizky is here." In a few
minutes, as usual, he had drawn to himself a circle
of listeners, who gave him the profoundest attention. Some one asked if there was any way to get
him to play. I answered that if going on my knees
would accomplish this, I would undertake it, and I
did. "It is not possible to refuse that," said
Leschetizky.

Amid much applause he went to the piano and
played with that splendid fire and grace and poetry
that was natural to him. He played Chopin on this
occasion, mazurkas, polonaises and nocturnes,
finishing with the "F Minor Fantasy." He had
looked tired at first, but all signs of fatigue soon
disappeared, and those who had never heard him
play before were astonished at the power of piano
playing under his fingers, to move them and at the
depth and variety of his interpretations.

CHAPTER XX

In 1907 I came home to America for the wedding of one of my sisters, intending to go back to Vienna, but several circumstances, including a long illness, prevented my ever returning. I did not see Leschetizky again.

All that I know of these last years, I have gleaned from his letters. On September 20, 1907, he wrote me from Wiesbaden:

"Your letter of the 3rd of September (you have for once written a date) I received in Ischl, where I spent one day only on the journey from Wiesbaden to Vienna. You do not know probably that I have been suffering greatly from rheumatism since July, and have tried to find relief in the sulphur baths of Baden, but have not found it. I came again to Wiesbaden with the greatest hopes of getting rid of my pains, but whether my hopes are to be realized is 'written in the stars'; certainly I do not know myself. I must be constantly attended by my valet Johann (whom you remember), and have him continually with me, as it is becoming difficult, almost impossible, for me to dress myself. And I am not allowed to be alone, or to travel alone. . . .

"Your letter, telling me of the two marriages in your family, was no great surprise to me. Young ladies, for whom art is not a substitute for other things must, particularly when they are beautiful, not only think of getting married, but really do so.

I do not know your other sister, but I want to congratulate both of them. . . .

"How about your concert affairs? You write nothing on this subject, which would have been of greatest interest to me.

"Forward, forward. *Plus d'energie, chère mademoiselle!* And I hope that you will return to Vienna crowned with successes. . . .

"Family is not a substitute for art, except when great love is in the play, and a true love marriage brings to a close the comedy of life."

On the 16th of March, 1908, he wrote from Vienna:

"As I have been looking for you every day in Vienna, I have not written to thank you for your letter, and for the charming present—the handkerchief with my initial embroidered by your own hand. As you haven't come, and no one has had a sign of life from you, I am writing now to send you my most appreciative thanks for such a gift.

"I have no special news to tell you, except that for several weeks now, I have been legally separated from Madame Eugenie. This process in the law courts has lasted eight and a half months. My health is far from good and I am still suffering from rheumatism. Some doctors (I have had ten) call it gout. But the worst is sleeplessness.

"I have many pupils, consequently have much to do, and remain indoors. For one and a half seasons I had not been to a concert until two days ago. . . .

"My principal amusement is playing cards between twelve and three o'clock at night. Almost every day I play a few games of Preference with an American here. My other diversion is the theater.

"I am expecting more news from you than I can give you in this letter. I am angry that you are not playing more in public, and that I do not read anything in the papers about you. I am waiting for this. Has the example of your sisters perhaps affected you? Are you perhaps going to be married?"

His next letter to me is dated May 23, 1909:

"My Poor Dear Friend:

"Your letter, which reached me to-day, I have read with heartfelt pity. You must have been suffering a long time, dear Ethel, if you are still so ill as you say. It depressed Marie [1] and me very much to know that you had not been well. How I should have liked to come to see you, dear friend, if we were not separated by such a terrible distance. We are very much with you in our thoughts, and we speak so often of you. How I should like to see you again! You have been away from here so long!

"I did not see Mr. Adams, as he was here during the fortnight which I spent with Marie (Madame Leschetizka) in Berlin. We were invited to Landecker's twenty-fifth anniversary by the committee as well as by Landecker himself. You will have read perhaps of this anniversary. You know that Landecker built the Philharmonic Hall in Berlin twenty-five years ago, thus founding the Philharmonic Society. He is owner of this hall, as well as of the Beethoven and Oberlicht Halls, all of which are in the same building.

"You must know these halls, because you have played with orchestra in Berlin, probably in the Beethoven Hall, which is not so large as the Philharmonic.

"We were received in Berlin in the friendliest

[1] In 1908 he married Marie Rorsborska, a young Polish lady, one of his pupils.

manner and fêted everywhere, so that we have
brought back with us only the pleasantest impressions.

"The journey might have done me a great deal
of good, as I was very tired from the lessons in
Vienna, but unfortunately the weather at the time
—the end of April and beginning of May—was
very cold, and my chronic bronchial trouble suffered severely from this. For six weeks I have
been coughing like a horse, and, since I have come
back from Berlin, like two horses. Only God
knows what will come of it. They want, that is,
the doctor wants, me to go south, and threatens that
otherwise there may be bad consequences. Unfortunately, I am not a rich man, not even in entirely
comfortable circumstances. *Ergo*—that means
earn as much as you can.

"There are now here some former American
pupils, whom I believe you must know, among them
the Dahl-Rich and Jeanette Durno, who wish to
replenish their repertoire with me. As I believe you
are again at home and no longer in the Buffalo
General Hospital, I shall send this to Whitney
Point. I hope to receive from you further details
of your health, and shall write more of ourselves,
and many others of your friends. Meanwhile, I
embrace you with heartiest greetings and best
wishes from us both.

"Your true friend,
"THEODOR LESCHETIZKY.

"P.S. Jane Olmsted Thaw also visited us. We
spent many pleasant hours together. I also had a
visit from Buhlig. Best greetings to your charming mother."

The last word I had from him was a letter sent
from Abbazia in October, 1911, congratulating

me on my birthday. But from Edouard Schütt I have some accounts of these years until 1915, when he died.

Schütt was one of his truest and most devoted friends. Leschetizky was always aware of this devotion, and, in spite of the fact that they often had violent disagreements, he always turned to this friend in time of trouble.

Schütt writes that on his eightieth birthday, that day that had been celebrated so often with all the festivity that loving friends and pupils could devise, Leschetizky preferred to see no one. His health was failing fast, and his old spirit was gone. The evening before he met Schütt at the Southern Station, where they drank a glass of champagne together, and then, Leschetizky accompanied by another true friend, his half-sister Madame Dunzendorfer, left for Abbazia on the coast. She always was and remained devoted to his interests, and with great love and patience supported him through many trials. "What a contrast," said Schütt, "to the cheerful and beautiful celebrations of former birthdays!"

In the following years he did give his lessons, but with effort. Now and then, at his beloved evening classes on Wednesdays, it would seem that the old fire and charm would revive and enchant his beloved pupils as of old. Every summer he still went to Carlsbad, and afterward to Ischl, and came back to Vienna, apparently somewhat strengthened. Often he would go again to his beautiful Abbazia for a few weeks in the autumn.

Then came the war. This deprived Leschetizky of the one joy of life, for it took away the youthful

and cosmopolitan atmosphere in which he breathed
most freely.   The Poles and Russians came no
longer to Vienna; then the French and the Italians
ceased coming, and lastly, the English and Americans.   This was almost unbearable to him.

In January, 1915, Schütt writes that he came
with his attendant and nurse, Pepi Praehofer, to
spend several months with him in Meran, in order,
as he said, to be once more with his best friend,
alone and undisturbed.   He was now physically and
spiritually very noticeably shaken, says Schütt, and
conducting a conversation with him was hardly
possible.

In March, 1915, I received the following from
his faithful attendant:

"Professor Leschetizky has instructed me, as his
nurse, to write to you, as it is not yet possible for
him to do so himself, because of an operation on
his eyes.   Unfortunately, up to this time he has not
gained the strength which he needs.   The doctor
says it will surely come, but it will take several
months to cure his impaired eyesight, injured by
the scars of repeated operations.   Herr Professor
is glad that you are again playing in public and
are having success.   The war affects him very un-
happily, and he hopes that it will soon be ended.

"Herr Professor greets you warmly.

" Most respectfully,
"PEPI PRAEHOFER."

In the spring of 1915, when the declaration of war
by Italy seemed imminent, Meran, so near the
Italian border, was a dangerous place to stay in.
Schütt had to attend to Leschetizky's safe return
to Vienna.   Leschetizky was most unhappy, but

there was no alternative. Schütt took him to Vienna, where he attended to him constantly.

The day before the 22nd of June, his eighty-fifth birthday, when they sat together in the Türken-schanz Park, was the last time Schütt saw him. Schütt speaks of him as tender, good and kind, but deeply embittered, and to the sorrow of all of his friends, very unhappy. At the door of his house in the Carl Luding Strasse they separated, and his attendant helped him into the house, as he was almost blind. The next morning, which 'was his eighty-fifth birthday, Leschetizky left his home in Vienna never to return. He went first to Carls-bad, and from there, wherever war conditions would permit.

Finally he went to his son in Dresden, where he was lovingly cared for by him and his daughter-in-law. He stayed first in a hotel, but, as his condi-tion grew worse, he was later removed to a sanato-rium. There he contracted an acute inflammation of the lungs, and one night quietly closed his eyes forever.

He had wanted to have his remains cremated, and requested that nobody attend his funeral. But this, in any event, would have been impossible, as passports were difficult to obtain, and the difficul-ties of traveling enormous.

A year later his only son, Robert, died, and to-day the surviving relatives of Leschetizky are Therese, his daughter, a very esteemed singer in St. Petersburg, and Madame Helene Dunzen-dorfer, his half-sister.

In concluding these recollections of a remarka-ble man, as well as an inspiring teacher, I cannot do

better than to append a charming letter from his
very dear and loyal friend, Edouard Schütt, giving
a few personal impressions of the master.

"When I recall our dear friend in the flesh, many
of his characteristic phrases come to my mind. For
instance, how often did he interrupt the playing of
a pupil, and say 'Don't play in such a bourgeois
manner! . . . I hate everything bourgeois!'
This expression, better than anything else, charac-
terizes the man, who all his life reflected the true
Bohemian spirit. He had all its sudden impulses,
and his soul seemed to be always restlessly seeking
contact with a friendly soul.

"How many other admirable qualities he possessed! For example, he was a wonderfully true
friend. What did he not do for the young artists
who came to him to learn, and for many of whom,
indeed most of whom, he became in time an affectionate friend. Everybody was truly devoted to
him: it could not help but be so. And even in cases
when he incurred only ingratitude and animosity,
he kept his poise and good temper.

"I remember distinctly every detail of our first
meeting in St. Petersburg in 1876. I had just completed my final examinations as pupil of Professor
Stein at the local conservatory, and had played as
pièce de résistance the first movement of the 'Concerto in D Minor' of Rubinstein. Leschetizky was
one of the judges of my performance, which pleased
him so well that he gave me the highest mark. I
was not personally acquainted with him then, and
I was, therefore, not a little proud, when he, already such a distinguished authority on music and
playing in St. Petersburg, came to me, and shook
hands with the words, 'You have played exceptionally well.'

"When, two years later, I heard from Madame Essipoff in Berlin that Leschetizky was going to transfer his residence to Vienna, I wrote to him at once, asking whether he would accept me as a pupil. By return mail I had his answer: If I would come, he would be only too pleased to be of any assistance or personal service to me in Vienna. Shortly afterward I knocked at Leschetizky's door at Währing in the little house in the Sternwarte-strasse that he had just acquired, and which he later let to Hans Richter, the famous Wagner director, who, in his turn, lived there for about fifteen years before he went to England. Little did I think then that this wonderful man and master should become in the future not only my teacher and adviser in all artistic matters, but also my best and dearest friend to thank for drawing me to Vienna, which has been my home for over forty years, and who never tired of advancing and protecting my interests.

"What a place of incomparable inspiration was Leschetizky's home for every young artist, and nobody understood so well as he how to receive in his house such men as Liszt, Rubinstein, Brahms, Tschaikowsky, Grieg, Massenet, and many other great masters, upon whom he exercised the most fascinating charm of the man of the world. Whoever has not seen Leschetizky on such occasions has not known fully this rare personality. Every subject he touched upon he illumined with an intellectuality that captivated the hearers. And, although in argument he defended with warmth his own point of view, he had the greatest respect for the opinions of his opponents. His perfect poise never forsook him.

"Until the eighty-second year of his life he remained continually energetic, worked indefatigably and was always an inspiring teacher. Then suddenly the life machine gave way. The tragic war dispersed his pupils in all directions, and it seemed that he could not live without this youthful circle. He grew ill and restless. In January, 1915, he came to Meran in the Tyrol to visit me, but the light in his eyes, the light that charmed everybody young and old, was gone forever.

"In the autumn of 1915 he closed these wonderful eyes forever. In Leschetizky the world lost a great master and a wonderful man."

Plate I. Leschetizky in 1843, one year after his first concert in Vienna

Plate II. Photo taken in 1913.

Plate III. Photo taken about the same time.

Plate IV. First row, left to right; Evelyn Suart (Lady Harcourt); Clara Clemens, daughter of Mark Twain; Katherine Goodson, English concert pianist, teacher of Clifford Curzon; Ethel Newcomb and Mary Newcomb. Top row; Elise de Bruckere, Jane Olmstead, and Constance Parrish.

THEODOR LESCHETIZKY
A Bibliography
compiled by
Frederick Freedman and Philip Solomita

Allison, Irl. "Miniatures of the Mighty; Some Notes on Piano Teaching Since 1880," *Musical Courier*, CLI/3 (February 1, 1955), 66–68.

(Anonymous)

———. "Advice to a Young Piano Teacher," *Woman's Home Companion*, XXXVIII/9 (September, 1911), 20.

———. "Death of Theodore Leschetizky," *Musical America*, XXIII/4 (1915), 3–4.

———. "Edwin Hughes Announces Fourteenth Annual Summer Master Class for Pianists and Teachers in New York," *Musical Courier*, C/20 (May 17, 1930), 8. (Includes facsimile of Leschetizky letter to Edwin Hughes.)

———. "Gallery of Musical Celebrities," *The Etude Music Magazine*, XLVII/7 (July, 1929), 511–512.

———. "Gravures Historiques 'Musikalische' Dokumente," *Disques*, 92 (October, 1957), 887.

———. "The Greatest Teacher of the Piano the World Has Ever Had," *Current Literature*, XLI/1 (July, 1906), 63–64.

———. "Leschetizky and His Pupils," *The Nation*, CI/2630 (November 25, 1915), 618–619.

———. "Leschetizky Tale," *Musical America*, LXXIV/3 (February 1, 1954), 6.

———. "Leschetizky Tells of His Method: Two Letters to Carl Stasny," *The Musician*, XIX/6 (June, 1914), 380; *Musical Standard*, V/127 (1915), 439–440.

———. "The Man Who Taught Paderewski," *The Outlook*, CXI/12 (December 1, 1915), 774–775.

———. "The Master Teacher," *The Etude Music Magazine*, XLVIII/2 (February, 1930), 85.

301

————. "Paderewski to the Defense," *The Piano Teacher*, V/3 (January, 1963), 4. (Reprint of a letter in *Musical Courier*, 1893.)

————. "Paderewski's Musical Father," *The Literary Digest*, LI/23 (December 4, 1915), 1285–1286. (Interview with Paderewski.)

————. "Passing of the World's Most Famous Piano Teacher," *Musical America*, XXIII/4 (November 27, 1915), 3–4.

————. "Passing of Theodor Leschetizky, Most Picturesque of Piano Pedagogues. A Biography—the Venerable Teacher as Seen by His Famous Pupils—Personal Tributes and Reminiscences," *Musical Courier*, LXXI/21 (November 25, 1915), 5–7.

————. "The Right Kind of Relaxation," *The Etude Music Magazine*, LX/8 (August, 1942), 507.

————. "Teachers Behind Leschetizky," *The Musician*, XXXVIII/7 (July, 1933), 10.

Antrim, Doron K. "Who Are the World's Greatest Piano Teachers?" *Etude*, LXXI/2 (February, 1953), 18.

Beaurain, Maria. "Theodor Leschetitzky," *Finsk Tidskrift*, LXXX/2 (March, 1916), 221–226.

Bisbee, Genevieve. "Is Leschetizky a Great Teacher?" *The Musical Leader and Concert Goer*, XI/8 (1906), 19.

Bisbee, Genevieve. "Leschetizky and His Method," *The Musical Leader and Concert Goer*, X/25 (1905), 19.

Bolte, Theodor. "Theodor Leschetizky: Ein Erinnerungsblatt anlässlich seines 80. Geburtstages am 22. Juni 1910," *Musikalisches Wochenblatt*, XLI/12 (June 23, 1910), 117–119.

Boyd, Mary B. "Between the Diploma and the Concert Stage," *Musical Courier*, CLVI/7 (December 1, 1957), 6–7.

Boyd, Mary B. "The Hammer Finger or 'Perfect-Finger,'" *Etude*, LXX/5 (May, 1952), 9.

Boyd, Mary B. "Just How Leschetizky Taught," *Etude*, LXVII/3 (August, 1949), 480.

Boyd, Mary B. "Sing With Your Fingers," *Etude*, LXIX/4 (April, 1951), 19.

Brailowsky, Alexander. "Master Secret of a Great Teacher," *The Etude Music Magazine*, XLIII/6 (June, 1925), 389–390.

Brée, Malwine. *Die Grundlage der Methode Leschetizky*. Mainz, B. Schott's Söhne, 1902.

Brée, Malwine. *The Groundwork of the Leschetizky Method; Issued with His Approval by His Assistant*, trans. by Dr. Theodore Baker. New York, G. Schirmer, 1902.

Brower, Harriette. "Fourteen Years with Leschetizky," *Musical America*, XXIII/19 (1916), 33.

Brower, Harriette. "Leschetizky and the Virtuoso," *Musical America*, XXIV/8 (1916), 17.

Brower, Harriette. "Leschetizky's Genius as a Teacher; Interview with M. G. Leschetizky," *The Musician*, XXIX/12 (December, 1924), 12, 40.

Charbonnel, Avis B. "The Disputed 'Method' of Theodor Leschetizky," *Musical Courier*, CXLII/4 (September, 1950), 6.

Cheridjian-Charrey, Marcelle. "Théodor Leschetizky," *Schweizerische Musikzeitung und Sängerblatt*, LXX/14-15 (August 1, 1930), 552–554.

Chumleigh, George. "Theodore Leschetizky," *Musical Courier*, XLVI/8 (February 25, 1903), 12–13.

Clarence, Violet. "Recollections of My Teachers: I. Leschetizky. II. Pugno. III. Philipp," *Monthly Musical Record*, XLIX (April, 1919), 79–81.

Cleophas, Gertrud. "Leschetizky Anniversary," *Music of the West Magazine*, I/11 (July, 1946), 7–8.

(Cleophas, Gertrud). "Teacher Pays Tribute to Leschetizky," *Music of the West Magazine*, IX/1 (September, 1953), 12.

Clymer, J. B. "Leschetizky, His Friends and Pupils—A Remarkable Photograph," *Musical America*, X/4 (June 5, 1909), 3, 27.

Copp, Laura Remick. "Leschetizky," *The Music Student*, IV/3 (1917), 69–75.

Ericson, Raymond. "Leschetizky Memoir; Moiseiwitsch Tells What He Learned from Teacher of 'Grand Tradition,'" *The New York Times*, (January 22, 1961), 9.

Feldman, Steve. "What was Leschetizky's Secret?" *Musical Courier*, CLIV/7 (December 1, 1956), 9.

Funk, Addie. "Europe's 'grand old man' of music: Leschetizky," *Musical America*, XIV/11 (1911), 21.

Gabrilowitsch, Ossip. "A Great Master of the Piano; Theodor Leschetizky," *Musical Courier*, CI/26 (December 27, 1930), 6. (Reprinted in *The Piano Teacher*, V/4 (April, 1963), 8–10.)

Gabrilowitsch, Ossip. "Memoir of Leschetizky; Ossip Gabrilowitsch Recalls Student Days with Great Master—Famous Pupils," *The New York Times*, (December 7, 1930), 8.

Garbett, A. S. "The Musical Scrap Book: Leschetizky at the First Lesson," *The Etude Music Magazine*, XLV/7 (July, 1927), 508.

Gardner, Roy R. "Leschetizky and His School," *The Musical World*, I/7 (August, 1901), 87.

Hale, Edward Danforth. "Leschetizky Again," *The New England Conservatory Magazine*, IX/5 (1903), 202–205.

Halski, Czeslaw R. "Theodor Leschetizky," *Grove's Dictionary of Music and Musicians*. Fifth ed. Eric Blom, ed. New York, St. Martin's Press, Inc., 1954, V, 144–145.

Hambourg, Mark. *From Piano to Forte*. London, Cassell and Co., Ltd., 1932.

Hambourg, Mark. "Leschetizky Days," *The Etude Music Magazine*, L/10–11 (October–November, 1932), 689–690, 768. (Extracts from the chapter on Vienna from Hambourg's autobiography, *From Piano to Forte*.)

Hambourg, Mark. "Tales of an Artist's Life: Viennese Memories," *The Piano Student*, Old Series XVI/12 (New Series III/3) (December, 1936), 50–51, 55.

Hopekirk, Helen. "Theodor Leschetizky: A Retrospect," *The Musician*, XXI/1 (January, 1916), 7–9.

Horowitz-Barnay, Ilka. "Bei Theodor Leschetizky," *Deutsche Dichtung*, XXVII/6 (December 15, 1899), 146–151.

Hughes, Edwin. (Article in) *Dunning Messinger*, (June, 1937), 5.

Hughes, Edwin. (Article in) *Human Life*, (December, 1908).

Hughes, Edwin. (Article in) *Music Teachers Review*, (January–February, 1941).

Hughes, Edwin. "Leschetizky Passes the Eighty-Third Milestone," *Musical America*, XVIII/11 (July 19, 1913), 2.

Hughes, Edwin. "Leschetizky's Pianistic Legacy; A Contemplation of the Master Pedagogue's Ideas and Personality—Artistic and Humane Aspects," *Musical Courier*, CIV/18, (April 30, 1932), 6–7, 15.

Hughes, Edwin. "Leschetizky's Young Wife," *Musical America*, X/22 (October 9, 1909), 15.

Hughes, Edwin. "Theodor Leschetizky: A Maker of Pianists," *The Musician*, XV/9 (September, 1910), 579–583.

Hughes, Edwin. "Theodor Leschetizky on Modern Pianoforte Study," *The Etude*, XXVII/4–5 (April–May, 1909), 227–228, 307. (Interview with Leschetizky.)

Hughes, Edwin. "Theodor Leschetizky, Pianist and Pedagogue," *The American Review of Reviews*, XLII/4 (October, 1910), 494–495.

Hughes, Edwin. "Theodor Leschetizky's Musical Heritage to America," *Proceedings of the Music Teachers National Association*, LIX/Ser. 30 (1935), 19–30.

Hughes, Edwin. "A Visit from Leschetizky," *The Musician*, XIX/4 (April, 1914), 234–235.

Hughes, Edwin. "With Leschetizky at 79," *The Designer* (February, 1910).

Hullah, Annette. "The Leschetizky Method," *The Musical Observer*, I/3, 5 (March and May, 1907). March, pp. [?] May, p. 6.

Hullah, Annette. "The Lessons of Theodore Leschetizky," *The Musical Observer*, II/5 (May, 1908), 4–5.

Hullah, Annette. *Theodor Leschetizky*. London, J. Lane Company, 1906.

Huneker, James. "A Comparison of Theodore Leschetizky with Other Great Piano Teachers," *The Musical Observer*, XVIII/3 (March, 1919), 13, 420.

Jenkins, Constance. "Four Years With Leschetizky," *The Musical Opinion*, LIII (July, 1930), 895–960.

Jenkins, Constance. "Leschetizky: A Great Teacher," *Music Teacher*, VIII/6 (June, 1930), 341–342.

Jenkins, Constance. "Leschetizky as Teacher," *Monthly Musical Record*, LX/716 (August, 1930), 236–237.

Jenkins, Constance. "Memoirs of Leschetizky," *The Musical Standard*, XXXV (June 14, 1930), 196.

Jenkins, Constance. "Theodore Leschetizky, 1830–1915," *The Musical Times*, LXXI (June, 1930), 504–506.

Kantz, John. "Leschetizkyism," *Musical Courier*, XLVII/7 (1903), 18–19.

Kardos, Kornelie. "Ein Klavierabend bei Leschetizky," *Neue Musik Zeitung*, XXIX (1908), 392–394.

Karpath, Ludwig. "Erinnerungen an Theodor Leschetizky," *Der Merker*, VI/23 (1915), 838–840.

Keefer, Austin Roy. "Leschetizky's Pianistic Philosophy," *The Etude Music Magazine*, LXVI/11 (November, 1948), 673.

Lafferty, Roger. "Carrying on the Leschetizky Tradition: Louis Finton, Apostle of the Viennese Master, Develops a Systematic Analysis and Synthesis of His Playing Methods," *The Musician*, XXXIX/9 (September, 1934), 7.

Leonard, Florence. "Why Was Leschetizky Great?" *The Etude Music Magazine*, LIX/5 (May, 1941), 307–308.

Leschetizky Association (of America). *News Bulletin*. New York, 1945–   . (An annual organizational publication which includes considerable material on Leschetizky, his pupils, and other members.)

Leschetizky, Marie Rorzborska. "Master Thoughts from the Life of a Great Teacher," *The Etude*, XLIII/10 (October, 1925), 695–696.

Liszniewska, Marguerite M. "Why Czerny?" *The Etude Music Magazine*, LIII/9 (September, 1935), 509.

Loesser, Arthur. *Men, Women and Pianos; a Social History.* New York, Simon and Schuster, 1954.

Marilaun, Carl. "Die Villa in der Karl Ludwigstrasse," *Der Merker*, VII/1 (1916), 31–33.

Mason, Lolita. "An Hour with Leschetizky," *The Etude*, XXX/6 (1912), 397–398; also in *Musical News*, XLIV (1913).

Melville, Marguerite. "Leschetizky and His 'Method,' " *Musical America*, XI/12 (1910), 2.

Merrick, Frank. "Memories of Leschetizky," *Recorded Sound*, III/18 (April, 1965), 335–339.

Moffett, Cleveland. "The Man Who Taught Paderewski," *The Ladies' Home Journal* (1898).

Moiseiwitch, Benno. "Impact—Leschetizky," *The Piano Teacher*, V/3 (January, 1963), 3–4.

Moiseiwitsch, Benno. "New Tendencies in Pianistic Art," *The Etude*, XXXVIII/5 (May, 1920), 295–296.

Mojeska, Helena. "Mojeska's Memoirs," *The Century Magazine*, LXXIX/3 (January, 1910), 363–380.

Monod, Edmond. "Hommage à Théodore Leschetizky," *La Vie Musicale*, III (1910), 380–381.

Navratil, Carl. "When Paderewski Sat at the Feet of Leschetizky," *Musical America*, L/20 (December 25, 1930), 42.

Nemeth, Carl. *Franz Schmidt; ein Meister nach Brahms und Bruckner.* Zurich u. Wien, Amalthea-Verlag, 1957, 29ff.

Newcomb, Ethel. *Leschetizky as I Knew Him.* New York, D. Appleton and Co., 1921.

Newcomb, Ethel. "Leschetizky: Man and Teacher," *Musical Courier*, LXXI/26 (1915), 11.

Niemann, Walter. *Meister des Klavier.* Berlin, Schuster & Loeffler, 1919.

Peczenik, Caroline. "Recuerdo sobre Teodoro Leschetizky," *Correo Musical Sud-Americano*, III/107 (1917).

Pohl, Hans. "Theodor Leschetizky," *Allgemeine Musik-Zeitung*, XLII/48 (1915), 556–557.

BIBLIOGRAPHY   307

Potocka, Angèle. "Anecdotes of Leschetizky," *The Century Magazine*, LXVI/6 (October, 1903), 933–938.

Potocka, Angèle. *Theodor Leschetizky, an Intimate Study of the Man and the Musician*, trans. by Genevieve Seymour Lincoln. New York, The Century Company, 1903.

Prentner, Marie. *Die Leschetizky Methode*. 1902.

Prentner, Marie. *The Leschetizky Method*. Seventh ed. London, J. Curwen & Sons, Ltd., 1903; Philadelphia, Theodore Presser Co., 1903.

Prentner, Marie. "Leschetizky's Vital Ideas," *The Etude Music Magazine*, XLV/9 (September, 1927), 645–646.

Prentner, Marie. *The Modern Pianist, Being My Experiences in the Technique and Execution of Pianoforte Playing, According to the Principles of Theodor Leschetizky*. English translation by M. De Kendler and A. Maddock. Philadelphia, T. Presser, (c1903).

Reijen, P. van. "De muzikale memoires van Ilka Horovitz-Barnay," *Mens en Melodie*, XX/6 (June, 1965), 176–179.

Rowbotham, John F. "Leschetizky, the Greatest Music-Master in Europe," *Good Words and Sunday Magazine*, XLI (1900), 599–604.

Schnabel, Artur. "Theodor Leschetizky. Zum achtzigsten Geburtstage," *Allgemeine Musik-Zeitung* XXXVII/25 (June 17, 1910), 599–600.

Schonberg, Harold C. *The Great Pianists*. New York, Simon and Schuster, 1963. (Chapter XX: The Lisztainers and Leschetizkianers Take Over; Chapter XXIII: Some of the Leschetizky Group.)

Schweisheimer, Waldemar. "Look Out for Your Hands! Neuritis, Neuralgia, and Temporary Paralysis Must be Watched," *Etude*, LXVII/2 (February, 1949), 85.

Sietz, Reinhold. "Theodor Leschetizky," *Die Musik in Geschichte und Gegenwart*, herausgeben von Friedrich Blume (Kassel, Bärenreiter, 1960) 664–665.

Silber, Sidney. "Leschetizky: the Man and Pedagogue as I Knew Him," *Proceedings of the Music Teachers National Association*, LXIII/Ser. 34 (1940), 267–274.

Slonimsky, Nicolas. "Musical Oddities," *Etude*, LXXV/2 (February, 1957), 4.

Smith, Fanny M. "Theodor Leschetizky (Prepared from a Biography Just Issued by the Century Co.)," *The Etude*, XXI/12 (December, 1903), 474–475.

Spencer, Eleanor. "Leschetizky's Stern Discipline Only an Armor to Shield a Deeply Warm Nature," *Musical America*, XXVI/4 (May 26, 1917), 9.

Spencer, Vernon. "Leschetizky: Man and Teacher," *The Music Student*, I/5 (1915), 14–18.

Thur, R. "Leschetizky and the Invalid," *The Etude Music Magazine*, XLV/5 (May, 1927), 348.

Trumbull, Florence. "Leschetizky as I Knew Him," *The Etude Music Magazine*, XLIX/2 (February, 1931), 87–88.

Unschuld von Melasfeld, Marie. *Die Hand des Pianisten. Methodische Anleitung zur Erlangung einer sicheren, brillanten Klaviertechnik modernen Stils nach Principien des Herrn Prof. Th. Leschetizky.* Leipzig, Breitkopf & Härtel, 1901. (Second ed., 1903.)

Unschuld von Melasfeld, Marie. *The Pianist's Hand.* Revised and augmented ed. New York, Carl Fischer, c1909.

Unschuld von Melasfeld, Marie. *La Main du Pianiste.* Leipzig, Breitkopf & Härtel, 1902.

Whitney, Julia B. "How I Studied the Piano Under Leschetizky," *The Ladies' Home Journal*, XXVIII/5 (March 1, 1911), 7–8, 76.

Wittgenstein, Paul. "The Legacy of Leschetizky," *Musical Courier*, CXXXII/3 (August, 1945), 13.

Woodhouse, George. "How Leschetizky Taught," *Music and Letters*, XXXV/3 (July, 1954), 220–226.

Woodhouse, George. "Theodor Leschetizky: His Contribution to Pianistic Art," *Musical Courier*, CI/20 (November 15, 1930), 18.

THEODOR LESCHETIZKY

A Chronology

(1830–1915)

1830 Born June 22 at Lancut, near Lemberg, in Austrian Poland. He and his parents—his father, Josef Leschetizky, Czechoslovakian, and his mother, née Thérèse von Ullman, Polish—lived on the estate of Count Alfred Potocka, where Josef Leschetizky served as musical instructor to Count Potocka's daughters.

1835 Began studying piano with his father.

1839 Made his public début at age of nine, in Lemberg, performing Czerny's *Concertino*, with orchestra directed by Wolfgang Amadeus Mozart, son of the immortal Mozart.

1840 Family moved to Vienna. Received first regular schooling at St. Anne's; entered the Gymnasium of the Benedictine Fathers.

1841 Began piano studies with Karl Czerny.

1842 Embarked on a series of concert tours which continued successfully through 1848.

1844 Began to teach the piano; studied law; studied composition with Simon Sechter.

1848-
1852 Continued to teach and perform; wrote his first opera, *Die Brüder von San Marco*.

1852 Went to Russia, September. Début at Michael Theatre in St. Petersburg, followed by command performance before Nicholas I.

1856 Married Anne de Friedebourg (singer); continued to concentrate on playing and teaching. In St. Petersburg, held post of director of music at the court of Grand Duchess Helen, sister-in-law of Emperor Nicholas.

1862 Opening of St. Petersburg Conservatory, Anton Rubinstein music director. Leschetizky headed pianoforte department from beginning to his retirement in 1878.

1864 Visited England for first time. Début at Musical Union Concerts, playing in Schumann's Quintet and performing his own pieces.

1867 His second opera, *Die Erste Falte*, first performed in Prague, October 9.

1871 Divorced from Anne de Friedebourg.

1878 Married Annette Essipoff (his pupil). Returned with her to Vienna. Continued performing throughout Europe, teaching.

1880 *Die Erste Falte* performed at Wiesbaden.

1881 Helped organize Tonkünstlerverein, an association of musicians.

1882 *Die Erste Falte* performed in Mannheim. Visited by Liszt.

1885 Arrival of Paderewski in Vienna to study with Leschetizky.

1887 Terminated his virtuoso career at Frankfurt-on-Main, playing Beethoven's E Flat Concerto under the baton of Dessoff. Devoted himself to instruction from then on, teaching many pianists who subsequently became world famous.

1892 Divorced from Annette Essipoff.

1894 Married Donnimirska (Eugenie de) Benislavska (his pupil).

1897 Visited London in September, gave last public performance there at Salle Erard, playing own compositions.

1908 Divorced from Donnimirska Benislavska. Married Marie Rorsborska (his pupil).

1915 Died at Dresden, Germany, November 14.

WORKS FOR PIANO
by
THEODOR LESCHETIZKY

(List from known published works)

Op. 1. Salut à la Nuit (Nocturne)
Op. 2.
      No. 1. Les Deux Alouettes (Impromptu)
      No. 2. Mazurka
Op. 3. Les Pêcheurs au Bord de la Mer (Chanson)
Op. 4. Souvenirs de Venise (Barcarolle)
Op. 5. Grande Polka de Caprice
Op. 7. Le Dialogue d'Amour
Op. 8. Two Mazurkas
      No. 1. In D Flat Major
      No. 2. In F Minor
Op. 9. Souvenir de Gräfenberg (Capriccio à la Valse)
Op. 10. La Cascade (Etude de Concert)
Op. 11. Six Improvisations
      No. 1. Le Doux Rêve (Impromptu)
      No. 2. Souvenir
      No. 3. Premier Amour (Impromptu)
      No. 4. Barcarole Napolitaine
      No. 5. Chant du Soir (Idylle)
      No. 6. La Petite Coquette (Scherzino)
Op. 12. Second Nocturne
Op. 13. Andante Finale de *Lucia di Lammermoor*
      (for left hand alone)
Op. 22. Valse Chromatique
Op. 23. Filigrane-Polka
Op. 24. Two Mazurkas
      No. 1. In E Minor
      No. 2. In E Flat
Op. 31. Deux Morceaux
      No. 1. L'Aveu (Improvisation)
      No. 2. Papillon (Intermezzo en Forme d'Etude)

Op. 35.
> No. 1. Le Bal d'Hier (Mazurka-Rêvérie)
> No. 2. Souvenir d'Ischl (Valse)

Op. 36. Quatre Morceaux
> No. 1. Aria
> No. 2. Gigue (Canon à Deux Voix)
> No. 3. Humoresque
> No. 4. La Source (Etude)

Op. 37. Valse-Caprice

Op. 38.
> No. 1. Menuetto Capriccioso
> No. 2. Mazurka-Impromptu

Op. 39. Souvenirs d'Italie. Suite de Morceaux.
> No. 1. Barcarola (Venezia)
> No. 2. Le Lucciole. Scherzo (Como)
> No. 3. Canzonetta Toscana all'Antica (Firenze)
> No. 4. Mandolinata (Roma)
> No. 5. Tarantella (Napoli)
> No. 6. Siciliana all'Antica (Catania)

Op. 40. A la Campagne. Suite de Cinq Morceaux.
> No. 1. Jeu des Ondes (Etude)
> No. 2. Consolation (Romance)
> No. 3. Primula Veris (Intermezzo)
> No. 4. Mélodie à la Mazurka
> No. 5. Danse à la Russe

Op. 41. Trois Etudes Caractéristiques
> No. 1. Etude Humoresque
> No. 2. La Toupie (Kreisel)
> No. 3. La Babillarde

Op. 42. Deux Morceaux
> No. 1. Fantaisie-Nocturne
> No. 2. Valse Coquette

Op. 43. Deux Morceaux
> No. 1. Serenata
> No. 2. La Piccola (Etude)

Op. 44. Pastels. Quatre Morceaux.
> No. 1. Prélude
> No. 2. Gigue all'Antica
> No. 3. Humoresque
> No. 4. Intermezzo en Octaves

Op. 45. Deux Arabesques
> No. 1. Arabesque en Forme d'Etude (Pas Trop Facile)
> No. 2. Arabesque à la Tarantelle

Op. 46. Contes de Jeunesse. Suite de Morceaux.
> No. 1. Berceuse
> > (to Miss Jane Olmsted)

Op. 46 (continued)

 No. 2. Ainsi Dansait Maman (Menuet all'Antica)
  (to Miecio Horszowski)
 No. 3. Affaire Compliquée (Canon)
  (to Arthur Schnabel)
 No. 4. Un Moment de Tristesse
  (to Miss Katie Goodson)
 No. 5. Toccata (Hommage à Czerny)
  (to Ossip Gabrilowitsch)
 No. 6. Impromptu en Souvenir de Henselt
  (to Miss Bertha Jahn)
 No. 7. Gavotte all'Antica et Musette Moderne
  (to Miss Dagmar Walle-Hansen)
 No. 8. Fantasiestück (Hommage à Schumann)
  (to Miss Ethel Newcomb)
 No. 9. Hommage à Chopin
  (to I. J. Paderewski)

Op. 47. Deux Morceaux
 No. 1. Nocturne
 No. 2. Scherzo

Op. 48. Trois Morceaux
 No. 1. Prélude Humoresque
 No. 2. Intermezzo Scherzando
 No. 3. Etude Heroïque

Op. 49. Deux Préludes
 No. 1. Chant du Soir-Prélude
 No. 2. Valse-Prélude

LESCHETIZKY ON PIANO PLAYING

Accuracy
worthless without expression 31;
wrong or missing notes 28, 129,
236, 238

Ear, playing by 5, 214–215

Fingering
bad in some editions 58, 98; differences in 12, 14, 45, 98

Hands
ailments 5, 9, 101–102; individual
differences 13–14, 101, 106

Interpretation
adjective playing 51; affected and
strained 63–64, 122, 175, 246, 249–
250; Beethoven 166; Brahms 247,
249, 252, 254, 260–262; Chopin
219; correctness of details 96;
depth and variety 285; *desinvoltura* 51; differences of, between
individuals 14, 45, 61, 253; ex-
aggeration 253; fantasy 51, 66,
160–161, 267; fire, abandon, grandeur 43, 185; intelligence 120,
236; knowing musical values 57;
meaning of music 61, 162; music
a dramatic art 162, 168, 173–174;
order in playing 223; piano playing and life 71, 239, 250; "play
ideally" 45, 207; refinement, emotion, poetry 66, 134; rhythm and
dynamics 129; self-expression 31,
39, 40, 44, 66, 233, 253; simplicity
252–253; temperament 11, 120

Keyboard sense 11, 100–101

Listening
importance of 29, 41, 43, 234; to
pedaling, style, taste 64–65; to
tone 20, 130–132; to own playing
129; training in 11–12, 17–19

Memory
away from piano 18, 96; by ear
14; for phrasing 215; method of
128, 130, 172; musical 55

Pedaling 58–59, 64

Phrasing and phrases
bad 29; breathing before long
40; changing 246; each dependent on preceding 17, 42; listen to
17–19; lack of inflection in 162;
memory for 215; motion of 133;
shading of 133; thinking over
50; unfolding of 139

Position at piano
awkwardness and eccentricity
222–224; deportment, good manners, 32; postures 232; sit as in
a saddle 193

Practice and study
analysis of difficult passages 98;
chords, visualizing 127–128, 132;
composition 228; concentration 5,
18; cure for illness 102–103;
finger exercises 132; harmony
and theory 16; late at night, danger of 102; playing etudes 127;
preparedness, thorough 7, 38, 45,
96, 151, 223; slow practice 12, 99,
125; study away from piano 18,
96; study hours 5–6, 189–190;
studying well 11–12, 45, 251;
thinking problems over 42, 153,
242, 249

Public performance
adjustments for 138, 153–154;
breaking down 15, 32, 136–137;
courage 49, 140; covering up
errors 171, 214; critics 155, 164;
growing accustomed to 15, 26–27,

35, 50, 149, 156; improvising to overcome nervousness 282; L. interested only in pupils preparing for 149; orchestral blunders during, 143, 152; preparation time for 27, 246; relation between performer and audience 31–32, 135, 138, 145, 155, 251; stage presence 32, 44, 55, 137–138, 144, 156, 171, 198, 229, 266; taste in repertoire 101; value of 26, 164

Rhythm
correcting faulty pauses 38; dramatic pauses 40; effect of 53; freedom and sureness of 31; L. on unrhythmic playing 23, 38, 199, 239, 246; listening to 130; problem of sixteenth note after dotted eighth note 130; ragtime 247, 250; repose 40; "rhythm is balance" 199; stiff and jerky 43, 53–54; stirring 32; rubato 251–252

Shading
accuracy of without expression worthless 31; bring out right sound, meaning 42; crescendos 234; fine 43; individual differences in 14; learned away from piano 18; top note 41; visualized 133

Style 7, 64

Talent
beware of pupils with 125–126; different grades of 240; natural vs. learned 120, 168, 242, 250, 252–253; of accompanist 122; of mind, eye, and ear 11; plasticity of 217; wide variety of 123–124

Technique
artistic use of 11, 219–220; correctness of detail in 96; Czerny studies 11, 127; dependent on study 53, 102, 129, 220; finger strength 6, 13, 39, 132, 234; getting to bottom of keys 11, 100; heavy, hard 231; methods in teaching 54–55, 99, 105, 107, 127, 243; polish 53, 218, 251; relaxation 101, 248; scales and etudes 125; substitution of hands 164; problems of different nationalities 129; tricks of 58; trill 251; variety of 102; views on 106; without expression, cold 65, 239; wrist motions 60, 106–107

Tempo
awkward and hurried 28, 38, 40–41, 236, 265; confidence in 56; graceful and smooth 38, 54, 58; individual differences in 14; learned away from piano 18; relation between dynamics and 60; "tempos are manners" 44; use of metronome 126

Tone and touch
bring out meaning 42, 61; getting touch of piano 27; hardness of 238; know how should sound 172; listen to 17, 20, 29; modulation in 233; pounding 231–232, 234, 236; study relation of tones 29, 234; tone, beauty of 32, 53, 162, 233, 250, 284; touch, lightness of 45, 54, 194, 244, 252; touch, variety of 102; wrist and arm motions 107

Index II

COMPOSITIONS DISCUSSED

Bach, Johann Sebastian:
Fugues, 37
A Minor Prelude and Fugue, 104

Beethoven, Ludwig von:
Concerto in C Minor, 161
Concerto in E Flat, 165, 167
Quartets, 167
Sonatas, 13, 16, 51, 62, 167, 240
Sonata in A Flat Major (op. 26),
51, 57–61, 65–66
Variations in C Minor, 60

Brahms, Johannes:
Brahms–Handel 'Variations', 246–
247, 249–254
Concerto in D Minor, 260
F Major Romanza, 262
'Horn' Trio, 167
Rhapsody in E Flat, 261

Chopin, Frédéric:
Ballades, 37, 219
Barcarole, 7
'Butterfly' Etude, 174
F Minor Fantasy, 119, 285
Mazurkas, 34, 285
Nocturnes, 215, 285
Polonaises, 285

Czerny, Karl:
Studies, Op. 740, 11, 92, 216, 236,
240

Dohnányi, Ernst von:
Concerto in E Minor, 119

Henselt, Adolph von:
Concerto, 260

Leschetizky, Theodor:
Arabesque, 53
Canzonetta Toscana, 162

Mandolinata, 162
Mazurkas, 16, 34, 282
Opera: *Die Erste Falte*, 240–241
'The Two Larks', 214

Liszt, Franz:
Hungarian Fantasie, 150
Rhapsodies, 16, 183, 265

Litolff, Henry Charles:
Concerto, 161

Mendelssohn, Felix:
Concerto in G Minor, 30, 49

Moszkowski, Moritz:
Etincelles, 37
Waltz, 39

Offenbach, Jacques:
Tales of Hoffman, 49–50, 150

Powell, John:
Sonata Virginianesque, 170

Rossini, Gioacchino:
The Barber of Seville, 87

Rubinstein, Anton:
Concerto, 266, 293
Nocturne in G Major, 130

Schumann, Robert:
Carnaval, 36, 38–46
Concerto, 24, 150–154, 172, 264
Fantasy, 19, 61
Quintette, 157
Variations (duet), 158
Songs, 47, 282

Schütt, Eduard:
Canzonetta, 216
Carnaval, 36–37, 40
Prelude in D Major, 37

Strauss, Johann:
'Blue Danube,' 276

Tschaikowsky, Peter Ilyitch:
   Concerto, 29–31
Verdi, Giuseppe:
   La Traviata, 87

Wallner, Leopold:
   Variations, 30
Weber:
   Concert Piece, 129

Adams, Mr., 288

Albert, Eugène d', 45, 185, 219–220

Americans (opinions about), 31, 37, 70, 81, 88, 103–105, 128–132, 164, 166, 200, 242, 247–248, 250–251, 272, 291

Auer, Leopold, 90

Barbi, Alice (singer), 34, 280–281

Beethoven, Ludwig von, 22, 47–50, 57, 166–167

Berger, Baron (director of Court Theater in Vienna), 280

Bird, Clarence (pupil), 201

Brahm, Otto (director of Lessing Theater in Berlin), 276

Brahms, Johannes, 108–109, 167, 247, 252, 254, 260–264, 294

Brandt, Marianna (opera singer), 281–282

Brée, Frau Malwine (assistant), 54, 92–93, 134, 183

Brieux, Eugène, 276

Buhlig, Richard (pupil), 289

Buxtehude, Dietrich, 166

Carreño, Teresa, 185, 251

Chopin, Frédéric, 21, 29, 260

Clemens, Clara, 186–187, 210–211, 280

Clemens, Jean, 187, 210–211

Clemens, Samuel (see Twain, Mark)

Clemens, Mrs. Samuel, 187–188, 210–211

Conne, Paul de, 267

Coudenhove, Count, 280

Cover, Virginia (pupil), 13

Czerny, Karl, 167

Dahl-Rich (pupil), 289

Diémer, Louis (teacher of piano), 63

Dohnányi, Ernst von, 119

Duncan, Isadora (dancer), 33

Dunzendorfer, Madame Helene (half-sister), 290, 292

Durno, Jeanette (pupil), 289

Dutschka, Madame von (friend), 280–284

Edward VII, 269

Emperor Francis Joseph, 49–50, 108–111, 114, 256, 258, 269, 277–279

Empress Elizabeth, 110–112

English (opinions about), 81, 200, 222, 249–250, 272, 291

Epstein, Julius, 118

Essipoff, Annette (second wife), 21, 157–158, 294

Flonzaleys, The, 284

French (opinions about), 167, 198, 200, 251, 253–254, 291

Friedman, Ignace (pupil), 161, 197, 234

Fulda, Ludwig, 275–276

Fuller, Loie, 33

Gabrilowitsch, Ossip (pupil), 15, 118

Germans (opinions about), 165–166, 185, 200

318

Goethe, J. W. von, 180–181

Goldschmidt, Paul (pupil), 122–124, 126–127, 133–135

Goltz, Alexander (portrait painter), 175, 276

Goltz, Madame, 175

Goodson, Katharine (pupil), 15, 102, 185

Grieg, Edvard, 294

Grünfeld, Alfred (teacher of piano), 24, 257

Gutmann, Mr. (impresario), 144–149, 151–152, 154, 252

Gypsies, 163, 183–186

Hamburg, Mark (pupil), 90

Hansen, Fräulein Walle (assistant), 92, 134

Hanslick, Edward (critic), 51, 145

Hauptmann, Gerhard (poet), 275

Haydn, Franz Joseph, 218

Hofmann, Josef, 251

Hopekirk, Madame Helen (pupil), 70

Horzowsky, Miecio [Horszowski, Mieczylaw] (pupil), 127

Hullah, Miss Annette (pupil), 128

Inness, George (painter), 202

Inness, Miss, 202–204

Italians (opinions about), 198, 200, 251, 291

Jahn, Bertha (pupil), 15, 27–28

Jews (opinion about), 213

Joachim, Joseph, 167

Johann (valet), 286

Kleeberg, Clothilde (pupil), 102

Krause, Mrs., 211

La Forge, Frank (pupil), 171, 284

Landecker (builder of concert halls), 288

Laszlo, Philip de (portrait painter), 276, 284

Laszlo, Mrs. (violinist), 284

Lehár, Franz, 274

Lenbach, 282

Leschetizka, Madame Eugenie (third wife), 22, 80, 90, 187, 203–204, 264, 272, 287

Leschetizka, Thérèse (daughter), 33, 157, 292

Leschetizky, Robert (son), 292

Liszt, Franz, 2, 40, 144, 162, 182–183, 294

Livinski (actor), 173–174

Löwenbergs (patrons of chamber music), 167–168

Lubomirska, Princess, 283–284

Lucca, Pauline (friend), 176

Mahler, Gustav (conductor), 150, 255–257

Marchesi de Castrone, Mathilde (voice teacher), 124, 198

Massenet, Jules, 72, 294

Melville, Margaret (pupil), 171

Mendes, Catulle (poet), 275–276

Minkus, Dr. (violinist), 22

Mütter, Fräulein (voice teacher), 87

Nawratil, Karl (teacher of composition), 170

Neusser, Professor (physician), 116

Newcomb, Mary (singer, sister of Ethel), 19–21, 84, 86–89, 91–93, 117

Ohnet, George, 276

Olmsted, Jane (pupil), 114, 187, 207 (see also Thaw)

Orientals (opinion about), 199

Paderewski, Ignace (pupil), 2, 45, 50–51, 126, 164, 167, 211, 255–256

Palpiti, Tante (aunt of Ethel Newcomb), 7

Patti, Adelina [?] (singer), 146, 251

Philippe, Isidor (teacher of piano), 63

Poles (opinions about), 199, 284, 291

Potocka, Countess Angèle (sister-in-law), vii, 114

Powell, John (pupil), 170–171

Praehofer, Pepi (attendant and nurse), 291

Prentner, Fräulein Marie (assistant), vii, 4–5, 7–9, 11, 92, 134

Prill, Dr. Karl (Concert-Meister), 148

Prince Henry, 181

Proctor, George (pupil), 15

Pruckner, Professor (teacher of piano), 1–2

Rauchinger (portrait painter), 276

Richter, Hans (conductor), 255, 263, 294

Rorsborska, Marie (fourth wife), 288

Rosenthal, Moriz, 45, 108

Rubinstein, Anton, 28, 40, 59, 130, 144, 158, 182–183, 264–267, 294

Russians (opinions about), 167, 291

Saint-Saëns, Camille, 72

Sanderson, Sybil (singer), 146

Sauer, Emil von (pianist), 42

Saville, Madame Frances (singer), 33, 149–150, 153–154, 257

Scala, Mr. de (museum director), 281

Schmidt, Martha (pupil), 36–37, 39, 258

Schnabel, Arthur (pupil), 15–16, 118

Schnitzler, Arthur, 268, 276

Schratt, Madame (actress), 110, 114

Schumann, Madame Clara, 259–260

Schütt, Edouard (pupil), 37, 46, 82, 90, 108, 114, 170, 290–293

Scotford, Jane (pupil), 132

Sechter, Simon (Leschetizky's teacher of composition), 169, 278

Shattuck, Arthur (pupil), 200

Sickescz, Jan (pupil), 33

Sieveking, Martinus (pupil), 203–204

Sinigaglia, Leone (composer), 273

Stein, Professor (teacher of piano), 293

Stepanoff, Madame (assistant), 243

Strauss, Edward, 269

Strauss, Johann, 108, 274

Suart, Evelyn (pupil), 90

Szalit, Paula (pupil), 40, 101–102, 127, 171

Thaw, Jane Olmsted (pupil), 289

Thomas, Ada (pupil), 239

Tschaikowsky, Peter Ilyitch, 294

Twain, Mark, 186–188, 210, 280–281

Ullman, Thérèse von (mother), vii

Viennese (opinions about), 37, 165, 167–169, 185, 227, 253, 261, 263, 268–272, 275–279

Welte-Mignon records, 159

Wienezkowska, Madame (assistant), 243

Wieniawski, 144

Wiesinger, Madame (painter of flowers), 276

Wilbrandt, Adolf (poet and director), 275, 280–281, 284

Wilbrandt-Baudius, Madame (actress), 281

Williams, Marie Novello (pupil), 221

Winkelmann, Hermann (tenor), 256–257

Wittgenstein family (music lovers), 167

Wolff, Erich (accompanist), 239

Wolff, Hermann (manager), 158

Wydenbruch-Esterhazy, Countess, 280

Ysaye, Théophile, 252

Zamoyski, Count Xaver (art patron), 283

Zeisler, Fannie Bloomfield (pupil), 38, 70, 108, 185